DOMESTIC ECONOMIES

DOMESTIC ECONOMIES

Women, Work,

and the American Dream

in Los Angeles

SUSANNA ROSENBAUM

DUKE UNIVERSITY PRESS

Durham and London 2017

Typeset in Quadraat Pro by
Westchester Publishing Services

Library of Congress Cataloging-in-Publication Data Names:
Rosenbaum, Susanna, 1972– author.
Title: Domestic economies : women, work, and the
American Dream in Los Angeles / Susanna Rosenbaum.
Description: Durham : Duke University Press, 2017. |
Includes bibliographical references and index. Identifiers:
LCCN 2017024179 (print)
LCCN 2017040972 (ebook)
ISBN 9780822372264 (ebook)
ISBN 9780822369974 (hardcover)
ISBN 9780822370024 (pbk.)
Subjects: LCSH: Hispanic American women— Employment
—California—LosAngeles.|
Women householdemployees— California—
Los Angeles. | Women foreign workers—California— Los
Angeles—Social conditions. | Working
class women—California—LosAngeles— Social
conditions. | Middle class women—California—
Los Angeles—Social conditions. | American
Dream. | Motherhood—California—Los Angeles.
Classification: LCC HD6072.2.U52 (ebook) |
LCC HD6072.2.U52 L674 2017 (print) |
DDC 331.4/816408968720979494—dc23
LC recordavailableathttps:// lccn.loc.gov/2017024179

Cover art: Ramiro Gomez, *Laundry Day*, 2015 (detail).
Acrylic on magazine, 11 × 8.5 inches. Courtesy of the
artist and Charlie James Gallery, Los Angeles.

For "Carmen"

and all of the women

whose stories

make up this book

CONTENTS

ACKNOWLEDGMENTS

Working on this project has taught me the intensely social nature of research and writing. Rather than a solitary process, this has been one of collaboration and support, and one to which numerous individuals and institutions have contributed. My deepest appreciation goes to the domestic workers and employers who welcomed me into their lives. They took me into their worlds, generously giving of themselves and their time. Although I can never do full justice to their stories, I do hope that this book conveys even a small part of their all-too-often unseen experiences. I would especially like to recognize the immigrant women with whom I spent most of my time in Los Angeles—the women I've named Carmen, Josefina, Doña Flor, Eva, Mercedes, Aída, Lucía, María Luisa, Raquel, and Julia. I cannot overstate my admiration and profound respect for the ways they have not only managed but triumphed under the most difficult of life circumstances. Their daily struggles and successes continue to humble me.

My work on this book began in the Anthropology Department at NYU, under the supervision of Faye Ginsburg, Tom Abercrombie, and Bambi Schieffelin. Their guidance, encouragement, and intellectual visions shaped this project in uniquely incisive ways. Faye Ginsburg's pioneering research on anthropology in the United States and on the anthropology of reproduction serve as crucial foundations for my work. From Tom Abercrombie, I learned to focus on domestic space and on the coproduction of seemingly separate identities, understandings that reverberate through this book. Bambi Schieffelin's work on the micro practices of socialization, her attention to detail, and her always sharp insights continue to guide my thinking. As fourth reader and scholarly inspiration, Rayna Rapp also provided invaluable perspectives that helped in shaping the book.

Various institutions supported this project in its multiple stages. Fieldwork in Los Angeles was funded by a dissertation research grant from the Wenner-Gren Foundation (6917), and NYU's International Center for Advanced Studies provided support for dissertation writing. A Mellon Postdoctoral Fellowship and participation in the Sawyer Seminar "Globalizing the Americas" at the University of Toronto afforded me the intellectual space to begin the long process from dissertation to book. Additionally, a position as Visiting Assistant Professor and Visiting Scholar at Columbia University's Center for the Study of Ethnicity and Race helped to refine my thinking. The final revisions to this manuscript were completed with support from The City College of New York's Division of Interdisciplinary Arts and Sciences, as well as The City University of New York's Faculty Fellowship Publication Program.

The opportunity to discuss this project with multiple academic audiences pushed me to sharpen my argument. I am particularly grateful for animated discussions at the Department of Women's and Gender Studies, University of California, Irvine; the Department of Anthropology, John Jay College; the Department of Anthropology, Temple University; the Department of Women's and Gender Studies, Rutgers University; the Department of Interdisciplinary Arts and Sciences at the City College of New York; and the Department of Anthropology, Binghamton University. This book also benefited immensely from the comments of Mary Romero and two anonymous reviewers. A special thank you to Ken Wissoker for his patience, for his excitement about this project, and for his expert stewardship in bringing it to fruition. I am also indebted to Olivia Polk for her assistance in the production of the book.

Previous versions of chapters 2 and 4 appeared, respectively, in *When Care Work Goes Global: Learning the Social Relations of Domestic Work*, edited by Mary Romero, Valerie Preston, and Wenona Giles (Ashgate Books, 2014); and in *Working USA: The Journal of Labor and Society* 19(2) (2016): 187–206.

During each phase of this project, I've relied on the generosity of friends and colleagues for both moral support and analytic acumen. In Los Angeles, Sammy and Nancy Berkowitz, and their entire family, eased my entry into the field, providing a home away from home and countless delicious meals. Through our daily walks, Jennifer Eler lightened the process of fieldwork. Linda Kite and Anayansi Prado graciously opened doors, generously sharing their experiences and contacts. At NYU, my dissertation writing group, Kristin Dowell, Danny Fisher, Aaron Glass, and especially Eleana Kim, provided critical and engaged readings. Shalini Shankar also served as a crucial interlocutor in early stages of this project. My colleagues at CUNY's Faculty Fellow Publication Program, Kafui Attoh, Melissa Borja, Lawrence Johnson, Devin Molina, Emily Tumpson Molina, Seth Offenbach, and Stephen Steinberg, offered much-needed perspective and indispensable insights as I finished revising this manuscript.

I am extraordinarily fortunate to work in the Department of Interdisciplinary Arts and Sciences at the Center for Worker Education (CWE) at The City College of New York. Thank you to Dean Juan Carlos Mercado for his support and for inviting me to participate in the many innovative initiatives that make CWE such a dynamic intellectual hub. As department chair, Kathy McDonald has fostered an especially supportive and collegial environment, providing both the encouragement and space so necessary for completing this manuscript. Over innumerable cups of coffee, Susanna Schaller and Alessandra Benedicty-Kokken generously shared their friendship, knowledge, and astute observations. I also thank Carlos Aguasaco, Marlene Clark, David Eastzer, Vicki Garavuso, Mary Lutz, Elizabeth Matthews, Justin Williams, Martin Woessner, and Danielle Zach for their solidarity.

A final note of thanks goes to my family, both chosen and obligatory, whose love and support made all of this conceivable. Rene Gerrets, the brother I never knew I needed, has been by my side every step of the way. Stephanie Sadre-Orafai continues to be a principal interlocutor, her generous and incisive readings challenging me in the best possible ways. My long-standing intellectual conversation with Ruti Talmor continually inspires me; her unexpected and illuminating perspectives make my work sharper than it could otherwise hope to be. Her friendship, along with Stephanie's and Rene's, carried me through all of the ups and downs of this process. In the final stages of writing, Steve Cohen knew when to encourage me and when to serve as welcome diversion, attending to both with abundant love and ridiculousness. My mother, Brenda Rosenbaum, and my sisters, Elena and Dora Lisa Rosenbaum, have lived with this project as long as I have, their patience and encouragement extending beyond all reasonable limits. Indeed, their love and laughter buoyed me through the length of this endeavor. My father, Fredy Rosenbaum, did not live to see this in final form, but his influence nevertheless remains. Both he and my mother made this possible: their unflagging belief in me, commitment to intellectual pursuits, and devotion to social justice propelled and sustained me on this journey.

Introduction

In January 2003, I observed two strikingly different versions of the "ten-chair exercise." Used to illustrate income distribution in the United States, this exercise calls for ten volunteers and ten chairs, each representing one-tenth of the country's population and wealth, respectively. The inequalities of our so-called middle-class society are then rendered acutely vivid: one person lounges on seven chairs, seven people fight over the remaining three, and two people are left standing. I first encountered this at a bimonthly gathering of mothers in an upper-middle-class neighborhood in Los Angeles. The moderator, an active member of the group, wanted her fellow mothers to pay attention to tax policies, to understand how deeply a seemingly arcane system influenced their daily lives. She emphasized how the tax structure squeezes individuals in the middle class, their economically precarious position objectified by the seven women scrambling to fit on three chairs. A few Mondays later, in a felicitous turn of events, I arrived at the weekly meeting of a domestic workers' cooperative and found the coordinator preparing to run through this same exercise. This time, however, participants would not recognize themselves in the seven women piled on three chairs, but rather in the two individuals with no place to sit. Members had been at odds lately, struggling to balance cooperative principles with a shrinking clientele, and the coordinator wanted to bring home the need for collective effort—only together would they be able to add another chair to the mix, to create a new source of wealth.

At first glance, this juxtaposition seems ironic, serving only to underscore the stark economic disparities between the two groups. In this exercise, native-born, middle-class employers and the Mexican and Central American women who worked in their homes clearly represented distinct sectors of the population. Nevertheless, as evinced by this activity, both agonized about their financial stability. Despite glaring inequalities of privilege, all of these women could easily envision the economic brink and fought to guard against it. The perils of economic failure magnified as they all defined themselves in large part through financial mobility, through achievement of the American Dream, for themselves and for their children.

Both groups of women turned to domestic service in pursuit of the American Dream, but for both the Dream remained just out of reach, hampered by the ever-present fear of economic collapse, as well as the difficulties of becoming proper and valuable "Americans." These concerns are of a piece, firmly linked through the continued devaluation of reproductive labor and its association with women. This book explores the different ways that native-born employers and immigrant domestic workers navigate this context, each locating personal value and success at the intersection of economic advancement, re/productive labor, and national belonging. Attention to both groups illuminates alternative, coexisting understandings of individual and social worth, and in turn, varying ways to conceive of social membership and belonging. In so doing, it situates immigrant women firmly inside the nation, underscoring them as critical and active players in defining and producing contemporary "Americanness."

American Dreams

In an 1862 essay denouncing slavery, Ralph Waldo Emerson wrote, "America is another word for Opportunity" (1862: 508). The America he extolled would be resolutely antislavery, allowing each man to own the fruits of his labor. Labor, he argued, was an essential component of morality and hence civility. Even so, his vision of America was also explicitly racialized (cf. Knadler 2002), composed of the correct kind of men—the civilized type, from "temperate" rather than "hot" zones. For Emerson's America valued labor, sharply in opposition to Indians and Africans, who understood neither its moral centrality nor its potential to transform the future.

Emerson's nineteenth-century ideal strongly resembles the contemporary American Dream. This Dream promises opportunity, holding that success and economic advancement are open to anyone who is willing to work hard. It is the very essence of this country—unfettered by her past, the driven, disciplined individual can become anything she desires. The Dream ostensibly rewards those who are worthy, while the less deserving languish. Placing the blame on individuals, it helps to constitute the moral borders of Americanness, since only those who have strength of character and determination will flourish. Of course, this version of the story is incomplete: emphasizing the individual helps to conceal the very limits that make the Dream possible. Not only is the American Dream increasingly elusive for its intended recipients, but it has always functioned through foreclosure. The labor of those not entitled to the Dream continues to subsidize the lifestyles of those who are. Further, these boundaries are still demarcated through race, even as the content of whiteness and its others has shifted over time.[1]

This ethnography examines how two groups of women seek to achieve the American Dream, however imperfect and slippery it might be. It takes domestic service as analytic entry point, illustrating how immigrant and native-born women struggle to realize the Dream; how each is indispensable to the other's quest; and the abiding importance of reproductive labor to this pursuit. This occupation provides a tangible intersection that brings together immigrant and native-born, foreign and "American," domestic worker and domestic employer. Although these categories exist only in relation to one another, their mutuality often remains invisible. The give and take of domestic service materializes these usually unseen connections, as it simultaneously facilitates, complicates, and transforms the processes of self- and nation-making for women on each side. Juxtaposing employers and employees reveals how these processes are neither smooth nor uncontested, and underscores how the Dream is not only racialized but also gendered. This view foregrounds how reproductive labor remains invisible but crucial—indeed, crucial in its invisibility—to shaping "Americanness." As such, it sheds light on an enduring cultural fault line, a struggle for personal worth and social recognition that centers the value and meaning of reproductive labor.

Checking the Dream: Gendered Exclusions and the Racialization of Immigrants

The inherent potential of the American Dream implies that everyone can become middle class. This category is fluid and almost meaningless in its alleged ubiquity, but it remains an important marker of self-identification, acknowledging that an individual accepts the terms of the deal—she is willing to put in the effort that the Dream requires. Yet, for the middle-class[2] women I met in LA, this bargain was neither satisfying nor viable. For this group, the American Dream was riddled with ambivalence and contradiction, pledging success but yielding mostly frustration. These women felt like individual failures, and yet they were set up by a system that continues to deny the economic value and social importance of reproductive labor. Although Emerson's belief in the moral value of work—of the worker—persists today, this view recognizes only paid employment, erasing reproductive labor and establishing an irreconcilable conflict for women.

In turn-of-the-millennium LA, female employers defined success as raising accomplished children as well as achievement in the paid workforce—in fact, the latter was vital to the former. Even so, these goals remained incompatible, both practically and ideologically. From a middle-class (primarily white) vantage point, proper motherhood is exclusively concerned with children, enacted through reproducing and caring for children. Fulfilling this requirement is paramount, for motherhood is inherent in womanhood, its most essential manifestation. These understandings clash with an analogous emphasis on self-realization through paid employment, and they collide with the urgent need to earn an income as well as with the ever-expanding reach of the workplace. The fact that neither the demands of the home nor the exigencies of work have abated creates an increasingly unmanageable situation. As Hochschild and Machung (1989) point out, after completing a full day at the office, most women return home to a "second shift."

Motherhood and paid employment thus exerted contradictory pulls, the first fulfilling the imperatives of femininity while the latter underpinned a socially recognizable and respected identity. From an employer's perspective, the domestic sphere remained ideologically distinct from the public domain, the world of *economic* value. Its association with the private sphere and with women rendered reproductive labor invisible, uncounted in the GDP, and unimportant (e.g., Budig and England 2001; Folbre 2001, 2012; Budig and Hodges 2010; Brooks and Rogalin 2014). Paid employment provided a way to counteract these erasures—allowing middle-class women not only the ability to maintain a particular standard of living and ensure their kids' futures, but also the opportunity to be productive and thus successful persons, (economically) valuable members of society.

The widespread availability of domestic service in LA helped to ease the tug of war between work and home. But this did not solve the conflict, merely papered it over, bringing other inconsistencies into pointed relief. Hiring a domestic employee forced employers, often for the first time, to grapple with the inequalities, inconsistencies, and complicities required to sustain their lifestyles. Bringing difference into the protected space of the home, domestic service forced employers to see their privilege and thus to reconsider the myths and meanings of the American Dream.

When I started my research, I expected that employers' concerns around domestic service would center on issues of family, motherhood, and social reproduction—for instance, who was raising their children, how they were raising their children, how to define motherhood, and how to think about work and women's work. Although these did arise from time to time, to my surprise, privilege emerged as the principal trope in employers' stories of domestic service, foregrounding its disruptive potential. For example, whenever I described my project to employers, especially those I met in passing, they responded the same way: they loved their domestic employee, who was "like family." Many would then proceed to elaborate the various ways they had helped her out. This script never varied, an almost instantaneous justification for me, as well as for themselves, that redefined their particular relationship as different and more equal.[3] More importantly, employers also often pointed out that the women who labored in their homes were immigrants. Their insistence on foreignness helped to construct an insuperable distinction and underscored just who is entitled to the American Dream and where the "shifting human extractive frontier" (Liechty 2003: 10) is located. As a result, they temporarily replaced gendered limits with national cum racial boundaries.

This displacement represents merely another iteration of the racialized and racializing foundations of the American Dream. Immigrants have been crucial to these processes, serving as both the cheap laborers and emblematic others necessary to defining national identity (e.g., Gordon and Lenhardt 2007; Johnson 2009). Engaging in domestic service further compounds these distinctions. Historically, racially marked women have provided the main supply of paid domestic labor in the United States. Although the ethnicity, race, or national provenance of the women who performed this work has varied according to region and historical moment, they have always belonged to groups "placed in a separate legal category from whites, excluded from rights and protections accorded to full citizens" (Glenn 1992: 8; cf. Barnes 1993; Katzman 1979; Tucker 1988; Palmer 1989; Dill 1994). The concept of "illegality," often projected onto all Mexican and Central American immigrants whether they have legal documents or not, further rigidifies these lines (e.g., Ngai 2004; De Genova 2005; Romero 2008; Goldsmith et al. 2009). In the present, the operative distinction is not one between full citizens and internal "others"; instead, we find "Americans" and (dangerous, encroaching, illegitimate) foreigners, outsiders who cannot expect any rights or protections.

See(k)ing Alternatives: Ethnography and the Unexpected

Their difference seemingly congealed and impossible to transcend, immigrant women nevertheless had a very different experience of the American Dream than their employers did. Despite the abiding indignities of immigrant life, these women consistently asserted their successes, their faith in the American Dream, and hence their claims on it. Certainly, the Dream has always been more myth than actuality, and especially in the years since the "Great Recession," its limitations have eclipsed its potential. Middle-class families, the very subjects of this Dream, increasingly doubt its relevance to their lives. How, then, could immigrants, who at best were afterthoughts, at worst the vehicle for others' attainment, of the Dream hold so steadfastly to it? Were they simply "duped," hoodwinked into upholding a system that exploits them?

This book argues that the American Dream was their reality—even as they were acutely aware and highly critical of the hardships they faced in this country. The promise of the Dream structured their daily lives and senses of self, and although they were most often on the wrong end of it, their stake in and demands on it pushed against its very boundaries. Initially jarring, and certainly humbling, this apparent incongruity gives shape to my ethnography. I begin by questioning its very dissonance: *Why did I see a contradiction?* The answer, I realized, required a shift in analytic framework. How does a focus on a specific occupation shape *how* and *what* we know about Mexican and Central American women in the United States? More broadly, what are we already assuming about individual worth and social membership if we begin from the premise that productive labor, self, and value are isomorphic?

The efficacy of ethnography lies in its ability to undermine the assumptions of the researcher, but she must remain open to this. Doing fieldwork "at home" easily confirms what we take for granted, and so when I started fieldwork, I accepted that "domestic service" would be a critical category of experience. After all, I supposed, there was no way that performing such unsavory work could have less than a fundamental impact on an individual's sense of self. The injuries of this job are multiple and well known: domestic workers earn little and often put up with abusive treatment, even as they perform crucial tasks without which the economy could not function. Crystallizing both global and local inequalities through backbreaking, poorly paid, and socially disparaged labor, domestic work *should* be a defining category for the women who engage it—or at least that is what I expected. What I found, however, was that domestic service was inseparable from the broader immigrant experience, the struggle for survival and success in a context of economic and social erasure.

This became increasingly clear in the first months of fieldwork, as I tried to find "domestic workers" for my study. Shortly after arriving in Los Angeles, I contacted the Domestic Workers Group, an association set up by and housed within a well-known immigrants' rights coalition. I spoke to their coordinator, and she invited me to their upcoming meeting. That Saturday, I attended my very first gathering, where I met a number of women. As the session wound down, I found myself in conversation with Blanca and Carmen and offered to drive them home. Carmen accepted for both of them, explaining that public transportation was particularly erratic on weekends, and since Blanca had to change buses, it would take her at least an hour to get home.

After we dropped Carmen off, Blanca asked if I wanted to get a cup of coffee. She directed me to a Salvadoran bakery near her apartment, and over coffee and sweet tamales, told me her life story—she left Honduras after discovering her husband had cheated on her, arrived in LA ten years earlier, initially worked in several homes, and now cleaned hotel rooms. I started to worry: Was Blanca a "real" domestic worker? Why was she at that meeting if she no longer labored in private homes? I tried to ask about work, but she wouldn't engage my questions, always shifting the conversation back to other stories—her neighbor whose husband had just left, her nephew who was gay and didn't practice safe sex, and her children who lived in Honduras.

We finished our coffee, and I took Blanca home. She promised to call me, and the possibility of further contact made me feel both relieved and increasingly anxious. I was pleased to be meeting more people but nervous that they weren't "real" domestic workers. Would it be okay to hang out with Blanca even though she no longer labored in this capacity? If I included her, did this mean that once a domestic worker, always a domestic worker? Did this job carry such force that it would mark you for life?

These same doubts plagued me when Carmen introduced me to Raquel, a teacher's aide at an elementary school. Raquel was a nanny when she first came to Los Angeles but had been at her present job for the past three years. Still, she cleaned homes with Carmen during school holidays, and a few months after I met her, took a weekend job caring for a newborn from Friday night to Sunday afternoon. All the while, she was attending night school, hoping to pass the GED, start taking college classes, and eventually become a teacher. I wondered: Was Raquel a domestic worker? I could classify her as a domestic worker, but is that how she would choose to identify herself? Just what made someone a domestic worker? Did this occupation override other, concurrently held jobs, uniquely defining individuals?

The longer I was in Los Angeles, the more I started to question whether the categories of "domestic worker" and "domestic service" were the appropriate lenses through which to make sense of immigrant women's experiences. This occupation is one of the few available to Central American and Mexican women, and it is usually their "best" choice, higher paid and more flexible than the other jobs they could find. It remains, of course, poorly compensated, and to make ends meet, individuals worked long hours, often at nights and on weekends, in multiple positions. They scratched out an income through any combination of cleaning a house, taking care of children, working in a factory, selling beauty products, or other informal labor.

Mexican and Central American women did not attribute definitional force to "domestic service," instead characterizing themselves as mothers. They took up paid employment as *tool for* achieving rather than as *source of* individual and social worth. Their work allowed them to provide for their children—and it was this endeavor, along with the personal transformations it required and catalyzed, that rendered them successful, achievers of the American Dream, valuable and valued social beings (cf. Coll 2010). As such, they knew themselves and their lives in the United States as much through inclusion as through exclusion, tempering the very real experience of marginality through the equally real experience of gain.

To get at this complexity of experience, I take domestic service as an important but not by itself defining category of immigrant women's lives in the United States. My perspective builds on an extensive and growing literature on paid domestic employment. This body of work draws on feminist analyses of globalization, which underscore how such processes place growing responsibility on women; increasingly, it is women's remittances that support both their families and the economies of their home countries (Sassen 2000). The travails of immigrant domestic workers are crucial to understanding these global movements, highlighting not only what Sassen (2000) has called "women's burden" but also the disparities that reproduce the privilege of Western women through the labor of those from the Global South. Accordingly, scholars have examined domestic service across a variety of sites, including Filipinas in Hong Kong (Constable 1997), Los Angeles and Rome (Parreñas 2001), Taiwan (Lan 2006), and Vancouver (Pratt 1999); West Indian nannies in New York (Cheever 2002; Brown 2008) and Toronto (Stiell and England 1999); Sri Lankan women in the Middle East (Ismail 1999; Gamburd 2000); Indonesian women in Saudi Arabia (Silvey 2004); African women in Italy (Andall 2000); and Mexican and Central American women in the United States (Repak 1995; Luz Ibarra 2000; Hondagneu-Sotelo 2001). They have explored the day-to-day of this occupation (e.g., Romero 1992; Hondagneu-Sotelo 2001); its links to global economic transformations (e.g., Bakan and Stasiulis 1997; Momsen 1999; Anderson 2000; Ehrenreich and Hochschild 2004; Zimmerman et al. 2006; Lutz 2008; Romero et al. 2014); and its effects on the children and families of domestic workers (e.g., Parreñas 2001; Gamburd 2008; Romero 2011).

These studies provide invaluable insight into an occupation that simultaneously results from and sustains global relations of power, calling much-needed attention to households as key sites in the production of broad-scale inequalities. My research is deeply indebted to this scholarship and, at the same time, seeks to expand the scope of inquiry; now that we know that domestic service is multiplying, creating new family formations, and reproducing global asymmetries, how can we understand the daily lives and perspectives of the women who perform this work? For as much as this literature tells us about the occupation and its attendant injuries, it tells us relatively little about the individual women who labor in this capacity. In fact, a focus on one mode of employment can blur other aspects of immigrant life. Reading paid domestic employees through their jobs, we highlight inequality, exploitation, and exclusion.[4]

This ethnography refocuses the relationship of immigrant women with their work to consider how poverty and upward mobility, exclusion and belonging, hopelessness and possibility exist simultaneously. Thinking through paid employment and motherhood as part of the same endeavor elucidates multiple ways of figuring an individual's value and social position. This view does not elide the harsh realities of immigrant life or the destructive consequences of capitalism. Unquestionably in the United States, neoliberal[5] policies increasingly define the parameters of belonging, shaping experiences of social membership through its presumed connection to work (cf. Greenhouse 2009; Muelebach 2011; Weeks 2011; Brodkin 2014). This form of belonging, accrued through productive labor, reinforces the of-courseness of neoliberal logics and is tied directly to the interests of a particular class (Harvey 2011). In the present, however, most people's potential to fulfill these goals has evaporated, producing a new and ongoing state of crisis—a pervasive sense of hopelessness and precarity (e.g., Berlant 2011; Povinelli 2011; Stewart 2012; Allison 2013; Muehlebach 2013; Roitman 2014; Hébert 2015). Yet it is the very urgency of this moment, when the future no longer seems possible, that forces us to begin imagining alternatives (e.g., Halberstam 2011; Allison 2013).

Biehl (2013) encourages us to use ethnography as a way into these concerns, but also cautions us to account for constraints as much as for newly found openings: "What about life *inside* capitalism. Why this investment in a counter-ideology to capitalism that rests on the imaginary of a capital's *outside*? How to make sense of contemporary realities of society inside the State and people who mobilize to use the state, forging novel, tenuous links between themselves, the state, and the market place?" (2013: 589). Without romanticizing their predicaments, I investigate how individuals newly inhabiting this precarity, as well those whose destitution is enduring, conceive of and exploit emergent possibilities, gaps that not only reinforce but also challenge normative definitions of nation and belonging.[6] I explore both the difficulties and the potentialities of the present, particularly for those women relegated to the margins, where often just "managing *to be*" (Allen 2011: 30) or "simply trying to find room to breathe beneath intolerable constraints" (Biehl 2013: 574) is a triumph.

Domestic Economies

Examining both sides of domestic service at once underscores how immigrant and native-born are part of the same process, both requisite in the making of the American Dream, of "Americanness." It also reveals the importance of reproductive labor to this same project. Indeed, paid employment is integral to but not exclusively defining of individual women's subjectivities and their efforts to become valuable and valued. All of the women I met in LA located success at the intersection of motherhood and paid employment. They defined individual achievement through their own economic mobility, but also through the ability to ensure their children's future accomplishments; together these would render them valuable social members, proper "Americans." Crucial to realizing the American Dream, economic independence, self-discipline, and upwardly mobile aspirations worked to identify the desirable national subject. Importantly, these qualities transcended the individual, for they would only retroactively be proven by the successes of the next generation. In the present, a measure of economic prosperity coupled with working toward that future evinced the appropriate attributes of "Americanness." An individual's worth and social value, her sense of belonging, therefore spanned several selves, temporal horizons, and categories of labor.

The chapters that follow discuss how immigrant and native-born women grapple with this always-mutable terrain, foregrounding the significance of reproductive labor to national belonging. This is not incidental, for the processes of reproduction highlight the values upheld, assumed, or contested within a society; they clarify what it means to be a (desirable) person as well as how personhood is constituted within a specific cultural context (Ginsburg and Rapp 1995). We see then how belonging is always already gendered. I use "belonging" for its ambiguity, to emphasize how particular dispositions and aspirations, along with the sense of a shared future, work to shape a desirable and proper "American." My analysis deliberately moves away from the notion of citizenship,[7] from an emphasis on rights, for as I found out in the process of fieldwork, citizenship is not in itself the ultimate goal for most women from Mexico and Central America. It is certainly important, indeed increasingly imperative,[8] but its value does not necessarily translate into economic stability, acceptance, or recognition. I am concerned instead with the attachments that immigrant women form to this country, and the ways in which their very being frays on a series of borders that seek to exclude them.

Thus, I draw on scholarship that attends to affective and temporal forms of belonging (e.g., Young 1989; Yuval-Davis 1997, 2006, 2007; Bell 1999; Hage 2003; Ahmed 2004; Ramirez 2007; Winarnita 2008; Gálvez 2009; Ho 2009; Coll 2010; Ramos-Zayas 2012). These authors underscore how "citizenship" exceeds legal definitions and is most broadly concerned with "the meaning and scope of membership of the community in which one lives. Who belongs and what does 'belonging' mean in practice" (Hall and Held 1989: 17; cf. Walzer 1983; Rosaldo 1994; Ong 1996)?

In the day to day, belonging is variegated, its experience refracted through diverse and overlapping categories of difference. And as feminist scholars have shown, gender remains pivotal to these processes (e.g., Pateman 1989; Young 1989; Yuval-Davis 1997; Werbner and Yuval-Davis 1999; Bosniak 2006; Caldwell et al. 2009), especially in relation to motherhood and reproductive labor (e.g., Colen 1995; Ginsburg and Rapp 1995; Schultz 2000; Kessler-Harris 2001; Herd and Harrington 2002; Bosniak 2006; Lister 2007). Further, intersectional analyses have shown us that differences persist between and within groups of women, for individuals must contend with multiple, cross-cutting forms of identity, exclusion, and belonging (Crenshaw 1991; Collins 1998). As Colen (1995; cf. Ginsburg and Rapp 1995) insists, the work of social and physical reproduction is valued and allotted differently depending on an individual's position within other social hierarchies, including race and class. Only those women whose children rank highly within a given economy of value are supposed to be mothers. In the United States, ideas about good and desired mothers follow ethnic and racial stratifications: white women are supposed to have children, while women of color, in this case Latinas, are tied to uncontrolled and uncontrollable reproduction (cf. Chavez 2008). We also find the abiding belief that the mothering instincts of women of color, often immigrants, are more profitably diverted into caring for the children of white, middle-class women. Proper supervision and care of their own children, who are also understood to be less desirable members of society, becomes secondary (cf. Romero 2011).

Accordingly, *Domestic Economies* situates the processes of "Americanness," of belonging, *inside* the home, in the everyday struggle to make a living and to make a life. In so doing, it illustrates the concomitant production of the domestic sphere—the quintessentially intimate domain—with domestic, or national, borders (McClintock 1995; Stoler 1995, 2002; Kaplan 1998).

Los Angeles, Immigration, and the American Dream

If home- and nation-making are concurrent and interconnected projects, the location of these homes in Los Angeles is also notable. LA serves as an exemplary site in which to examine the simultaneous making of "Americanness" and difference—especially of the interplay between Americanness and the labor of immigrants from Mexico and Central America. Indeed, from the inception of U.S. control, Mexicans have been a key foil to Americanness-as-whiteness in LA. The Treaty of Guadalupe Hidalgo, which ended the Mexican-American War, specified citizenship for Mexicans wishing to remain in territories conquered by the United States, but in application never lived up to its spirit (Menchaca 1993; Gutiérrez 1995). Individual states could legally impose restrictions on citizenship, and they availed themselves of this freedom to ensure that the right type of people would maintain political control. The new state of California, consciously working to erase any trace of its Mexican past, to *become* "American," allowed only white males to vote, thereby denying rights to most Mexicans, who were Indians or mestizos (Menchaca 1993: 588).

This move further ratified the presumption that Americanness was whiteness, rendering Mexicans as immutable foreigners—a project that secured both the ideological and material grounds of difference. For middle-class status anchors both Americanness and whiteness, and especially in LA, class privilege has always relied on the labor of immigrants. Conveniently, classifying Japanese, Chinese, and (the majority of) Mexican inhabitants as nonwhite created the necessary workforce to sustain LA's "American" population (e.g., Lowe 1996; Ngai 2004).

Immigrants, especially Mexican immigrants, have been crucial to each of the city's economic booms, but their reception has been ambivalent at best. Often invisible, immigrants were seen as a necessary ill in times of prosperity and a pernicious presence during economic downturns. These (racialized) perspectives joined with immigrants' economic contributions to mold a white Angeleno identity.

First, the city itself expanded through attempts at "Protestant racial purification" (Scott and Soja 1996: 4). Originally part of Mexico, LA grew by over 200,000 people in the last quarter of the nineteenth century (1996: 4); most of these new arrivals were WASPs, often retirees, from the Midwest, lured through concerted efforts to whiten the city (Davis 1990). The majority of these new settlers were white, economically prosperous individuals who wanted to escape the perceived deleterious effects of large, overcrowded cities like New York or Chicago.

LA's Anglo elites, themselves fairly recent arrivals, had set out to build a paradigmatically "American" (read: white) city, and this required a particular demographic (cf. Hise 2004; Deverell 2005; Molina 2006). Accordingly, they promoted LA as an Eden—a place of health, wealth, and leisure—successfully targeting large numbers of relatively well-off, white Protestants. These migrants sought space, privacy, and homogeneity, convinced that this would prevent the conflicts that plagued contemporary urban areas (Weinstein 1996).

Initially, LA prospered through agriculture, real estate, and leisure services. The depression of the mid-1890s, however, forced a rethinking of the economic base, and at the turn of the century, Angelenos increasingly turned to industrial production (Scott and Soja 1996: 5). The years between 1900 and 1920 witnessed unprecedented economic development, fueled by the growth of the ports, aircraft manufacturing, and oil refineries. Importantly, it was immigrants who provided the labor force. Mexicans began arriving in droves to work in the railroads, agriculture, and the city's fledgling industries; by 1920, they comprised the largest immigrant group in LA (1996: 6).

During the 1920s, the economy continued to grow, as did the number of immigrants, prompting increased unease about their presence.

The 1924 Johnson-Reed Act, which instituted national origin quotas, further compounded this discomfort. Although this law did not set quotas for Mexicans, it established a legal regime, maintained through paperwork and surveillance at the border, that effectively rendered large numbers of them "illegal" (Ngai 2004). Fears about this "illegal," dangerous population only intensified after the stock market crash in 1929, when economic anxiety led to increased xenophobia and, by 1930 to the forced deportation of Mexicans; between 1930 and 1933, LA lost one-third of its Mexican population (Valadez Torres 2005).

World War II led to a strong resurgence of LA's economy and with it renewed Mexican migration. During the war, the Bracero program brought Mexicans on temporary visas to work in agriculture and railroads (cf. Daniels 2004; Hayes-Bautista 2004; Ngai 2004). The war, however, also reinvigorated racism in Los Angeles, culminating in the Zoot Suit riots in 1943 (cf. Sanchez 1993).

In the postwar era, LA's economy flourished once again—gaining particular strength from Hollywood, an expanding housing market, electronics manufacturing, and a newly powerful defense industry (Scott and Soja 1996: 9)—and with it the population of immigrant laborers. In addition, business owners, especially large agriculturalists, lobbied successfully to extend the Bracero program, for the continued presence of imported and undocumented Mexican workers kept wages low (Ngai 2004). Yet, as before, the growing number of immigrants was greeted with suspicion; increased alarm over "illegals" resulted in Operation Wetback, which saw the deportation of about 1 million Mexicans, whether citizens or immigrants, between 1953 and 1955 (Valdez Torres 2005: 32).

The end of the Bracero program in 1964 and the Immigration Act of 1965, which restricted Mexican (and Latin American) immigration for the first time, created a surge in undocumented migration, especially to Los Angeles, whose thriving economy continued to rely on cheap, immigrant labor. For the first time, more women than men began to arrive in LA, shifting the balance away from farm work and industrial manufacturing to service sector and sweatshop labor. Beginning in the 1970s, global economic transformations altered the nature of LA's economy, splitting the workforce into well-paid, high-skilled "managers, business executives, scientists, engineers, designers, and celebrities and many others in the entertainment industry" (Scott and Soja 1996: 12), and their low-skilled counterparts whose labor in the service sector enables middle- and upper-class lifestyles. The economic calamities and civil unrest that swept through Central America in the 1970s and 1980s also precipitated the influx of Central Americans into LA. Always "illegal" in the public imagination, Mexicans and Central Americans are seamlessly folded into a single category, the "foreigner-within" (Lowe 1996: 5).

This "re-Latinization of Los Angeles" (Soja and Scott 1996: 16) began in the late 1960s with increased migration, but reached critical mass only in the 1980s with the rapid influx of undocumented Mexicans and Central Americans. In 1970, LA's population was 70 percent Anglo (Soja and Scott 1996: 14). However, by 2008 Anglos were in the minority, 48.7 percent, while the Latino population had grown to 47.7 percent.[9]

Fueling LA's economic miracle, the presence of immigrants has therefore been crucial to the city's white inhabitants from the start. As "illegal" or permanently foreign, immigrants provided the obverse of an Anglo identity. Equally important, this group has made possible the prosperity that defines white middle-class subjectivities. At the turn of the millennium in LA, employers in large part derived their sense of self from their class position and subsequent efforts to reproduce it, and this continued to depend on the availability of immigrant (domestic) workers. Yet the perceived dangers of immigration from Mexico and Central America endure: the media, scholars, and politicians still characterize these immigrants as a contagion that threatens the very existence of the American way (cf. Huntington 2004).

Los Angeles, then, has always been exceptional and a preview of what's to come for the rest of the country; its very roots imagine it as the definitive "American" city, one that assessed the mistakes of older places and used these lessons to produce an authentically "American" place. However, in its present and future forms, LA's destiny, and the fate of "Americanness," is never secure. It remains exposed to increasing numbers of outsiders, threatened by its own "foreign" past. It is in this way that, in the contemporary moment, LA most stands for the national future.

Fieldwork and Fieldworker

Carmen greeted me excitedly through a small window as she jangled the keys to the front gate. She and I had arrived in Guatemala City two days earlier and each headed off to our respective homes. This morning, my sister had walked with me from my grandmother's house, three blocks away, to meet Carmen, who always stayed with her former employers when she came to Guatemala. Finally landing on the right key, Carmen threw open the gate and gave me an emphatic hug. I introduced her to my sister, who wasn't staying, and after assuring my sister that she would take care of me, Carmen directed me to follow her in. We had planned to go for a walk, but she had to get ready first.

Inside, Carmen led me directly to Don Mario, whom she'd known for fifty years and frequently referred to as her other father. At the age of twelve, Carmen ran away to Guatemala City; there, she landed a job working as a maid for Don Mario and his late wife Doña Clara, who were kind to her, always sympathetic and supportive. A few years later, she got pregnant and had to leave them, but Don Mario and Doña Clara continued to help her out, providing both advice and practical assistance whenever possible. Even after Carmen departed for Los Angeles, they continued to be close, as Doña Clara kept an eye on Carmen's sons. Now, when Carmen returned to Guatemala on her yearly pilgrimage, she went directly to Don Mario's.

Introducing me to Don Mario, then, was the first thing on Carmen's agenda that morning. Opening the door to the house, she called out his name, grabbed me by the hand, and pulled me into his office. She explained that I was a friend from LA and that she was going to show me the neighborhood. We exchanged greetings, and then Carmen gave me a tour of the house, taking me through the living room, dining area, kitchen, and bedrooms. Walking into the kitchen, she pointed directly to the new microwave, which she'd purchased the previous day after noticing that the old one was emitting sparks. It was top-of-the-line, she assured me—only the finest for Don Mario.

Carmen's place in this house had shifted greatly over the years: from servant to guest with the wherewithal to purchase expensive items for her former employers. Nevertheless, she had not been able to shed her previous self entirely, for she still slept in Alma's, the maid's, room when she visited. This tiny room, a narrow space with two twin beds, a television, and its own bathroom, was the archetypical maid's quarters, smaller and starker than the parts of the home occupied by employers. Such spatial distinctions reproduce relations of power, reminding all the inhabitants of the house of their particular locations within social hierarchies. But Carmen found herself in an interstitial place: simultaneously welcome as guest and relegated to the maid's room, she remained less than equal, yet she was more than she had been before LA.

Carmen's new position, her changing location within local regimes of value, was enabled by her experiences in the United States. This became ever more clear on our walk that morning. After showing me the house, brushing her hair, and reviewing everything she'd done for the last two days, down to the coffee and bread she'd eaten for breakfast, she was ready to "*salir a vagar*" (go out and wander). She was feeling restless, and besides, she wanted me to see her neighborhood.

Our walk took us away from her quiet street, across a busy thoroughfare, past McDonald's, and toward some tourist shops. These were located a short distance from several major hotels and next to an expensive shopping area, restaurants and boutiques frequented by the wealthy. We visited several stores, looking at Guatemalan textiles and other souvenirs. Every time we walked into a store, a salesperson would scurry over, eager to help us. And each time, Carmen delivered the same response: we were only looking around, she had just arrived from LA, and she was staying nearby. This unchanging refrain foregrounded her new self—she was different now, a successful visitor from the north. Carmen was keen to show off this achievement, expecting that a Guatemalan audience, unfamiliar with life in the United States, would be more easily impressed than her peers in LA.

More than that, as an accomplished immigrant, she interacted differently with these shops; once a maid, supermarket clerk, and waitress struggling to find food, she now walked through these places, the domain of tourists and well-to-do Guatemalans, as a potential customer; she had become someone who *would* enter these stores and *could* buy something there. Her transformation also manifested palpably in the ways Carmen strolled through the city. After thirty years in Los Angeles, Guatemala City looked, felt, and meant something completely different to her. The streets were now small, dirty, and unfamiliar, a temporary inconvenience, not a daily cross to bear. She walked gingerly, trying not to get her white sneakers dirty and looking over every new store, always comparing it to Los Angeles. Her comments, her movements, her attitude—all of these marked her as a visitor, as no longer of this place. And it was this new status, gained through migration, that afforded her these possibilities in the first place.

I experienced a similar shift, as the meaning of each place and of myself in it, changed with Carmen's presence. I knew this neighborhood well, for my grandmother lived there, but I had always occupied it as an upper-class-Guatemalan-cum-*gringa*.[10] What this meant, effectively, was a well-developed fear of the streets, since insecurity suffuses the imaginations of wealthy Guatemalans, who live behind gates and barbed wire, protecting their homes with elaborate alarm systems, dogs, and, at times, armed bodyguards. From this outlook, walking leaves you prone to attack and is thus to be avoided—the street is best navigated in a locked car, preferably armored or protected by bodyguards. Although no one in my immediate family lives under such dire protective measures, I was nevertheless socialized into this sense of constant danger. With Carmen, however, the fear dissipated, for I was no longer myself—at least not the self usually highlighted in this context. Instead, I was a fieldworker, an "American" student, learning about a new place. If Carmen's triumphant return allowed her to move about in different ways, my newfound role as researcher also altered, at least momentarily, my relationship to these streets. Through migration, then, Carmen and I came to occupy radically different places, both physically and metaphorically, the ground literally shifting beneath our new selves.

The possibility for us to converge here, blocks from where we both started out, required that we each travel a tremendous distance; migration and life in the United States transformed us into different kinds of people, presenting options not readily available in Guatemala. Carmen was able to make a better living and to fulfill her lifelong dream of learning to read. I became an anthropologist, studying "maids," assuredly a topic in which I would have had little academic interest without the distance provided by the United States. Only in the United States could we have met in this way. Of course, our experiences in the United States have also varied enormously: even as there are more opportunities here, inequalities persist, and your social location continues to shape who and what you can become: I became an academic and at sixty-five Carmen continued to clean houses.

I bring up this story to emphasize my background, which played a major role in the ways I understood and interacted with the subject of domestic service and immigrant women I met in LA. Born in Guatemala and raised in a household with servants, I came to the United States at the age of eight. In upstate New York, I quickly learned English and became as "American" as the rest of my friends. However, becoming a full-fledged *gringa* required more than letting go of my Guatemalan ways; in the United States, my Guatemalan privilege became an encumbrance and an embarrassment, something that I couldn't shed fast enough, although, of course, it was impossible to separate myself from it. I highlight this only to explain how it shaped my interest in domestic service and how it inflected all of the interactions I had while doing fieldwork.

Conducting fieldwork, I found myself not only doing research between two very different worlds, those of native-born employers and immigrant domestic workers, but occupying an in-between place in each of these. I do not mean in-between as in between these two sides; finding domestic workers and employers who had no relationship to one another, I avoided becoming an intermediary. Rather, sharing both similarities and differences with each of these groups, I constantly had to negotiate myself and my position, especially among immigrant women.

While my research examined both domestic workers and their employers, the bulk of my time in Los Angeles was spent with immigrant women, whom I met in a variety of ways. I began with two different organizations, the Domestic Workers Group (DWG) and the Sparkle and Shine Cooperative (the Co-op), a group of six women who cleaned houses together. When I arrived in LA, I was determined to meet domestic workers on my own, but soon found out that it was not always so easy. It therefore became more practical to go through these groups and to get to know their members, who then introduced me to friends and family.

I spent a considerable amount of time with each of these organizations. Aside from attending DWG meetings and events, I regularly accompanied Josefina, the group's organizer, on her outreach efforts. Together, we would the ride the buses, visit domestic employment agencies, and hang out in parks where nannies congregate with their charges. We handed out information on the rights of domestic workers and listened as countless women related their particular stories. This experience proved invaluable, teaching me about the occupation itself but also about different ways of moving through and inhabiting the city. I also became a regular presence at the Co-op, sitting in on weekly meetings, participating in their yearly retreat, helping in the office, providing rides to work, and translating during job estimates.

As I became closer to members of both organizations, I started spending time with them in other contexts and meeting their friends and family members, many of whom I got to know quite well. In the main, my time in LA revolved around the concerns of daily life. The immigrant women I knew told me all about their jobs and employers, tried to sell me beauty products, gossiped about friends, demanded to know about my social life, and confided in me about their husbands, boyfriends, and children. They called me with daily updates and generously invited me to their homes for meals, coffee, or just to hang out. They also took me to parties, friends' houses, and meetings of other organizations to which they belonged. I drove people to the store when they needed to purchase things in bulk or just buy something heavy. We shopped across the city, at the 99-Cent Store, Target, the alleyways of the garment district, and Costco, among others. I also took people to work, where they would often let me watch but would rarely allow me to lift a finger.

Ironically, perhaps, it was the fact of being Guatemalan, especially my native Spanish skills, that made my research possible. Speaking the same language and sharing a claim to another world, however different our claims might be, gave me an in, a way to relate and to be recognizable to immigrant domestic workers. Yet, while there was something familiar about me, I was also patently different: my skin was lighter, I spoke English fluently, I was in graduate school, and I had a car. My privilege was evident, but not as easy to characterize as it would have been in Guatemala. In the United States, social hierarchies are differently organized, and for Mexican and Central American women in LA, the operative experiential distinction remained immigrant versus native-born. Growing up here, knowing English, having an American passport—these reflected my "American" privilege, but my accession into this position was fully informed by my social standing in Guatemala. And so I remained firmly in between the two worlds; I wasn't so much Guatemalan or American as a strange admixture of both.

The whole time I was in the field, then, I found myself playing a game of bait-and-switch: offering up my Guatemalanness to reassure people that I wasn't just another *gringa*, but asserting my *gringa*-ness to negate my Guatemalan upper-class status, which I naïvely imagined was possible. At times I successfully walked the line between the two, but often I fell flat on my face. In these moments, it was clear that I was fooling no one but myself and that my privilege, however it was defined, was always visible. That they sometimes chose to overlook it did not mean that they were not acutely aware of my difference.

These uncomfortable situations wound up being incredibly instructive. Through them, I was able to see just how immigrant women constituted themselves in relation to upper-class Latin Americans and to *gringos*—what they valued in each and what was to be repudiated. In their reactions to me, I learned a lot about who these women were and who they wanted to be; in particular, the need to assert themselves as moral, valuable, and intelligent seemed especially relevant in relation to their marginality.

The other side of my work, research with employers, produced a different set of concerns. While the initial approach proved easier, sustaining durable relations with these women was more difficult. Most of them worked and had young children, leaving them little free time. Since I did not connect with them through their jobs, my time with them was more limited.

I met employers through personal contacts, as well as through two women's organizations. The first, a networking association for professional women, mainly provided a venue for meeting individuals, while the second, a mothers' group, became an important site in itself. I joined this mothers' group, attended bimonthly meetings, participated in their book club, was on their email loop, and helped out at a few special events. The only member with no children, I certainly stood out, but the mothers were very open to my presence, generously telling me about their daily lives and concerns, at times even thanking me for my interest.

I spent a lot of time with several couples in their thirties; all of them had children under two and were just reentering the workforce after completing professional training. As such, they were trying to figure out who they were as individuals, as they struggled to reconcile a new family with the pressures of the working world.

If my privilege informed the ways I interacted with domestic workers, it also shaped my relationships with employers, whose lives seemed both terribly familiar and radically different from my own. There were a lot of commonalities, as I was working with women who were well educated, had professional careers, and belonged primarily to my generational cohort. On the other hand, we inhabited separate realities: while I was in graduate school, accustomed to life in New York, and completely distanced from the world of work, these women had high-powered jobs, husbands, children, and houses. Because of our sameness and because at first they seemed unaware of their privilege,

I found myself being critical of their choices. As I got to know them better, however, I began to appreciate their points of view. Most of all, I realized that they were themselves conflicted and felt reined in by social expectations, economic anxiety, and concern for their children. Like the immigrant women who worked in their homes, they were just trying to get through each day as best they could.

I originally conducted fifteen months of ethnographic fieldwork from 2002 to 2003, fully immersed in the daily lives of the women whose stories make up this book. In the intervening years, I have kept up with a number of individuals through frequent phone calls and less-frequent visits to Los Angeles. This long-term perspective lends analytic distance and added context to the immediacy and intensity of the initial research. This book is about the crunch that both groups of women experience as they try to make a living, define themselves as successful, and raise accomplished children. The lives of these women have undergone transition since I met them, as they and their children have moved through different biographical moments. Yet they continue to jostle against these constraints, albeit in different manifestations. Childcare, for instance, fades as a concern as children attend school and become old enough to care for themselves. Nevertheless, just as finding the time and income to support this necessity wanes, parents begin to balance the schedules and costs of after-school activities, college preparation programs, and so on. Eventually, especially for middle-class families, the skyrocketing costs of college take center stage, placing an even more unreasonable squeeze on finances.

While the local and national terrains have been transformed in the wake of the financial crisis and subsequent recession, I argue that the tightening economy only heightened the everyday struggles and experiences that I followed so closely from 2002 to 2003. For employers, middle-class status became even more insecure, as individual families now had to balance the same requirements on a tighter budget. Immigrant women, on the other hand, had to contend with job losses, as their employers found that cutting back on household work or childcare was a relatively convenient way of reducing spending. If the financial crisis aggravated the already precarious economic position of most immigrants, an increased focus on immigration, "illegality," and deportation only exacerbated it. Many domestic employers became concerned with legal documents for the first time. Additionally, a surge in workplace raids encouraged factories to tighten hiring restrictions. In the last ten years, everyone's hold on the American Dream has become more tenuous, the "immigration crisis" has captured the national dialogue, and these two have become progressively interlinked in the public imagination. Thus, the worries and stresses I first observed in the early 2000s have only magnified for everyone.

Overview of the Book

This book attends to both immigrant and native-born women, individuals on either side of domestic work. However, my discussion of immigrant women's lives is more intimate, delving beyond the immediate pressures of paid work, household management, and children. This reflects both deliberate choice and methodological constraint. The vagaries of fieldwork are well known. The process is uneven, serendipitous, and improvisational; every opening piles on every obstacle, lending particular shape to our knowledge. Access, then, is crucial—the type of access especially so. As I indicate above, my time with employers was more limited than my time with immigrant women. Both were generous with their time, but immigrant women were more so. Perhaps they were more amenable to my presence because I had something to offer, such as rides that would help them avoid the drudgeries of public transportation, if only for one morning or afternoon. As well, this could be a consequence of their social invisibility. Individuals who feel acutely erased, unrecognized, are perhaps more willing and open to sharing their stories when someone expresses interest in listening (Myerhoff 1978). On the other hand, access was harder to negotiate with employers, individuals whom I could not accompany to work and to whom I could only provide a sympathetic ear. Further, as multiple scholars have remarked, it is often much more difficult to find a way in when "studying up" (Nader 1972) or "sideways" (Ortner 2010).[11] Powerful individuals and institutions tend to guard their boundaries more carefully, knowing all too well the vulnerabilities entailed in being a subject of academic inquiry. Of a higher or equal social standing relative to the anthropologist proposing to study them, members of these groups feel no obligation to please. I experienced this firsthand: both groups of women were harried and overextended, but employers more easily said no.

Despite these disparities in access, the story that emerged was one of remarkable parallels, underlining similar preoccupations and aspirations. Throughout these chapters, the invisibility of women, of immigrants, and of reproductive labor recurs again and again, as does their continued importance to processes of U.S. nation-making. To be sure, immigrant domestic workers and native-born employers inhabit distinct positions within these processes, and therefore my approach to each varies. Even as native-born women wrestle with gendered exclusions, nobody challenges their place *within*. Racial, national, and class privilege conspire to render their "Americanness" a certainty. While the erasure of reproductive labor creates persistent hurdles, they can wield their economic and racial privilege to mitigate these pressures. By contrast, immigrant women do not have the economic or racial capital to cushion the effects of gendered inequities. They live on the margins, with seemingly little recourse for improvement. Still, as I argue above, analyzing their lives solely through the lens of abjection—their poverty, the abuses they endure at work, their racialization as immigrants—works to fix them at the margins. Therefore, I provide a more intimate view of these women's lives, exploring their hopes, dreams, and stories in fuller detail, to stress their centrality to as well as their position inside the American Dream. Their commitment to and assertions of belonging foreground that they are already "American," actively shaping and reshaping the meanings of this term.

The five chapters that follow consider different aspects of the give-and-take among invisibility, inequality, and belonging. They argue that the processes of "Americanness" require inequality, but that this inequality has to be invisible. In other words, the American Dream is only possible if we classify certain people and particular types of work as less worthy and less valuable. However, these processes will not function smoothly if we admit this, and thus we must find ways to disavow, or at the very least to ignore, these disparities. Focusing on the unseen and unrecognized, I seek to illustrate not only the underside of the American Dream but also the different ways in which putative outsiders make claims on this Dream.

I begin by looking at racialization and then shift into an examination of gendered exclusions, moving from the marginalization of particular types of people to the devaluation and revaluation of reproductive labor. The first two chapters sift through the coincident production and erasure of immigrants' difference, situating these processes in the city and inside middle-class homes. Chapter 1 considers Los Angeles, the material context of this study, discussing how each group of women conceives of and inhabits the city. Homing in on the immigrant version of Los Angeles, it shows how everyday spatial practices reflect, challenge, and affirm social hierarchies—how immigrants' difference is simultaneously materialized and hidden. Chapter 2 scrutinizes how middle-class employers understand the American Dream: how they define success, how they have an increasing reliance on domestic workers to achieve their goals, and how the presence of an immigrant inside the home disrupts and reproduces the logics of belonging. Forced to see inequality, employers reinscribe immigrants' difference, thereby reproducing the very processes of middle-class and the borders of Americanness.

I center the remaining chapters on the in/visibility of reproductive labor, discussing diverse renderings of the relationship between self, work, and social value. Chapter 3 inquires into how neoliberal forms of belonging, which negate the value of reproductive labor, confine the choices available to middle-class, native-born mothers. These mothers aspire to success in the workplace as well as to raising accomplished children, but these aims increasingly conflict with each other. Further, even as they devote time and effort to their children, these women are embedded in a system that erases the import of their endeavors, rendering hollow their value as persons.

The final two chapters analyze how immigrant women, twice marginalized by their immigrant status and the devaluation of their labor, simultaneously reproduce and interrupt the logics of their alterity. Focusing on reproductive labor, they strive to make themselves visible and to affirm their value as Americans. Chapter 4 points out that, unlike their native-born counterparts, Mexican and Central American women define themselves through their roles as mothers rather than workers. I investigate two separate efforts to organize domestic workers, demonstrating that these women locate success in providing for their children rather than in paid employment. Chapter 5 argues that this alternative reckoning of success produces a more expansive version of "Americanness." Underscoring personal stories of success and hardship, I trace how immigrants claim their place within the nation, how they experience belonging and exclusion.

CHAPTER 1

Producing In/Visibility
in Los Angeles

Monday morning. I was supposed to meet Josefina at the metro stop on Wilshire and Vermont, two busy commercial streets that intersect just west of downtown, on the edges of Koreatown, an area filled with Mexican and Central American immigrants. A Mexican immigrant in her mid-forties, Josefina had worked in various homes as a live-in nanny before becoming an organizer at the Domestic Workers Group. As organizer, she rode the buses several times a week, handing out information about the organization and about workers' rights. She also visited domestic employment agencies and spoke to women looking for a job.

Over the course of fieldwork, I frequently accompanied Josefina on her morning rounds, but this would be my very first trip, and I was eager to get going. She had told me to be there at 8 AM, but when I arrived, she was nowhere to be seen. Impatiently, I watched three buses stop on Wilshire and a couple on Vermont. People got off a bus and scurried onto another bus or ran down the escalator into the metro. I also noticed a number of street vendors sitting behind makeshift tables or just standing with bags. They were selling tamales, *pan dulce*, bread, *atole*, *champurrado*,[1] and Spanish-language newspapers. After twenty minutes, I began to worry that I'd been stood up, and I was about to give up when I saw Josefina squeeze out of an overflowing bus. She was incensed: she'd waited half an hour, watching two packed buses go by before a third finally stopped to pick her up.

But she was here now and didn't want to waste any more time. She grabbed my arm and led me down the escalator. We'd almost reached the metro when I remembered that I didn't have a ticket. I headed back up toward the automated ticket machines, but Josefina stopped me, pointing instead to a row of vendors. The tokens were cheaper, she explained: at a dollar a pop, I would save twenty-five cents with each one. I purchased two tokens and dropped one into the automated machine, getting myself a ticket with a transfer.[2] We hurried back to the escalator and reached the platform just in time to get on the train to Universal City.

The metro ride took about twenty minutes, and at Universal City we switched to a bus. As we waited to board, Josefina distributed flyers to the people standing near us. Then a policeman or maybe a transit guard joined the line, and Josefina stopped. She seemed nervous, glancing at him repeatedly. Luckily, he walked away after a few minutes, just as the bus opened its doors. We got on, and I handed the driver my transfer. Josefina was not happy: I wasn't supposed to *give* him the transfer. We were getting on another bus after this one, and without the transfer I would have to use my second token. We walked to the back of the bus, sat next to a woman on her way to work, and began chatting. After exchanging the obligatory complaints about public transportation, she told us about her job cleaning hotel rooms, and we gave her a pamphlet detailing workers' rights.

At one of the stops, a transit guard got on the bus. Josefina and the other woman flashed him their monthly passes without really looking at him. I showed him my ticket and, without thinking, said something to him then turned and said something to the other two in Spanish. Josefina stared blankly into space and neither she nor the other woman responded, sitting quietly until the following stop, when the transit guard left.

Half an hour later we reached Ventura Boulevard, where we would transfer to *another* bus. Getting off the bus, I spotted a Coffee Bean[3] and, nodding toward it, told Josefina that I needed caffeine. She frowned and shot me a look that said this wasn't a place where we should/could/ would enter and then informed me that we'd be there soon. A woman approached to ask if we helped people find work. Josefina handed her a pamphlet and told her that the organization's members sometimes helped each other with job referrals, although that wasn't the group's primary aim. Our bus pulled up, and to Josefina's dismay, I had to use my remaining token. We found seats next to Silvia, who was on her way to the very agency where we hoped to hand out information. Silvia hated going to this agency; the owner was always rude and usually sent more than one person to the same job to make extra commission. She didn't know why she bothered to go, especially since it seemed that no one was hiring.

This last leg of our trip took about fifteen minutes—the whole trip, about two hours. But, finally, we arrived. We landed further up Ventura Boulevard, in Tarzana, in front of a discount clothing store and the entrance to the 101 East, across the street from a gas station. Then we crossed the street and walked to a mini-mall about halfway down the block. The agency was on the second floor of this otherwise unremarkable strip mall. I saw an International House of Pancakes (IHOP), a cell phone store, and a dry cleaner; it looked just like every other mini-mall in Los Angeles—and they are everywhere. Josefina suggested that I follow Silvia into the agency; Josefina couldn't go in, because they would recognize her as a troublemaker. So I stepped into the agency but lingered by the door while Silvia looked for a seat. The place was awful: there was no bathroom, no privacy, no pay phone, nothing. It was one room, and it didn't have enough chairs. Some women sat and others stood while they waited, often for hours, to see if a job became available. The owner presided over the room from her desk in the back corner. She interviewed everyone who came in, reviewing each person's application, taking the ten-dollar fee, and asking questions. Since the room was open, everything was public and every last detail of every conversation was audible. One woman came in hoping to find work for her two granddaughters, who had just arrived from Mexico. Embarrassed that everyone could hear, she looked around the room and shrugged, appealing for understanding. Her plea elicited no sympathy, only raised eyebrows and a series of clucks: What was this woman thinking? The poor girls were sixteen at most. Unmoved, the owner accepted their applications—and their twenty dollars.

After thirty minutes or so, I left to find Josefina, who was sitting around the corner. She couldn't wait at the mini-mall, as the last time she'd been there the mall's security guard had asked her to leave. We headed to the gas station across the street, where we could use the bathroom and the pay phone. I mentioned coffee and gestured to the IHOP, but Josefina shook her head and kept walking. This refusal reminded me of her response to the Coffee Bean. She had looked through both places as though they didn't exist at all, as though she couldn't imagine going into either one.

Inside the gas station, I found the coffee while Josefina ordered food from the taco stand. This surprised me at first—a taco stand inside what otherwise looked like every other gas station mini-mart I'd ever seen, complete with maps, trinkets, postcards, junk food, cold drinks, coffee, and so on. We paid $3.50 for a beef taco and two cups of coffee and went outside to enjoy our breakfast. We sat in front of the store, facing the gas pumps, at one of two round cement tables with umbrellas on top to shield you from the sun. Once again, I was a little thrown off, as I realized that we had *walked* to a gas station and were sitting there, eating and hanging out. I'd never spent more than five minutes at a gas station before, but then I usually drive to gas stations.

We spent some time at this spot, running to catch up with a few women as they got off the bus and talking to women who had been at the agency all morning and popped out to use the bathroom or to grab a quick taco. I watched as a stream of cars, mostly Toyotas and Hondas but also some luxury models, came in and out of the station. Drivers stopped, pumped their gas, sometimes ran inside to get coffee or maybe to use the bathroom, and then drove off. They didn't seem to notice us, and after a while I was so focused on finding women going to the agency (especially after repeated visits to this place) that I stopped looking at drivers or cars.

I tried to strike up a conversation with a woman sitting at the table next to us, but she seemed distracted and uneasy; she didn't want to talk, and she definitely didn't want to take the pamphlet I offered her. As I walked away, a beige Lexus SUV drove up, and she climbed into the front seat. Josefina shook her head and sighed, "Pobrecita, está encerrada"[4] (Poor woman, she is a live-in). Suddenly, I understood: she didn't want her employer, who came to pick her up, to find her talking to me or to see her with information about workers' rights. Josefina explained that gas stations are often close to bus stops, which in many neighborhoods are a long walk from residential streets, so some employers will arrange to meet their employees there.

After a couple of hours at the gas station, Josefina decided that she was done, and we made our way back to the bus stop, where we waited for twenty minutes. Having used my two tokens, I had to pay full price for this ride. Displeased, Josefina chided me, again, for squandering my tokens and made sure that I requested a transfer. We got off after four stops and waited for the express. It was clearly not our day, though; our bus didn't show up for half an hour. As we waited, standing in the hot sun, we chatted with a woman who was with her four-year-old grandson. They were on their way home from work; she only cleaned one house on Mondays, because she had to babysit her grandson that day. The bus finally arrived, and it took us another twenty minutes to get to the metro, and once on the metro, another fifteen minutes to get back to Wilshire and Vermont. We had spent nearly two hours in transit, but Josefina had to keep going; she had to take another bus to get to her office. Fortunately, her bus pulled up almost immediately. We said goodbye and made plans to go out again later in the week.

I begin with this story to underscore the importance of urban space to daily life—how the layout of Los Angeles and everyday struggles to navigate the city help to structure social life and to re/inscribe relations of power (cf. Lefebvre 1991). In particular, I want to punctuate the sense of distance that separates the experiences of domestic workers and their employers. In his much-cited history, Fogelson (1967) aptly labels Los Angeles "the fragmented metropolis." The city certainly feels disjointed, its denizens inhabiting discrete galaxies whose orbits apparently never converge. These pieces create distinct but overlapping versions of the city, an immigrant LA that coexists with the LA of middle-class employers. For even as they seem completely separate and separable, these fragments form part of a deliberate whole, a mosaic that outlines the boundaries of both the city and the nation. As the introduction clarifies, Mexicans and Mexican labor have been and continue to be (now along with Central Americans and their labor) central to the making of Los Angeles as a categorically "American" city.[5] Los Angeles, then, serves as reference for the contemporary American moment— our need for labor from Latin America must remain unseen. We cannot accept that the American Dream hinges on social and economic inequality, and we conceal this truth either by criminalizing immigrants or by erasing their very presence. This chapter focuses on the latter: asking how Mexican and Central American women's difference materializes through their engagement with the city, how this difference is erased (how they are erased) from the "American" imagination, and in turn how this erasure reaffirms their inherent difference. Examining how employers and domestic workers occupy and move through LA, I analyze the literal grounds upon which "immigrant" and "native-born," "domestic worker" and "employer" are made.

Rendering the In/Visible

Rancière (2006) elucidates how in/visibility is firmly embedded in a particular politics; "the distribution of the sensible" within any system defines what we see and hear, what (and who) counts as part of the social world. These processes locate people in a social system, empowering particular positions while disqualifying others "based on a distribution of spaces, time, and forms of activity" (2006: 12). Indeed, "at stake in the division of the sensible is rarely the formal question of visual perception but the social organization and control that is mediated by it" (Mirzoeff 2009: 5). The invisibility of particular bodies therefore highlights the power relations inherent in seeing and being seen. These relationships are always constructed in and through space[6]—for the question is not one of invisible bodies but rather *when* and *where* particular bodies are (or *should be*) invisible.

Los Angeles is a city of distances and of erasures, both literal and figurative. The sprawl, "spatial apartheid" (Davis 1990: 230), overdependence on cars, and minimal public space that characterize it abet the separation of different groups of people, allowing them not to have to see one another. These physical separations lend a particular shape to the city, a built environment that creates and maintains disaffection, exclusion, and class, racial, and gender inequalities (e.g., Soja 1989, 1996; Davis 1990; Fulton 1997; Keil 1998; Bobo et al. 2000; Valle and Torres 2000; Cuff 2000; Low 2008; Deverell and Hise 2010; Sullivan 2014). Yet these gaps are also metaphoric, for as I note in the above story, a sense of detachment exists even when various groups occupy the same place.[7] These erasures are necessary to creating a sense of wholeness[8]—exclusion is crucial to maintaining LA as both a geographic and an imagined place. Nowhere is this more evident than in the often-disproportionate responses to breaches of in/visibility (e.g., Zilberg 2011; Deener 2012). As Zilberg (2011) illuminates, post-9/11 security concerns and neoliberal imperatives converged in a spatial politics that sought to harness the mobility not only of gang members but of Latino immigrants more broadly. Janitors, for example, became problematic when they came together in public to make themselves and their demands visible. Similarly, attempts to regulate (or remove) street vendors (e.g., Bhimji 2010; Rosales 2013) and day laborers (e.g., Esbenshade 2000; Cummings 2011) reflect a violation of the norms of in/visibility. Drawing attention to the unseen, these ruptures underscore spatial expectations. Here I consider the flip side of disruption, asking instead how immigrants remain unremarkable as they inhabit and move through the city, and how this reinscribes their difference. I do so in three parts, looking at residential segregation, different modes of transportation, and distinct habitations of the same places.

Neighborhoods and Mental Maps

Los Angeles[9] is highly dispersed: in 2015, its population of 10 million spread out over four thousand square miles.[10] More importantly, LA is highly segregated by race, ethnicity, and income level. [11] This creates a logic of the city that marks neighborhoods according to who lives there, defining an area's desirability or imagined level of danger by the income levels and racial backgrounds of its residents. In turn, the neighborhoods that individuals inhabit categorize them and locate them in the social hierarchy. These spatial distinctions hold up existing regimes of value, not only reflecting differences but actively producing marginality.

The domestic workers I knew lived in immigrant neighborhoods, just to the west of downtown, primarily in Koreatown, Westlake, Pico Union, and Hollywood. The boundaries between these are porous—each of these areas blends into the next—but they are quite distinct from the wealthier neighborhoods where employers reside. A trip along Santa Monica Boulevard, one of the city's main east–west thoroughfares, highlights the differences between employers' neighborhoods[12] and those inhabited by domestic workers. We begin at the water's edge, in Santa Monica, in front of exclusive hotels that have come under criticism for not paying their cleaning staff a livable wage. We pass Santa Monica, West LA, Beverly Hills, and West Hollywood. This a commercial street, so we do not see private homes, but we see many fashionable restaurants and some fast food places, including a Koo Koo Roo that offers valet parking, office buildings, an art house movie theater, and many Starbucks or Coffee Bean shops. We drive in front of the Century City Mall, a good place to spot celebrities, and past Madonna's record label. We notice at least two Trader Joe's and a Whole Foods, two specialty food stores. Thus far, the only people we have seen on the sidewalks are probably jogging, waiting at a bus stop, or selling flowers or fruit on a street corner. If we were to turn off into a residential street, we would see large houses or expensive apartment complexes with well-manicured lawns.

As we go farther east, past Fairfax Avenue, past the second Trader Joe's, we notice a new Target. Approaching Western Avenue, we begin to see more people walking on the streets, signs are now in Spanish, and the strip malls now have donut shops, 99 Cent stores, and Guatemalan, Mexican, or Salvadoran bakeries. The air is heavier, the smog more visible. The streets are dirtier, the buildings are more run down, and the stores are clustered together. The cars parked on the street and in mini-malls look older. We pass by a Sears and the entrance to the Hollywood Freeway. The farther east we go, the more people we see on the street, walking, waiting for the bus, selling any number of things—fresh fruits and vegetables; homemade tamales, tortillas, or *pupusas*; bus tokens; clothes. Turning onto a side street, we would find apartment buildings that are cheaper, have fewer amenities, and are not as well kept as those on the Westside; there are no swimming pools in these buildings. In a couple miles' distance we have traveled from stylish West Hollywood, filled with popular eateries, bars, gyms, and upscale supermarkets, and into a neighborhood reminiscent of a Central American city.

These changes in the landscape are more than picturesque. Social and economic inequalities work to produce, and are reproduced by, these distinctions. Street vendors, for example, signal economic need: individuals who are out of work or do not earn enough at their jobs supplement their incomes through street sales. People are on the street because they do not have cars; they must walk or use public transportation. Those who do drive generally own older, used, less expensive cars. In addition, pollution gets worse as you travel east; the mountains and the beaches have much better air quality than low-lying interior areas. To make matters worse, housing in these areas is overcrowded, dilapidated, and increasingly overpriced. People must move farther and farther away from the city's center to find affordable housing. A friend whose mother works as a domestic worker told me that to find an apartment where she could pay the rent, her mother had to move to

Pomona—on the eastern border of LA County and about an hour from where she used to live, and even farther from her work.

If immigrant neighborhoods are characterized by their proximity to bus routes and stores, by overcrowded apartments, busy sidewalks, and street vendors, employer neighborhoods are notably quiet. The more secluded they are, the more desirable; someone who lived in the Hollywood Hills explained to me that her house was an "escape" from the madness of the "city." Houses are not as close together in these sections of LA, and the majority of residents live in single-family homes. In addition, these areas have no public space—residents do not want the "city" encroaching on them, and public space would only encourage the (visible) presence of the people they seek to escape. Moreover, the bus does not reach many exclusive neighborhoods, especially those in the canyons or the Santa Monica Mountains. As well, there are no sidewalks in many of these zones, because nobody walks—at least not anyone who lives there. Walking through Beverly Hills early in the morning, the only people I saw on foot were joggers, power walkers, and paid domestic employees on their way to work.

Attached to these tangible distinctions among neighborhoods are ideas about each place and those who inhabit it. How individuals link danger and ease/comfort to particular areas of the city is closely connected to where they live. For example, residents of wealthier areas assiduously avoid the city's downtown. I was surprised when a lifelong Westside resident asked me for the best way to get to the courthouse, downtown, for jury duty. She rarely visited this area and worried about finding suitable and safe parking. She also chastised me, more than once, for putting myself at "risk" by spending time in "those" parts of town.

Similarly, most of the immigrant women I knew preferred to spend time in those neighborhoods where they felt "safe," where Spanish was spoken, where stores were affordable and familiar, and where they were surrounded by others like themselves. For undocumented immigrants, "safety" depends on the ability to blend in, to pass unnoticed. Invisibility is crucial here, and I learned this the hard way: when I spoke to the transit guard and then said something to Josefina in Spanish, I unwittingly made her visible, calling attention to myself, to her, and to the fact that we were not speaking English. Luckily, the moment passed quickly, if uncomfortably, but potential danger lurks behind any such encounter, behind any exchange that can transform a faceless immigrant into an individual.

This sense of discomfort goes beyond the fear of somehow getting "caught." Even among immigrants who have papers, it shapes everyday interactions, or lack thereof, with people from different parts of the city, from different racial, national, and economic backgrounds. Members of Sparkle and Shine, a domestic workers' cooperative (the Co-op), made this abundantly clear when a group of students from a local university came by to interview them. The researchers asked a series of questions about the Santa Monica Mountains National Recreation Area (SMMNRA), federally owned parkland on the Westside, wanting to find out why more people of color do not use that park. All of the women responded that although the parks closer to their homes were not always well maintained, the SMMNRA was too far from where they lived. It would take too long, even for those who drove, to get there. Also, one of the members added, she did not like to go to places filled with *gringos*, that is, Anglos, because she and her family, like other Latinos, "*hacemos mucho relajo*" (make too much noise), and they would not want to disturb anyone. The other women nodded emphatically, agreeing that they were put off and intimidated by such places.

Each neighborhood, then, felt off-limits to people from certain sections of the city. More than others, domestic workers had to cross these borders, but when they did, they usually inhabited different places than the area's residents. Thus, Josefina did not want to go into the Coffee Bean or IHOP. Those are not the types of stores she patronized—because they were too expensive, because she did not speak English, and because she felt uncomfortable in a place filled with people who are not like her, that is, (probably) white, wealthier, and not immigrants. Instead, she found locations, like the gas station mini-mart, where she was surrounded by Spanish speakers and could afford the food. Walking around employer neighborhoods with Josefina and other immigrant women, I often felt that we were looking for the few actual places that existed in a sea of emptiness—restaurants, stores, homes that we did not even look at, as though they were not there.

Everyone charts the city according to familiar and unfamiliar places, safe and unsafe areas, habitable and uninhabitable sites—constructing personal "mental maps" that guide their movements (Lynch 1960).[13] As a result, we find multiple, incommensurable versions of the city: clearly the Los Angeles of immigrant domestic workers varied fundamentally from the Los Angeles of their employers. The ways in which individuals talked about the city and, especially, their movements gave concrete expression to these cartographies. Each group defined its own boundaries and made them tangible through physical avoidance of particular zones. In this way, they did not have to see one another, avoiding the discomforts attached to the recognition of difference. These erasures concealed inequality while deepening the distinctions that sustain it.

Modes of Transportation: Cars and Buses

Along with the neighborhoods in which people resided, individuals' experience of Los Angeles turns on the mode of transportation they use. How people move through the city defines how they know Los Angeles, and it gives form to their daily lives and social relationships. Cars and driving, for example, frame the lives of drivers. LA is notorious for its traffic and freeways; the first thing many people think of when they think about LA is cars. As I prepared to leave for fieldwork, everyone I talked to about my project asked if I liked to drive. I always brushed off the question, assuming it was not a big deal. I understood that I would have to drive in LA, but I did not expect it to become such an important part of my life. Five minutes into my LA experience, however, I was caught in a traffic jam, and suddenly I got it. Driving would become a central and defining practice of my life in Los Angeles. It was not just driving, but everything around it—calculating traffic and distances, complaining about rising gas prices, listening for Sigalerts (accident and traffic stoppage reports), finding suitable parking, and making all of my important phone calls while driving—that came to structure my life.

Driving plays a crucial role in the lives of Angelenos. The city is so spread out that people work far from where they live, and drivers spend a good part of their day in traffic or thinking about how to avoid traffic. One employer regularly left his house at 6 AM, before the morning rush hour, to cut his commute by half an hour. There was no way to escape traffic in the afternoon, however, and dinner conversations at his house were often peppered with talk about his ride home or things he heard on the radio while stuck in traffic. Indeed, people seem to conduct their lives from the car. Wherever you look, drivers are busy talking on the phone. More surprising, perhaps, was a friend's report that her co-worker pumped her milk in the car—a perfect way to save time.

The geographic layout of Los Angeles produces a heavy dependence on the car, creating a very specific kind of sociability or, I should say, lack of sociability. There is little public space in Los Angeles, and people who drive everywhere have little contact with one another. A friend told me, for instance, that after living in LA for about six months he started to get depressed: he was always at work, in the car, or sleeping. He felt that he rarely interacted with people outside of work, and he missed human contact. In a car, even while stuck in traffic, people are detached. They cannot really pay attention to the street, and they do not look at one another. All too often, while driving, I would look into passing cars and see drivers picking their noses. After a number of times, it struck me that people think of their cars as their own private worlds. Sitting in a car makes them feel separate and invisible; they do not look at anyone and they expect that no one looks at them.

As individuals drive from home to work and other private places—supermarkets, shopping malls, restaurants—in parts of the city where they feel safe and at ease, they hardly ever come into contact with people from different social classes or ethnic/racial backgrounds. They drive over uncomfortable, "dangerous" areas on raised freeways that are not integrated into neighborhoods and that, in a sense, render those neighborhoods invisible (cf. Wachs 1996; Avila 2004). If they must take surface streets and actually pass through "undesirable" areas, their cars work to separate and therefore protect them from local residents. For the most part, then, drivers manage to avoid seeing and interacting with people unlike themselves.

If driving defines one way that Angelenos engage with the city and with one another, riding the bus (and walking) provides another perspective on the city as well as a distinct type of sociability. Certainly, getting from one place to another also structures the lives of bus riders, but it does so in an entirely different manner. Bus riders arrange their daily routines according to bus schedules and bus routes. They map the city as a series of bus and metro stops and describe places through their geographic proximity to public transportation. For example, whenever Estela spoke about the houses she cleaned, she would tell me what buses she took to each one, what time she had to leave her house, and how far she had to walk after getting off the bus.

The city also looks different to drivers and bus riders. Walking gives you another view of the built environment. In the car, you notice certain markers—intersections, lights, stop signs—but are moving too fast to look at details. By contrast, when you are on foot, people, houses, front yards, and even sidewalks become meaningful. One morning, I drove Eva to work, and she missed the house that she had been cleaning every week for over a year. When she realized that we had driven past the house, she laughed and explained that she did not recognize it from the car, that the street looked completely different when she was walking.

More importantly, on the street and on the bus, you talk to people. Individuals often take the same buses every day, so they become friends and tell each other about their lives, their work, and everything in between. That is why Josefina rides the buses in the mornings; she meets people in a place where it is not uncommon to strike up a conversation with a stranger, as long as the stranger looks like you or someone you would know. She tells them about her organization, and their stories come pouring out. Every time we went out, we met women who were eager to talk about their work and their lives.

Because people spend so much time on buses, their lives and their stories are intertwined with bus rides. Carmen, for instance, found a job through someone she met on the bus. She and Susana started talking on the bus one morning and became fast friends. They would talk every day, and when Susana had to go back to Honduras for a few months, she asked Carmen if she wanted to take over her job. Twenty years later, they were still friends, and Carmen was still cleaning that house. Carmen also met her ex-boyfriend on the bus. At the time, he was living with someone else, so he wooed her on different buses. Later, she was confronted by his then-girlfriend on a bus. And, much later, she learned from a woman she befriended on the bus that he was cheating on her.

In addition to shaping social interaction and people's daily movements, the differences between driving and relying on the bus highlight a huge disparity. Buses are overcrowded and often not in the best condition. They are slow, and they do not reach all neighborhoods. The bus is read as undesirable and dangerous, because the majority of riders are poor and nonwhite. Tracy, an employer who lived in Beverly Hills, once told me that she thought I was brave, because she would be afraid to get on the bus. When I pressed her further, she could not recall any concrete story or news report, but she was sure that buses were crime-ridden. This is a popular perception, and people who live in affluent areas, those who seek to "escape" city life, do not want bus service near their homes. This means that domestic workers, who already live far from their jobs, spend up to two hours commuting in each direction. Furthermore, since buses do not go to the most exclusive neighborhoods, at the end of a long trip, often on more than one bus, domestic workers have to walk a mile or more, sometimes uphill, to get to work.

Bus service and bus riders are not a priority for the city, in large part because the people who ride the buses are the most disenfranchised and the most invisible. While many immigrants have cars, it is also true that most of the people who ride the bus are people of color and live in lower-income neighborhoods: in 2003, the median income for bus riders was twelve thousand dollars (Streeter 2003: B3). What's more, undocumented immigrants cannot drive, because they are not allowed to have driver's licenses. Many do drive, but the inability to obtain a license presents another hurdle for these individuals, who must opt for the bus or drive without a license and car insurance.[14]

Rising Bus Fares and a Bus Strike

LA's Bus Riders Union (BRU) fights against these inequities and constantly challenges LA's Metropolitan Transportation Authority (MTA), demanding better and expanded bus service. The BRU—a multiethnic coalition whose meetings are simultaneously translated into Korean, Spanish, and English—argues that the MTA is racist and purposely shifts resources away from low-income areas and communities of color. For example, in early 2003, just as the MTA was preparing to unveil its new Gold Line, from downtown to the wealthy suburb of Pasadena, it announced a planned rate hike for buses. The BRU opposed the Gold Line because it cost $869 million, arguing that the MTA was raising fares to pay for rail service to a wealthy community.[15] The proposed increase, to take effect in 2004, would raise the price of monthly passes from $42 to $52, raise the price of tokens, and eliminate transfers.

Whether or not this fare hike was intended to subsidize the Gold Line, it would definitely make life even more impossible for bus riders. For most people who relied on public transit, a ten-dollar increase in the price of a monthly pass presented an unimaginable expense.

Many of the transit-dependent already found bus fares unaffordable, and they used assorted combinations of bus tickets, tokens, and transfers to save as much as possible. This is why Josefina insisted that I purchase tokens rather than buying metro/bus tickets directly, to save twenty-five cents on each ride, an already significant margin that becomes even more meaningful with each additional trip.

Bus riders struggling to make ends meet grew increasingly dismayed about the proposed fare hike. But the MTA appeared to remain indifferent. At the MTA's public hearing on the price increase, the audience was packed with worried bus riders and social activists, but only a handful of the board members were present. Before the meeting started, the chair of the MTA board announced that each person would be given exactly one minute to speak, including time for translation. Of course, anyone who did not speak English was immediately placed at a disadvantage. BRU members complained, and after some arguing, the meeting began, rules unchanged—individuals were called to the microphone for exactly sixty seconds. Everyone who addressed the board conveyed a sense of desperation, pleading as they explained that the changes would break an already too fragile balance. One woman wept as she described how even now, she could not afford two rides, so she had to buy herself a ticket and purchase a transfer for her daughter's ride. She did not know how she would manage if transfers were eliminated.

Mainstream, English-language media coverage of the MTA's plan also exhibited indifference to the plight of bus riders. A few weeks after the MTA's public hearing, Carmen and I attended a BRU press conference about the proposed increase. The room was fairly empty, and even though the BRU had invited people from all the news media, there were no television cameras present. The next day, I looked in the LA Times and saw no mention of the event. Three days later, the Times published an article, on the third page of the Metro section, reporting that the MTA planned to vote on the issue that afternoon.

If the rise in fares went unnoticed by the majority of Angelenos, the bus strike in October and November of 2003 was harder to miss. On October 14, MTA mechanics walked off their jobs over a contract dispute, and bus drivers honored their picket line. The strike lasted thirty-five days, leaving approximately 400,000 people without transportation (Streeter et al. 2003: A1). Traffic was a nightmare, as people crammed into friends' cars, makeshift taxis, and the DASH bus system, which runs on limited streets and remained in service. Bus riders often arrange their days around bus routes and schedules, but during this time, finding alternative transportation dominated their lives. They missed work or wound up having to walk miles, ride bicycles, or find other creative ways to get to their jobs.

Eva, for instance, managed to get rides to work every day but otherwise stayed "*encerrada en mi casa*" (locked up in my house). She missed church and was unable even to get to the bank to cash her paycheck. This worried her, as rent and other bills were coming due. Similarly, Mercedes found rides to her various jobs, but her fifteen-year-old daughter had no way of getting to school and missed almost a month of classes. Eva and Mercedes had it relatively easy, however. For the duration of the strike, Carmen's son left his house at 5:00 AM, walked to Alvarado Street (about two miles), caught a DASH bus downtown, and finally took a taxi to his job in Montebello—and then repeated this on the way home.

This work stoppage only accentuated the major disparities in the system. While employers, and drivers more generally, could sit by, fretting about their employees getting to work on time and their houses being cleaned, bus riders had to rearrange their whole lives. They bore the brunt of the difficulties, both physical and economic, scrambling to get to their jobs and missing out on school, social gatherings, and opportunities to make money.

Although most drivers knew about the strike, especially because the streets and freeways were more congested than ever, few seemed to appreciate the severity of the situation for nondrivers. For instance, a couple of days into the strike, I ran into an employer who did not know that it was going on. As an article in the LA *Times* conveyed, while transit-dependent neighborhoods were hit hard by the strike, everyone else remained unfazed: "To be sure, hundreds of thousands of people have seen their lives disrupted by the transit strike. . . . But for the majority, the strikes pose a detour, not a derailment" (Streitfeld 2003: A1).

Either way, employers expected their domestic employees to show up—and to arrive on time. Some were demanding and inflexible. During a previous strike, one of Carmen's employers had paid for her to take a taxi to his home, but much to her surprise, he deducted the price of these rides from her subsequent paychecks. Others were more understanding. Many customers called the Co-op to inquire about the strike and how it was affecting members. Cristina, the Co-op's coordinator, was convinced they called only to make sure that their houses would still be cleaned. Still, whatever their motivation, many picked up their domestic employees and drove them to work.

Moments of crisis, like the strike, emphasize how ease of movement remains the prerogative of select groups, how rights to the city are varied and unevenly distributed. They expose the workings of difference by illuminating who is a (valued) member of society and whose struggles remain outside of (invisible to) public concern.

Shared Places: Employer Neighborhoods

These inequities remain tenable precisely because they go unseen; residential segregation and unequal access to driving obscure the disparities they generate through physical separation, removing one group of people from the other's line of sight. This is trickier to maintain in the context of domestic service, for every day, immigrant women traverse imagined and material borders as they cross into employers' neighborhoods and homes. Still, they remain invisible. How is this possible? Employers and domestic workers inhabit these sites in such radically different ways that they very often do not see one another. Low (2000) explains:

> The concept of spatial boundary often elicits an image of a physical or social barrier, a metaphorical fence or wall that separates and defines space and its use. It seems equally possible, however, that boundaries as such do not really exist and that what we are describing are locales where difference (different people, different ideas, different activities, different land uses) is evident. . . . This reconceptualization of spatial boundaries implies that territories of influence . . . are perceived to be bounded or distinct because the activities and people within the territory are distinct from the people and activities outside it. (2000: 154)

Following Low, we can make sense of my gas station experience. Josefina and I made the gas station our "office," and we were so intent on talking to women who were getting on and off the bus that we did not really notice people who drove into the station. I do not think the drivers paid too much attention to us either. As a driver, I rarely look beyond the gas pump when I pull into a gas station, except on the rare occasion when I go inside to buy a quick cup of coffee or bottle of water. "Well-trained" consumers, we do not expect people to spend much time at gas stations; like airports and train stations, they are "non-places" (Augé 1995), spaces of supermodernity that lack "any organic society" (1995: 112) and are characterized by coming and going. In addition, Augé notes that people have a "contractual relationship" with these non-places, especially in "the way the non-place is to be used" (1995: 101). Josefina and I did not keep up our end of this contract; by making it our office, a place to conduct our work, we no longer used the gas station for its primary purpose. Furthermore, although we often bought coffee, sometimes even food, we stayed far longer than the expected amount of time, taking advantage of seats and shade where there was no public space that provided them. We made this place ours, shaping it to our needs. It was a place we shared with drivers, but because we used it so differently, our paths never crossed with theirs.

Similarly, there is a busy bus stop on Wilshire Boulevard in Westwood. In the mornings, many women get off at this stop to wait for a local bus, transfer to a north–south bus, or walk to work. People waiting for the next bus gather and gossip, and on occasion, I saw individuals selling food or *atole*. About ten feet from the bus stop is a gym with a big window that faces the street. As you get on and off the bus, you can watch people working out inside, and they can see everyone who passes by. However, the individuals who are in the gym, exercising, live nearby and are in a place associated with home and recreation, not work. On the other hand, for the people at the bus stop, this is merely a transit point, a step to their destination, and a spot in a part of the city where they work, not where they live or spend much leisure time. So, even though they are literally right in front of each other, the two different groups of people are not in the same place. They are divided by a boundary, separate from and invisible to one another, because each is engaged in a different form of activity and habitation. Like the gas station, this corner of Westwood is layered with multiple users and multiple uses, and those inhabiting the separate layers do not see or interact with one another.

At the gas station and the bus stop, we can trace domestic workers' alternative mappings, their "counter-habitation[s]" (Borden 2002: 181), of employer neighborhoods. These counter-habitations tend to remain invisible, precisely because they are different, and, as such, work to reproduce difference.

In the mornings, in employer neighborhoods, domestic workers gather in donut shops, Burger Kings, 7-11s, or the like, meeting before work to have coffee, gossip, eat breakfast, and sell their wares. There are well-known places—a Burger King in Westwood or a McDonald's in Santa Monica—as well as impromptu gathering spots. Josefina and I sometimes visited a donut shop in Tarzana that is close to the intersection of two busy streets and to a number of bus stops. It is also, notably, across the street from a Coffee Bean, where most domestic workers probably would not go. The donut shop is smaller, cheaper, and has no bathroom, whereas the Coffee Bean has a bathroom, outdoor seating, and looks a lot shinier. Every morning, starting at six, immigrant women would stream in and out on their way to work, lingering over their breakfast as they talked, drank their coffee, and passed around an Avon, Shaklee Vitamins, or Mary Kay catalog, sometimes delivering previously placed orders. One woman always brought several garbage bags full of new clothes that she sold to the others. She took over a corner of the shop, where people would look through her merchandise and sometimes try something on over their clothes. Moreover, there was usually someone selling homemade food, primarily *pupusas* and tamales accompanied by homemade *curtido* (pickled vegetables). This donut shop, then, took on the feel of a market, a place to buy and sell goods, as well as to sit and gossip about boyfriends, husbands, children, and employers. The women who met regularly were good friends. One of them told me that she had been very depressed after her husband left her, but that her friends at the donut shop—along with the three hundred dollars in Shaklee vitamins she had purchased from one of them—had helped her.

That they were buying and selling food inside a private establishment struck me as disjunctive; they were using a place defined in one way in a completely different manner. I kept wondering when they would get kicked out, but nothing happened. And they seemed completely unfazed and unaware that this was something out of the ordinary. The domestic workers who patronized this shop, like the ones who hang out at the gas station, seemed not to recognize the "rules" or "contractual relationships" that customers are supposed to have with each of these places. Rather, their counter-habitations transformed unwelcoming parts of town into places where they felt comfortable. In a city with little public space, they carved out room for social gatherings wherever possible. In the process, they changed these places, altering them in ways that bridged their current needs, understandings of life in LA, and expectations they brought from their home countries. In so doing, they created new, alternative places that both remind us about and ask us to question social norms.

Yet this process also reinforced invisibility, alterity, and social hierarchies. Lefebvre (1991) posits that abstract space, the space of capitalism, defines itself through homogeneity, seeking to erase difference as it actively creates it. When domestic workers enter employer neighborhoods, they are marked as different because they are in a place in which they do not belong; they stand out as other. An (intentional) dearth of public space means that they must take their difference into the private realm, in a sense making their difference less visible. They are then doubly differentiated, because they cannot as readily afford the restaurants, coffee shops, and stores that their employers patronize. Difference is simultaneously constructed and concealed, as domestic workers are relegated, and relegate themselves, to "other" places, where people speak Spanish and things are less expensive. Therefore, as they change the meaning of these places and challenge assumptions about private space, these women also reproduce their own alterity. More importantly, social and economic inequalities premised on specific valuations of this difference remain untouched.

Employer Households

A similar process occurred in employer homes. Domestic workers engaged in counter-habitations of these households but did not erase the distinctions or power dynamics between themselves and employers. In a sense, the employer household mirrors the sociospatial distinctions of the city, and, as in employer neighborhoods, domestic workers disrupt spatial assumptions without undermining their own position of marginality. Again, invisibility plays a central role. Since the nineteenth century, the bourgeois household has been characterized by its separation from work and the outside world. And, in fact, this perspective prevailed in the minds of most employers I met, even though domestic workers effectively bring the "city" into employer homes, transforming these places through their presence, work, and modes of habitation. Domestic workers' invisibility allows employers to hold on to this view, sustaining the fiction that household work is not real work and erasing the value of those who perform it.

When employers and domestic workers are not in the house at the same time, they can easily remain invisible to each other. This is the ideal situation, allowing both sides to avoid discomfort and effortlessly masking the inequalities of this exchange. When they are alone, domestic workers make employer households their own, occupying different parts of the house; using the phone, the television, the computer; and doing things besides cleaning. All of this changes, however, when they have to share the house with its owners. When employers are home, domestic workers must head back into the shadows, remaining in rooms reserved for them—rooms like the kitchen that are tied to work—and occupying other areas only to clean them.[16] They stay out of the way, and remain invisible, by inhabiting the house in a different manner from their employers. If a domestic employee is working, she is invisible, because she is in her place, literally and figuratively. On the other hand, if she were to try to sit in the living room, watch TV, or lie down in one of the bedrooms, she would stand out, because she would be in her employer's place, a place where she does not belong.

In other words, for the transaction to work successfully, the domestic worker must remain invisible. She does this by erasing herself, by occupying only particular parts of the house or by the way in which she inhabits "living," not working, rooms. For example, María Luisa, who lived in, always used the house where she worked as her own—so long as her employer, Mr. Bill, was not at home of course. I was visiting one day, when she asked if I could help her send a fax. As we waited for the transmission to go through, she rifled through some papers on Mr. Bill's desk but stopped suddenly when she thought she saw his car. She jumped up, grabbed her document from the machine, and hurried me into the kitchen. Not surprisingly, she didn't want him to know that she'd used his things without permission, but even when she was being "transgressive," María Luisa gravitated back to the kitchen almost as soon as she heard Mr. Bill pull into the driveway. Although she was free to move about the house, she preferred to stay out of his way and tried never to enter his study or bedroom, even in his absence. Her avoidance of these was clear acknowledgment of the power differential between herself and her employer: it was *his* house, and she could not enter certain rooms without his consent.

At the same time, this avoidance is strategic, a deliberate way to avoid potential problems or the inherent awkwardness of this intimate, yet power-laden and economically delineated, relationship. Staying out of sight is simultaneously compulsory and practical, and as in the city at large, this invisibility reproduces the distinctions that predicate social hierarchies. Although this difference is hidden, it rises to the surface at extreme moments, particularly around sexually charged situations. Over lunch one afternoon, María Luisa and her friend Esther started telling stories about the men in the families where they'd worked. At one job, the *patrona* had asked Esther to clean up her bedroom. Esther did as she was told, and while she was making the bed, the *patrona*'s husband came out of the bathroom, naked. Esther jumped and said she would leave, but he told her not to worry and continued to walk around without any clothes. Esther still shuddered when she told the story. Now she knew to be vigilant, announcing herself before going upstairs and always making sure she knew where the man of the house was before setting out to clean the bedrooms. Her current employers thought her peculiar and overly cautious, but she didn't care—she was *never* going to let that happen again.

Conclusion

Accenting the discomforts of contact between different kinds of people, Esther's traumatic encounter underscores the importance of invisibility to domestic service. Both domestic workers and their employers, immigrants and nonimmigrants, feel more at ease when they do not have to see or interact with each other. Although this invisibility can be tactical, it nevertheless remains a function of difference and inequality. The economic, social, and racial disparities that make domestic service possible are also crucial to the processes of "Americanness"—but they are only useful insofar as they remain invisible. That is, "Americanness" relies on the simultaneous construction and erasure of difference. This chapter has shown how these processes play out in and through the built environment. In chapter 2, I turn to the ways in which native-born employers wrestle with notions of difference and inequality as these are made manifest through domestic service.

CHAPTER 2

Middle-Class Dreaming

and the Limits of "Americanness"

After running through the ten-chair exercise with the members of her mothers' group (see the introduction), Tanya explained that in Los Angeles, the top 10 percent of earners made $300,000 or more per year, but that income levels for the top 1 percent were much, much higher. Intrigued, Amanda asked about the country as a whole, for she was certain that national levels were lower. The previous year, she had used TurboTax to do her taxes, and the program calculated where her income ranked nationally. Finding herself in a much higher position than expected, she was taken aback and thought, "Whew, this can't be." Then she realized that the cost of living was higher in Los Angeles and, therefore, that a middle-class lifestyle in LA required more income than in other places. The other mothers nodded knowingly, and Mary jumped in, saying she always wondered just how "middle class" was defined. Tanya explained: "There is no economic definition of middle class, so everybody's middle class. I know very, very wealthy people who insist that they're middle class, you know, people who make $500,000 a year who insist that they're middle class." Mary pressed her: "So, it's a state of mind?" "Absolutely," Tanya affirmed, "it's a state of mind. It's *absolutely* a state of mind." She went on: the "middle class" has always been undefinable. It was easier to pinpoint in the 1950s and 1960s, when people owned their own homes, didn't incur large debt, and could still send their children to public schools. However, "I don't think it's ever been defined in economic terms; I think it's always been defined as quality-of-life terms."

This exchange foregrounds several points central to discussing class in American society, and in turn, to thinking about employers' relationship to domestic service. First and foremost, Amanda's comments and Tanya's explanation show that the term "middle class" reveals little in terms of income levels, since almost everyone identifies as such. At the same time, the enduring significance of this label—its purported all-inclusiveness that serves to deny difference—emphasizes its continuing importance to the ways we envision ourselves as individuals and as a country. Calculating her taxes, Amanda was astonished to discover her own relatively powerful economic position, and she quickly rejected this version of herself by remembering that it was more expensive to live in Los Angeles. This almost reflexive repudiation of privilege allowed her to continue defining herself as middle class, regardless of her actual location within national rankings. The surprise, and discomfort, she experienced before reminding herself that she was still middle class reflect the disruptive nature of class privilege to both the individual and national consciousness.

In the United States, "middle class" remains an amorphous and ideologically all-inclusive category, since almost everyone claims this status. Classifying oneself as middle class serves less as a predictor of income level than as an indicator of being a full and respected member of society (cf. Brodkin 2014). Thus, middle class and the American Dream are mutually defined (cf. Ortner 1998b): being middle class is crucial to fulfilling the American Dream, and this accomplishment recursively reveals that an individual is the right kind of person, in possession of the fundamental qualities of "Americanness."

The American Dream posits an open middle-class society and promises upward mobility in exchange for effort, a return in direct proportion to individual input. It also defines "Americanness" as enthusiastic engagement with hard work, the gumption to reach for the stars, and an uprightness that precludes moral laxity. Presuming equal and limitless opportunity, the Dream places responsibility on the individual and attributes any failure to personal deficiency (e.g., Fischer 2010). As such, it binds middle-class status to national belonging, distinguishing the proper national subject through her aspirations. In this formulation, middle-class identity is less about a particular level of income than a set of goals, or, as Ortner (2003) terms it, a "project":[1] an open-ended and enthusiastic quest for a better life, regardless of financial status.

This ongoing pursuit spans generations, as each cohort must outdo its predecessor, part of an assumed *progression*, a forward movement that continually enhances and expands the prerogatives of Americanness.

Often unquestioned, this national mythology belies the inequalities required and constructed to maintain it, for it is the physical labor of those on the outside that sustains the lifestyles of those on the inside. That is, the borders of middle class are directly constructed by foreclosing entry to specific religious, ethnic, racial, or national groups (Sennett and Cobb 1973; Lowe 1996; Lipsitz 1998; Ortner 2003). These boundaries are necessary and necessarily invisible, erased through the fiction of equal and infinite opportunity. The processes of middle class, then, produce Americanness by separating those who achieve from those who do not—who *cannot*—into "Americans" and "others," internal or otherwise. In this chapter, I explore how domestic service highlights, disrupts, and ultimately reinforces these processes by forcing employers to see, recognize, and somehow disavow the privileges so crucial to their own middle-class projects.

Holding onto (and Reproducing) Middle Class

The employers I met in Los Angeles, primarily women in their thirties, forties, and fifties, worried about their financial well-being, evincing a "fear of falling" (Ehrenreich 1989; cf. Newman 1988; Ortner 1991; Bledstein 2001) that has come to characterize the middle class in the United States. Whether they were actually pushed to the financial brink or not, employers felt broke, afraid that they would not be able to sustain their standard of living. Indeed, as we discussed the ten-chair exercise, Samantha, a white, thirty-six-year-old mother of one, declared: "My husband and I keep going back and forth. Okay, he has a good job at a law firm, and still we feel like we can't pay for everything—so strapped. How do we save for college and everything?" Samantha's comments echo the question I posed at the beginning of this chapter: how is it possible to earn a good living and still feel constantly "strapped"? Amanda's remark about the high cost of living in Los Angeles provides a way into this question, but it must be pushed further. Certainly, life in LA is more expensive than in other parts of the United States, but that does not clarify why it is less expensive for immigrant domestic workers than it is for their middle-class employers. In addition, it does not explain why employers imagine that ten dollars an hour is sufficient to live on, when they themselves can't make do with their much higher incomes.

The key lies in examining just where individuals locate this financial precipice, just what is indispensable to a particular lifestyle. As Bourdieu (1984) reminds us, the process of distinction, the competition for status, is often enacted through consumption and consumption practices. Specific tastes and dispositions set different groups apart, naturalizing relations of power by appearing idiosyncratic. However, these are not arbitrary but rather the essential trappings of a particular habitus. "Necessity," then, is relative, defined through one's particular class, or class project.

For middle-class employers in turn-of-the-millennium Los Angeles, class projects revolved around children, around providing for them in the present and ensuring their future success. Relating how she and her husband felt strapped, Samantha specified just one preoccupation: "How do we save for college?" It is not coincidental that Samantha's concerns fixed on saving for college. Middle-class status is not automatically reproduced; since parents cannot pass it on to their children, it must be attained all over again by the next generation (e.g., Ehrenreich 1989; Ortner 1991; Devine 2004). Preparing children for the future therefore gains added urgency (cf. Nelson 2010).

These concerns loomed large for most employers: everything they sought to provide—from intellectual stimulation and academic enrichment, to participation in team sports, to a nice house and vacations to far-flung places—would furnish their kids with the tools necessary to making a good life for themselves. Unfortunately, what it took to prepare children kept expanding, and parents confronted a swelling set of requirements that made their lives increasingly harried, complicated, and expensive. Shuttling children around from one activity to the next had become the norm, and it was exhausting. It was also a frequent topic of conversation and grumbling—a recurring theme in all of my interactions with parents. Soon after arriving in Los Angeles, I contacted Danielle, a white, fifty-year-old corporate lawyer and divorced mother of two teenagers. A friend of one my East Coast relatives, Danielle invited me to dinner the following Friday. I arrived to find Danielle, her fourteen-year-old daughter Lisa, her next-door neighbors Michael and Carol, and the family who lived across the street, Linda and Steve, their seven-year-old son Adam, and their twelve-year-old daughter Molly. Over dinner, we chatted about the neighborhood: street paving, sidewalks that needed repairing, potholes, and whether the new speed bumps were a success. We also discussed college admissions, as Danielle's son was a junior in high school and already thinking about the application process. It was a warm night, and we lingered over our meal, enjoying the balmy weather and the peacefulness of their quiet neighborhood on the southern edges of Beverly Hills. Over dessert and coffee, Steve asked Lisa if she still played soccer. Danielle burst out an enthusiastic "no," and, realizing that she had interrupted, sheepishly added that she did not miss having to get up so early on Saturday mornings. Lisa explained that she had given up soccer the previous year to dedicate more time to swimming. Steve, who had smiled knowingly when Danielle jumped into the conversation, lamented that he and Linda spent all of their free time driving Adam and Molly to their many afternoon and weekend activities. Both Adam and Molly had recently started a new private school, and they were busier than ever. After school, Molly had soccer practice, or Hebrew school, or music lessons, and weekends were spent at soccer games. On top of that, she had hours of homework every night, often staying up until 11 PM. Talking about this reminded Steve that they should probably get home—it was past 10, and they had a soccer game early the next morning. After they left, Michael noted how much Adam and Molly had grown. I commented that they seemed very serious, almost like little adults. Michael, Carol, and Danielle quickly agreed, asserting that it was "crazy" how much those kids did and assuring each other that their own children had not been as overextended.

This conversation did not strike me as particularly significant until months later, when I began to notice a pattern. All of the employers I encountered rattled off a long list of activities in which their children took part, including different sports, music lessons, and academic enrichment. While they bemoaned the social pressures that fed this kind of lifestyle—as well as all the extra driving it forced upon them—they also explained that these activities were important. They wanted to make sure that their kids had as many opportunities as possible, and, read as educational experiences, all these pursuits served as preparation for the future. By extension, parents who could not or did not provide a full array of possibilities would be risking their children's future. Marilyn, a white, forty-three-year-old systems analyst with two kids, explained: "I also think there's a lot of emphasis on how your children are developing. I mean, don't you feel like there's a constant, you have to spend more time with them. I mean, there's a constant expectation—you gotta do stuff with them. You gotta teach them a different language, or, you know what I mean. There are all sorts, a hundred different things that they say you should be doing with your kids. So I do think there's the, the expectation that you're trying to achieve something."

Marilyn described a preoccupation with "development," although she could not quite pinpoint what this development should lead to, what parents were trying to "achieve." From the rest of her comments, however, it is clear that she was talking about reproducing social class. Marilyn had recently joined the PTA board at her daughter's elementary school in Studio City and was learning a lot about how public schools worked. While she lived in a school district where it was still "okay" to send her kids to public school, the schools were not perfect. Therefore, the PTA—whose members wanted to guarantee that their kids received the best, most comprehensive education—put together programs to fill in what the schools could not provide. Education was imperative for Marilyn: "I guess from my perspective, it gives people options; the more education that you have the more successful you are, um, provide somebody with the ability to make choices about what they want to do with their life, um, and so, that's, you know, I want my children to be able to have as many choices and options as possible. So I guess that's where I see, uh, that education is so important." A good education would open up possibilities for Marilyn's children, helping them to achieve the kind of lifestyle to which they were accustomed and that she wanted for them.

Yet, Marilyn acknowledged, this emphasis on development/education could get out of hand: "There are all sorts, a hundred different things that *they say you should be doing* with your kids." It didn't matter who "they" were; what mattered was the "hundred different things" necessary to (re)producing a successful child. Where did one draw the line? How much was enough? How much was too much? One of her friends who worked in an exclusive private school told Marilyn that many families employed tutors for their children, even if the kids were not having any difficulties; these parents just wanted to be certain that their kids were getting the proper intellectual stimulation. Marilyn both lamented the increasing pressures and recognized herself in the picture she was painting. Some parents were over the top, but she also admitted that she would probably start pushing her kids harder in school once they reached the fifth or sixth grade. The lower grades were a time to develop, but at some point, they had to learn good study skills.

Of course, school was not the only place where kids could or should "develop"; extracurricular activities served as another avenue to success, exposing children to different interests and simultaneously preparing them for college. Many of the children in Marilyn's neighborhood were "completely programmed" with activities: tennis, soccer, chess, piano, other instruments, and so on. One of the girls on her daughter's soccer team, for example, also played basketball, karate, and participated in a second soccer league. Aware of these potential excesses, Marilyn tried to limit her kids' activities, but it was hard to know what was enough, especially because there was a lot of pressure to "program" kids in that way.

Making matters worse, there was increasing pressure to start younger, as competition was getting stiffer—within each particular field as well as overall—to get into college. It was important to specialize much earlier in life now; to be really good at something, kids had to start as young as possible, and of course, as more parents jumped on this bandwagon, what it meant to be "young" kept getting younger and younger. This held true not just for playing sports or a musical instrument but also in terms of academic development; hence the need for special tutors even for children who had no trouble with school. Marilyn knew a lot of people who made it a point to talk to their kids about college at a young age, to get them used to the idea that college was "something you go to." She also felt strongly about this subject and had brought it up with her daughter, who, at the age of eight, already knew that she was going to go to college. Marilyn noticed that people in her area all seemed to have "the same mentality": "where I grew up and the environment I'm raising my children in, the people are very into, and their families, everybody goes to college." They set their expectations higher and wanted not just to make college inevitable for their children but to start getting them motivated.

Marilyn suspected that "the higher economic folk in LA" pushed their children a lot harder. She differentiated the expectations of her well-to-do neighbors from those of the "lower class": "I do think that is an issue, and I don't mean, well yes, in the lower class . . . unless they thought about it, it seems like they have a different set of expectations." As if uncomfortable with this statement, she quickly amended it, reasoning that parents who were not middle class were probably busier, working more jobs, and didn't have the time or education to help their kids with their homework. Aside from Marilyn's unease, her remarks are significant for two reasons. First, despite the fact that Marilyn lived in a fairly wealthy area, she continued to identify as middle class. Acknowledging class differences, she nevertheless placed herself in the unmarked, unprivileged position of middle class. In addition, her comments serve to remind us of the impossibility of defining middle class solely in economic terms. Other employers also identified as middle class, even though they were not as well off as Marilyn, and they too emphasized the need to provide every available opportunity for their children, from intellectual stimulation to consumer goods, so as to facilitate future success.

The first time I met Kristen, a white, thirty-eight-year-old mother of two who worked as a legal secretary, she spent the better part of an hour complaining about poorly performing public schools, the difficulty of finding adequate childcare, and the high cost of living in Los Angeles. Kristen and her husband, who worked in a bank, lived in Highland Park; they had a daughter who was in kindergarten and a son who was just turning three. Working full-time, she spent much of her energy—and salary—trying to find reliable childcare. She was quite frustrated, afraid that her children were not getting adequate education or care. Before starting kindergarten, Kristen's daughter had attended the preschool where her son was still enrolled. Now she was in kindergarten, which only lasted three hours a day, so they had taken on a French au pair to care for her in the afternoons. Kristen was highly displeased with the quality of the public schools; she and all of her friends agonized over what would happen to their children once they had to start school:

> We were all biting our nails, going "what the hell are we doing," because we were all working mothers. We were all sitting there going "how is this gonna work out and what effect is it gonna have on our kids," and none of us have been terribly pleased. The ones who

sent their children to private school with private after-school care are the happiest but the poorest, because it costs *a lot of money*. . . . The ones who sent their kids to public schools with after-school care—nobody's happy with that. Because we all have, by the nature of where we work and how, you know, where we are, we have *very high* expectations for our children, and our goals for what we want for our families are *very high* as well.

Like Marilyn, Kristen had "high expectations" for her kids, including "academic success, integration into their environment, developing self-awareness and self-sufficiency." Disappointingly, the public schools did not necessarily prepare children properly, and she could not afford a private school or to move to an area with a better school system. This caused a great deal of consternation, especially when Kristen realized that in moving from private preschool to kindergarten, her daughter had had to backtrack. The presumed path to success was full of potential pitfalls, every step a potential misstep that could forever ruin your child's future. Transitioning from private to public schooling, Kristen's daughter had experienced a setback, leaving Kristen angry and distressed. She felt like a bad mother; even though she worked full-time and had a good job, she could not pay for the kind of education and childcare that would best ensure her kids' successes:

This is pretty much a lot of the lives of people I know here. . . . I can't tell you one parent I know who wakes up and says: "oh I see the end. My life's all set up, don't worry about it. My kids are fine." I talk to my other coworkers, and one of them I was talking to the other day, she's having to hire a babysitter to come in in the afternoon to be home with her thirteen-year-old and ten-year-old son. They're old enough to be home alone, but they're, they're almost like latchkey kids. Their parents work. So it's like, what do they do all day? Who's there to supervise them? Who sits there and helps them with their work? No one. So she has to hire somebody to do that. It's this weird system where because we are so big as a city, we have no support that's easily found. There are some out there, but they're not easy to find, and they're not accessible, *especially to middle-class people*. . . . It's a constant cobbling, mixing of this with that and trying to make it work, and if it doesn't, *damn, your kids are screwed*.

The sense that her children's futures were up in the air was a source of great anguish for Kristen as for her peers. The system had no built-in safeguards, no way to guarantee that kids would do well. Instead, each family had to patch together some sort of workable, though always imperfect, solution. Otherwise, "your kids are screwed." These anxieties were never-ending—no one felt that "my kids are fine," and they often focused on education, revealing the urgency and insecurity of reproducing class status.

Both Marilyn and Kristen planned around, worried about, and worked for their children's futures. Like all the parents I met, they wanted their children to have opportunities and to excel.[2] As such, a child's achievements were measured not just in terms of her ability to outperform her peers in as many different arenas as possible, but also retroactively: did she get into the "right" college, find the "right" job, buy a house in the "right" neighborhood? Significantly, failure or success did not bear just on the child but also on the parent—for parents' own class projects were invested in their children's ability to reproduce a particular class position. Moreover, the ability to provide for one's kids was a central necessity to, and a key marker of, middle-class status. The difference between Marilyn and Kristen, then, was not in their goals but in what they could feasibly provide for their children—and the varying ways this reflected on their own class status and on themselves as "successful."

Thus, "middle class" did not refer to a specific social or economic position, but rather to a particular set of aspirations and to the processes through which individuals sought to achieve these. Consumption was critical to these endeavors. Parents had to do more than ferry their children around LA; they had to pay for tutors, private school if necessary, homes in "acceptable" school districts, trips to museums, fees for sports teams, music lessons, art classes—not to mention school uniforms, team uniforms, computers for kids to do homework on, and so on. The list was endless.

As such, social reproduction rested on the ability to consume. Parents imagined relationships with their children through the things they could provide, measuring their own efficacy through buying power. Being able to give their kids "everything" produced the parents themselves as successful, as did their children's subsequent achievements. Nancy, a fifty-two-year-old Asian American graduate student and mother of four, argued that some parents push their children into activities because they just want "trophy kids." Marilyn added: "people feel strongly that somehow their kids, I think, have to be successful, because it's a reflection of what they did and what they raised." She admitted that she wanted her kids to do well in everything—in fact, to be the best. However, she also knew that she would have to change this expectation, because she did not want to pressure them too much. Still, letting go of this standard would be tough, and she wondered where this competitive streak came from:

> I'm wondering if it has to do with the kind of life we have chosen to create in America, where we want to be the best. We want to have the most money. We want to have all these toys. We want to take the great vacation. You want to show all that to your children. And so you kind of live with that in mind, with that idea or idealism. So I think that, um, I know that I struggle with that, and I know, I just, I have to find some way to take a step back and not get too over the top about what my kid's working on. But I can't, you know, I just, you know, I just, when I went back, I dropped my kids off at school on Monday, while they're there, so they can meet me, 'cause like, you know, the nanny takes them. So I went in and I immediately went up to the teacher, and said "Hi, how's my son doing?" "Oh he's doing very well." "Oh really? I want him to do really well." You know, what I mean? I could tell. I was like, you know, I want to know. Is he having fun? I didn't ask that.

Marilyn's comments illustrate the complicated feelings that animated parents. She wanted to have the best of everything so that she could "show all that" to her children, for their sake. Yet their successes were hers also, adding an extra layer of motivation. She had to learn to separate the two. Realizing that she had not asked her son's teacher if he was enjoying himself, she acknowledged that she had to moderate herself, to remember that it was just as important for her kids to be happy.

Regardless of the underlying desires, parental ambitions called for increased time and energy, particularly because accomplished children required constant stimulation, attention, and care. For example, Jennifer, a white, thirty-three-year-old mother, had recently hired a nanny to watch her nine-month-old son, while her two-year-old daughter attended a preschool close to their Culver City home. Jennifer and her husband had initially opted for center-based care over a nanny, because they felt that social interaction was very important. However, she realized that even though her daughter was by no means neglected in preschool, "it's still one teacher to three babies. . . . You just know there's a lot of sitting around in a bouncy chair going on, whereas if, if you've got one nanny, one baby, you're just gonna be held more, and played with more, and talked to more."

Getting a nanny was therefore preferable, the best way to provide the right kind of attention and intellectual stimulation for her son; this way, he would not be wasting valuable time "sitting around in a bouncy chair." As for her daughter, Jennifer and her husband had looked at better preschools, but these were far away, easily a thirty-minute drive in each direction. They opted against these because of the distance, convinced that it was better to spend that time at home, "enriching" her themselves, than to waste an hour a day sitting in traffic. That hour would be utterly unproductive; instead, they would take more initiative to supplement what she was getting at school, providing her with "stimulus, computer programs or museum trips."

This expectation of continuous, quality attention for kids, however, conflicted with parents' need to work, as even two incomes seemed insufficient to sustaining the ever-expanding requirements for raising successful children. More and more, paid employment was a requirement for this increasingly expensive middle-class lifestyle; many women told me they would have liked to stay at home with their children, but they were not willing to sacrifice their standard of living. Christine and Paul, African Americans in their mid-forties, also expressed this quandary. Paul explained:

> If you're really, you know, affluent, as far as, you know, you make enough money to where one of the parents can stay home, then ob-

viously the ideal would be, you know, for one of the parents to be there with the child, take him to school, participate in school—we try to do that as much as possible—but I think that's not the case for the lifestyle that people want to live. And it's a choice, I mean, if you want to live in a smaller house and you want to have a different lifestyle and you feel that that would be the "sacrifice," which I don't necessarily see as a sacrifice that you would want to make as a parent, that one parent stays home, because the kids grow up so quickly. You look up and you know those years are gone. You know, ten, twelve years old, and then they are in school, and I know some, some families do that and then the mom goes back to work or something like that, but if you cannot have that ideal or if you choose not to, because anybody can say we'll just have one income and we'll just have the one car and this, that, and the other, but you know if you choose to be a two-income family and to have that lifestyle.

Paul conceded that they could make do with less income if they changed their expectations and reduced their standard of living. However, they were not willing to make this "sacrifice," so both he and Christine had to work.

Many parents felt that they really had no choice. Everyone was increasingly pulled from two directions, between the exigencies of work and home. The amplification of both only aggravated the already stressful time crunch facing working parents (e.g., Rudd and Descartes 2008; Ochs and Kremer-Sadlik 2013). Kristen's description of her daily schedule illustrates the precarious, and intricate, balancing acts required to manage these competing demands. In her house, the day began around 6:00, when her husband usually woke up, got ready, and fixed breakfast. Kristen tried to sleep until 6:30, although her kids often got her up earlier. She got the kids ready for school, somehow finding the time to shower and eat breakfast in between. By 7:30, Kristen, her husband, and her son were headed out the door. Kristen dropped off her son, took her husband to his office, and arrived at her job by 8:30. Her daughter stayed at home with the au pair, who took her to school independently and picked her up at 11:30 when kindergarten let out. Kristen spent the whole day working, catching up on personal phone calls, appointments, and errands over her lunch break. At 5:30, she left work, swinging by to pick up her husband and son, and finally returned home between 6:45 and 7:00. She then heated up one of the meals she had prepared and frozen over the weekend, and the family sat down together to eat. After cleaning up from dinner, Kristen and her husband had to bathe the kids, change them into their pajamas, and try to get them to sleep. This was no easy task, however, as the kids hadn't seen their parents all day and wanted to stay up and hang out. Kristen and her husband usually managed to coax their children into bed by 9:30, leaving Kristen an hour or so to catch up with her husband and take care of loose ends. By 10:30, she was exhausted and ready for bed. Saturdays and Sundays gave her more time with her children, but she also had to find time for the tasks she had neglected during the week—going to the supermarket, making meals for the upcoming week, doing the laundry, or cleaning.

Trying to keep up with both work and home left Kristen exhausted and slightly embittered. Her life was a "constant battle": "This is where a big chunk of the dilemma comes from—being a parent and living, living in this city and trying to raise your children in the best way you can. . . . What you're saying, the juggling, the balancing, there is no balance. Something is always giving. Whether it's me giving myself up, whether it's my kids giving up their parents, whether it's the schools giving up on the kids. Something is always giving, and as time goes on, you find that more and more things are giving."

Part of the problem was the conflicting demands—the impossible choice between earning a sustainable living and spending time with your children: "You can't be expected to be there and not be there at the same time but that's what we are expected to do as parents. . . . It's this total line between what we in society are saying, these are our expectations of you as a parent, despite the fact you're working full-time, you still have to do these things."

Although she was unhappy that the au pair did not help out more at home, Kristen did rely on a "housekeeper," a Mexican woman who came twice a month and did the heavy cleaning. This freed up an extra four or five hours every week, time Kristen could devote to her children. Unfortunately, she could not afford to have the housekeeper more often, as this would have further lightened her load.

Kristen's experiences point to the growing importance of domestic service in maintaining and reproducing a middle-class lifestyle in Los Angeles. Employing a nanny or someone to clean helped to fill in the gaps left by the contradictory pulls of work and home. Scholars maintain that hiring a domestic worker is itself a sign of wealth, lending employers a particular class position and status (e.g., Romero 1992; Gill 1994). In LA, I found that domestic service seemed less important as status symbol than as a tool, something that afforded employers the time and flexibility to pursue other markers of middle-class identity. For instance, hiring a nanny permitted individuals to go to work and families to have two incomes. In the absence of broader state supports or legally mandated maternity leave, many women had no choice but to return to their jobs a few months after having a baby. They had to find suitable, affordable childcare, and often center-based care was more expensive than hiring a nanny. Further, preschools and day care centers closed at a certain hour, while nannies could often work late, even live in. Finally, nannies came to you, saving you the additional driving time.

Teresa, who worked for Christine and Paul, not only drove to their home in Santa Monica, arriving before they left for work at 8 AM, but also chauffeured their eight-year-old daughter Debbie to and from school. She took care of Debbie all afternoon, and when Christine worked late, Teresa made Debbie dinner and put her to bed. Christine and Paul knew that they would never be able to manage their busy work schedules without Teresa, whom their daughter loved and they trusted completely. Christine explained:

> You know, sometimes I can work from 7:30 until 7:30 in, in you know, one day. There are a couple of times that I didn't see her, you know, um, or, or the other kids, and traveling. There was one point where I was traveling a lot, but now it's more regular and I'm not traveling hardly at all now, um, so um, it's nice to have someone here to, um, as a stable entity, because she, she always picks her up, makes her feel more comfortable. She knows that if we're not around, Teresa's going to be there, and that works.

Teresa's presence eased Christine and Paul's stresses, permitting them to work late or travel for their jobs without having to worry about who was watching their daughter. Teresa also took care of most of the housework, liberating Christine and Paul from these tasks. Now they did not have to make time to clean on the weekend or at night, and they could spend this extra time with their family or pursuing other interests.

Paying someone else to clean, whether once a month or every day, also mitigated the time crunch, allowing employers more time to work, enjoy their families, or take up additional leisure activities. All of these helped to produce and reproduce a middle-class habitus, constituting and reflecting privilege. Marilyn, for instance, spent Saturdays running errands and attending to everything she had ignored during the week. On Sundays, however, she and her husband usually took the kids on a family outing—a museum, the beach, Disneyland. She could do this because she knew that her nanny would clean the house on Monday morning while the kids were at school. Otherwise, Marilyn would have had to set aside time to clean, making their Sunday excursions less feasible.

Especially for women, who continued to bear most of the responsibility for housework, the ability to hire a domestic worker created a new range of possibilities. It afforded them more time with their children and, on rare occasions, more time for themselves. Paying someone else to clean also eased potential conflicts between partners. Many women reported that housework was a source of friction, for men never did enough, even when they thought they were contributing equally. As one employer explained, she finally hired someone to clean after she realized that continuing to argue over cleaning was ruining her relationship. Increasingly, then, middle-class womanhood in Los Angeles—defined through a particular standard of living, a continued ideological association with motherhood, childcare, and housework, as well as the desire for and possibility of engaging in paid employment—relied on the availability of domestic service.

Home Work

Soaking up the burdens of housework and childcare, domestic service granted working parents the one thing they needed most—time to work, to spend with their children, and to pursue other interests. In addition, domestic service advanced employers' class projects precisely because of its focus on the house itself. A proxy for the American Dream, the middle-class home is a nexus of middle-class identity (e.g., Clark 1986; May 1988; Hornstein 2005; Arnold et al. 2012; Harris 2013), not only representing its owners but also working to constitute them. Seemingly unconnected to the public sphere, the home provides a refuge from and counterbalance to the amoral world of politics and markets. It is the locus of morality, a primary site for crafting appropriate middle-class Americans. That is, the type of house one owns, where it is, and how one decorates and maintains it says a lot about who a person is, reflecting not just individual taste but a particular class position.

Your house, Belinda informed me, was a reflection of who you were, or your "inner self." An interior designer in Los Angeles, she found that when women asked her to make over their homes, what they really wanted was to make themselves over. For her part, Belinda continually worked on her house, a two-story, two-bedroom townhouse in a new development on the western edges of the San Fernando Valley. She sought to ensure that it was comfortable, welcoming to visitors, and, in her own words, "well appointed." All of this required constant upkeep, but the reward made it worthwhile: "I'm proud of my home, so I'm proud of myself," she declared.

I first met Belinda at an open house for a group of mothers in the Valley. She invited me to her home to see her work in action, and so, as soon as I arrived, took me on a complete tour of the house, a modest two-story condo in a newish housing development in the San Fernando Valley. Looking at it from the outside, I expected that it would resemble many of the houses I had seen in LA, with clean lines, minimalist décor, bright colors, and a lot of light. The interior, however, was completely different, with a somber, almost heavy feel to it. Despite its many windows, the house was so dark that when I left, I was surprised to find that it was just 3 PM. All the furniture was wooden, dark, of an ornate, antique style. Belinda's office, for instance, contained a scroll-top desk, a wooden chair, and shelves lined with hardcover books. She made sure to point out her first editions, explaining that she had recently thrown out her ugly paperbacks. In the kitchen, a painting of a woman set in an antique-style wooden frame hung above the mantel. The table was dark wood with matching bench-like chairs. The living and family rooms were decorated in a similar vein. The living room had two dark couches, a wooden coffee table, and matching end tables. Like many

LA homes, this house had wall-to-wall off-white carpeting, but in the living room, a large Oriental rug covered the carpet.

The carpet stretched over the stairs and onto the second floor; this story was decorated in much the same vein. The family room held two overstuffed chairs, each with its own footstool, a television and entertainment center, and a wooden rack displaying a knitted blanket that looked very old. The baby's room was done in pink: there was a pink chair with an ottoman, a wooden changing table for the baby, and a large crib decorated with pink. The four-year-old's room was more elaborately decorated; the focus of the room was a queen-sized bed set on a wooden frame and covered with pillows. Next to it hung a poster that looked like a page from a nineteenth-century catalog or advertisement. The opposite wall held two shelves: the top one displayed four antique hats and the bottom one four antique dolls. Underneath these shelves sat a small table set up for a tea party. To its left, there was a play area, the toys put away and out of sight. Finally, the master bedroom was even larger and reminded me of a room from a small New England inn. The king-sized bed was quite tall, resting on a wooden frame and against the wall, against a blue curtain that was gathered in the middle. There was also a chair and desk and dresser, all dark wood, matching the downstairs furniture.

Initially, Belinda's choice of furnishings seemed jarring, but as she told me her story, I began to understand its logic. She explained: "I always sensed that I wanted a nicer home. We were very middle class, not poor. . . . My momma is, has always been like a decorator, but kinda always on that lower Kmart, J. C. Penney level, where it was always homey and clean, and there's nothing wrong with that. I wanted different in the sense of the choices that I can make. I knew that I wanted better maybe than I grew up with. . . . I knew I wanted the morals and principles and the hominess that I grew up with."

Belinda *had* done better, and her house and the ways it was decorated stood as tangible proof of her accomplishments. She was proud of her hard-won achievements but insisted that this added wealth had not changed her core self; she had retained her parents' honest, hardworking values. Filled with amenities yet—as she put it—always "cozy" and "welcoming," her home revealed both her financial accomplishments and her modest ways. It indicated that she was a good person, a worthy American—that she was living the American Dream.

More than that, her choice of décor revealed just how she defined and imagined a more successful life, the tastes that were part and parcel of her new social position. "Class" and "sophistication" were crucial here, and her understanding of both were displayed in her dark, somber, antique-style furniture. This fit with the other trappings of her upwardly mobile sensibility:

[My husband's] parents traveled. They drank wine. They ate cheeses. They experienced life. They went to fine restaurants. They were members of the opera and the ballet—foreign to me. . . . I knew the home but I didn't know about Paris, Europe. His parents drank wine, you know, my family didn't drink wine, which opened up a whole cultural thing to me, which brought in different styles. It wasn't just country, now I wanted Italian. I wanted French paintings. I wanted Baccarat crystal. I wanted to experience all of that. So it's that, it's just a different kind of home, where his parents literally did set the table with Haviland china, and Baccarat crystal, and Reed and Barton silver and candles, and you sat down, and his mother made duck à l'orange and sherry every Christmas.

Belinda's house and its furnishings foregrounded her successes, not just for visitors but also importantly for herself and her children. When her four-year-old daughter wanted a large bed, Belinda bought it for her, seeing this as a sign of her daughter's ambitions: "She would rather have a big overstuffed ottoman, which I have for her to step up on, to reach things; it's almost like this person who always has this goal, this aspiration that's bigger than herself, which I love. She loves it that she has to climb into this huge, look-at-this-pool-I-can-just-swim-in kind of bed." Belinda's stress on the word "climb" was not accidental, for this was exactly what she wanted her daughters to do—to move up in the world, surpassing her, as she had surpassed her own parents. Thus, Belinda's (newfound) worldliness was not only evident on special occasions, when she ate duck à l'orange and drank sherry, but more importantly, objectified, made visible, (re)produced in the everyday, in the ways she decorated and used her home.

Similarly, Karen described her house, and its location, as proof of having "made it." Karen grew up not far from LA, in a "rough area." Her parents did not have a lot of money, and her two older siblings never went to college. Although her parents did not press her, Karen was internally motivated and worked hard to get into college. She was accepted at a well-respected state school, and with her parents' financial support, completed a degree in architecture. In retrospect, she realized that college had been a major turning point: "That's when I realized what kind of life I wanted to have, as I started to learn more about myself, you know, I didn't want to, I wanted to have a better life. I wanted to, you know, live in a nice area. Um, I wanted to do better than my parents. That's the American Dream."

When I met Karen, a white, thirty-four-year-old mother of two, she was a successful professional and lived in the well-to-do neighborhood of South Pasadena. She was proud of what she had accomplished and read her achievements through her house—so much so that she was concerned when her parents didn't seem to like it:

> I used to think when we bought this house . . . and I told my husband, I said, I don't know. They act like they don't like our house, you know. It wasn't until they brought some of their friends. They drove all the way down here with their friends. They were going somewhere else, but they brought their friends by, gave them a tour, showed them everything, and then I realized: my parents are *proud* of me. They're *proud* of my house. They're *proud* of me, and you know, they don't really express it all the time, and so I didn't know, you know. Uh, I mean, they, they think it's kind of a, you know, ritzy area. They go to the grocery store—"I can't believe how much everything costs here." Well, you know, this is South Pasadena, I'm sorry. What can I do, you know, that's just how much it costs. When you live in a, yeah, groceries are more expensive. They charge more. They gouge you. I mean, you know, but you're shopping in a, in, in Pavilions, you know, rather than in a grocery store that's not as nice.

For both Karen and Belinda, the house signified and reproduced a desired class status. Karen's parents clearly understood this, showing off Karen's house to their friends, even if it meant they had to drive two hours in each direction. It was only in that moment, when she saw how proud they were of her house, that Karen realized that her parents were actually proud of her. Belinda echoed this sentiment: "I'm proud of my home, so I'm proud of myself." Here we see that a clean and orderly house was more than just a measure of comfort; it was central to middle-class projects. And paid domestic work helped employers with little time or inclination to clean to maintain this aspect so important to their identity.

Making Class Visible

Allowing individuals to invest in the relationships, activities, and commodities necessary to their class projects, domestic service thus worked to reproduce privilege; it also, importantly, forced employers to consider this privilege, not only to see class difference but to recognize themselves in the more powerful position. As a result, most employers expressed deep discomfort with this occupation. After all, to be middle class is to be ordinary, to be ambitious, hardworking, and successful, but to remain disciplined and modest. While the belief in American exceptionalism emphasizes the singularity of the nation vis-à-vis the world, "ordinariness" remains crucial to being a desirable member of the nation (e.g., Lamont 1992, 2000; Kefalas 2003; Devine 2005). And it is this defining principle that domestic service throws into question: the presence of a domestic employee, usually a Spanish-speaking immigrant woman, forces middle-class employers to see the economic and social disparities that uphold their lifestyles.[3] Confronted with these inequities, most employers sought to dissolve the gap between themselves and the women who worked in their homes. Their unease took many forms, ranging from unsolicited, flat-out denials of difference to more nuanced perspectives, but always revealing a necessary struggle to redefine the self as "ordinary." They grappled with their privilege, seeking ways to deny, assimilate, or displace it without having to alter their fundamental sense of self.

The (Moral) Value of Class

For many, just the ability to employ a domestic worker signaled a shift in social status away from an unmarked, unprivileged location to one with which they did not necessarily want to be associated. Being middle class was more than a set of aspirations and practices. It also implied a particular moral code, for "middle class" defined individuals through the "American" ideals of egalitarianism and hard work. On the other hand, "upper class," as seen from below, seemed to embody the opposite: privilege engendered laziness and moral lassitude.

Karen, for instance, confided that although she could well afford to hire someone, she felt quite uneasy at the thought of doing so. It was just not something she was accustomed to; in fact, when she was growing up her family didn't even have a dishwasher. Her father always joked that he didn't need one, because he had three—his three children. She laughed as she recalled this, adding that she had just recently gotten a dishwasher. Although her house was filled with all sorts of amenities that her parents did not have, she considered the dishwasher a needless luxury. It was only in the last few months, as she prepared to give birth for the second time, that she had succumbed to this "luxury"—and only because she dreaded the thought of having to wash bottles by hand. Here, "luxury" did not mean something unaffordable, but instead referenced something unnecessary or perhaps undeserved. Too many indulgences, such as taking on a domestic worker, would turn Karen into someone she did not want to be.

While she was pleased with her upward mobility, which she had earned through considerable effort, Karen did not want to lose her modest and hardworking principles. This seemed an especially critical concern for people from working-class or lower-middle-class backgrounds; they emphasized that they did not want to lose the "values" with which they grew up, often grounding differences between lower and upper classes in terms of morality.[4]

For employers, the possibility of inequality, the idea that their success was somehow less than fully earned, was disruptive—so much so that many struggled even with the decision to take on a domestic employee. For instance, Kate, a white, forty-year-old stay-at-home mother, recalled that she had had to convince herself to bring in someone to clean. Kate hated housework, and as the mother of a two-year-old and a nine-month-old, had little time to devote to it. Nevertheless, it felt "strange" to hire someone, and her husband had to talk her into it, pointing out that she would have more time to enjoy her kids if she did not have to worry about cleaning. He understood her hesitation, for he had felt the same way when he first paid someone to mow the lawn:

So the same kind of internal dialogue that I had with myself for internal, you know, cleaning, household cleaning, that he had for himself. I guess giving up that was kinda like, I don't know, like he would be much better than, kinda like a doctor, and I was the same way, like why should, you know, do I deserve this luxury of having somebody come in? And I even feel bad that they're cleaning my house, even though I'm paying them and helping them. . . . No, I guess I don't . . . I guess I feel good, I mean they're probably making a decent living. They seem like they are. I guess I would have to kinda catch myself, because like why would I feel . . . meaning like I don't respect that work? I mean who likes to clean other people's dirt, but they do a really good job and . . . I'm just so happy with them, 'cause I'm like "oh my house is clean."

Realizing that they could turn to domestic service, both Kate and her husband had experienced a shift in the ways they thought about themselves. This was unfamiliar territory, as they had both grown up in middle-class families where their moms did the housework and their fathers tended to the lawn. In hiring someone, both experienced a moment of unwelcome recognition that had required, and continued to call for, a reworking of the terms. After all, neither was used to such "luxury," and neither wanted to feel "much better than, kinda like a doctor." Kate had accepted her newfound position as employer simply because it made her life much easier. Still, a twinge of discomfort remained as she wrestled with her newfound status, and she struggled to remind herself: "I guess I don't feel . . . I guess I feel good, I mean they're probably making a decent living."

Similarly, Allison, a thirty-nine-year-old African American lawyer and mother, was reluctant to hire a domestic worker because of her family history. I met Allison when the Co-op did an estimate for her home. Pregnant with her second child, Allison knew she needed help but was not entirely confident that she would actually employ the Co-op on a regular basis. When I spoke with her about it a couple of months later, she explained that her two grandmothers, African Americans who had moved from the South to a mining town in Pennsylvania, had worked as domestic servants. Her own mother, a single mother, had struggled through a series of low-paid positions to raise Allison and her three siblings. To ease this load, Allison's mother had hired a woman to clean and to care for her children in the afternoons. Allison, however, was anxious about becoming an employer, even though her mother had done the same:

I don't think that she had the same struggle with it, primarily because, um, because she was totally financially marginal herself, and so it wasn't, it wasn't like this point of, um, she was not in the same position I am. I have sufficient, I have vastly more earnings and buying power than my mother ever imagined. And so it's not the same situation because she was financially marginal, marginal, and she was, you know, she was a single parent and all this other stuff, and my life is just entirely different from hers. So, in a very, very different sense, I have, I *am* the middle class that she never, she never really was. You know, she had some of the, some of the, um, trappings of middle class, in particular, they bought a, they bought a house, our parents bought a house. And so she always felt very, um, fortunate that she actually owned a home. And that made it much easier for us, I think, when they got divorced, because we didn't have to do a lot of moving around. We had, you know, some central thing, right? But for her, it was really more, I just need a break, and since I can't kill a kid or walk out on my kids or something like that, I need something to help. . . . She just didn't have, I mean it was just sort of like this needs to happen. It's a real problem for me. I can't handle going to work and working all the time and coming home and the house is a mess, and it's not really. It's not going to work.

Allison believed her case differed significantly from her mother's, as Allison was in a more privileged financial position. She felt inadequate for not being able to handle less than her mother or grandmothers had had to manage. Her life was not that hard, and she couldn't quite accept that: "I've got one stinking kid, a husband, and a job where frankly, I mean, okay, I like to think that I'm a little thoughtful about it, but it's not really that hard. I mean, it's not like I'm going out and really working hard, physically working hard all day, and sort of the notion that I can't maintain when it's so clear that so many other people can maintain. And so I'm sort of feeling like inadequate, right, especially in comparison to these other really strong-willed models." Given her mother's and grandmothers' struggles, she felt there was something wrong with her if she could not do everything she had to do—almost as if a middle-class lifestyle had made her indolent, "soft." Allison was proud to be in the middle class, but she felt conflicted, worried that this position of privilege would erode her hardworking values and lead to excess. She feared losing her moral center, and importantly, she wanted to make sure that her daughter learned the proper values. Thus, she always watched that line, careful not to step over it:

I'm not about being grand or being, you know, I want my things to be nice, and I worked hard to be in the middle class. It wasn't obvious that I was gonna be here, and I'm not ashamed of it or embarrassed about it, but it's not like, you know, I didn't need to have the biggest house on the block or the fanciest deck and a new car, and all that kind of stuff, right? It's important to me that my house, that we behave in ways that are civil to one another and that we talk to each other. . . . We say thank you and please to each other. You know, that kind of stuff, and I think it's important that you maintain that kind of thing. . . . It's nice to say thank you if somebody pours you a cup of coffee, even if that's your husband, and he's been pouring you a cup of coffee every day for the past ten years. And so then I can say to my daughter when she does something, we don't talk to each other like that. You know, you don't see that behavior from us.

Maintaining civility and good relationships with family were important to Allison, attributes and practices too easily discarded in an increasingly harried upwardly mobile lifestyle. She carefully guarded the boundary between "ordinary," hardworking values and the (moral) degeneracy of privilege. That is why she had to be honest with herself, probing her decision to hire a domestic worker:

I really think it's sort of this thing like other people I actually know and have seen and have lived with managed all this, and so, am I just being, um, the question is, is the expectation, um, that I can do more, um, inappropriate or is the expectation that I should be able to do less because I have income inappropriate. Right? It's like they say I'm making enough money that I don't have to fucking clean now, or is it, you know, I can't possibly do all this. I have too many demands on me to do all these different things, right? And it feels more like the, you know, I don't have to do this because I have money, than it feels like it's really unreasonable to think that you'd be able to care for one child and a modestly sized home without help.

Was she really overwhelmed or was it mere laziness? Allison could not quite decide, and this question haunted her. That she could turn to the Co-op eased her conscience to a certain extent; at least she knew that the women who cleaned her home would be earning a fair wage. Still, she continued to wrestle with the issue and was not ready to commit herself fully. She would reconsider her decision after the baby was born.

Confronting Privilege

If weighing the option to hire a domestic worker prompted would-be employers to examine who they were and who they wanted to be, these questions become more salient as individuals navigated the day-to-day of domestic service. Middle-class employers with little or no experience of domestic service had no clearly defined rules for these interactions; moreover, many sought to put some distance between themselves and the role of the powerful, potentially exploitative employer. This often collided with the expectations of their employees. The immigrant women that most employers hired came from countries where domestic service is a dominant, long-standing institution, and where an individual's position as employer or employee clearly locates her in the social hierarchy with little hope for upward mobility. The roles of upper class and lower class, or employer and employee, are clearly defined, dictating how each person should act toward and interact with the other. In these exchanges, employers unquestioningly assert their privilege, for the substance of these relationships helps to mold and fix their elite status and subjectivities.

This lack of familiarity with the situation, discomfort with their position as employers, and (usually unsuccessful) attempts to collapse class differences, created awkward situations and a fair amount of anxiety. Noah and Jessie's experiences punctuate the discomfiture of coming face to face with privilege. Graduate students in their mid-thirties, Noah and Jessie were both raised in Jewish, middle-class homes. They had middle-class goals, dispositions, and educations, yet, financially, they were on the edges of this class position. They certainly did not think of themselves as privileged, at least not until they set out to hire a nanny for their eight-month-old.

Shortly after I met Noah and Jessie, they hired Lupe, from Mexico, as a part-time nanny for their daughter Violet. When she began working for them, they were uneasy, feeling strange about having a nanny and not sure how to trust anyone. Noah was so nervous the first day that he had followed Lupe out of the house when she took Violet for a walk. In fact, it took him a good two months to trust Lupe, as it would have with anyone they hired. Jessie, on the other hand, got over that initial fear sooner, because she took her cues from Violet, who got excited whenever she saw Lupe.

Noah and Jessie did not feel comfortable being employers. They were unused to seeing their privilege and wary of performing it. This discomfort was pervasive, and the fact that they couldn't pay her enough continued to trouble them. Even though ten dollars an hour was a lot for them, Noah knew that it was nothing "for what she does for us . . . meaning, too little for her to survive in any real way." One of his colleagues had assured Noah that since Lupe didn't pay taxes, she was making the equivalent of fourteen dollars an hour and therefore earning a competitive wage. Noah did not entirely buy that argument, knowing that Lupe did not earn enough, had no benefits, and spent three hours a day on the bus commuting to and from their apartment. They had tried to help, recommending Lupe to two friends. Now, Lupe was working part-time for three families, but Jessie also worried about this state of affairs. Although Lupe had the equivalent of a full-time job, she had no paid holidays and earned no benefits.

Money aside, they had also had to figure out how to interact with Lupe in a way that was comfortable for all of them. They certainly did not want to define the relationship through power differentials. Thus, they had stipulated from the start that Lupe was only there to take care of Violet, that she was not, as Noah put it, "our maid." Noah had also endeavored to get to know her better, going out of his way to start conversations with her. She wouldn't really engage him, however, quickly answering his questions and then changing the subject.

Finding that class differences were not so easily dissolved, Jessie and Noah constantly had to navigate unfamiliar situations. For instance, inviting Lupe to Violet's birthday party had been unexpectedly problematic. They wanted to ask her, so Jessie broached the subject one afternoon, unaware that it would put Lupe in a bind. Lupe didn't want to say no—felt that she couldn't say no—so she equivocated; since the buses ran so infrequently on Sundays, she wasn't sure she would be able to come. Sensing Lupe's unease, Jessie realized that it would be a hassle for Lupe, and she didn't want Lupe to feel pressured, as though it were part of her job. They were not hiring Lupe for the party but asking her as a guest—yet that also felt strange, since Lupe wasn't really a friend. So Jessie had to backpedal, stressing that it was an invitation, not an obligation, and that it was okay if Lupe couldn't make it.

The birthday party was one example of countless similar moments; Jessie and Noah were never quite sure how to behave, because they did not know how to define their relationship with Lupe. They tried to subvert the differences between themselves and Lupe but were never entirely successful. According to Jessie, this left them "in this gray area where there are no rules, because I think that certainly, the other women I know who really do have much more money than I do. They think nothing of hiring somebody. They've got, you know, their thing and their woman, who comes, and you know."

Noah added, "And they think of her in a way that we think we're not supposed to think of her in that way, and we try not to." Knowing what they didn't want, however, did not make it easier to understand how to find a workable balance, a relationship that acknowledged their own position of privilege but one that did not make them completely uncomfortable. This weighed heavily on Noah, who held that

> the weirdest thing about having a nanny is that there can be a lot to think about, and every day, I actually do think about our relationship as I'm interacting with her, but there isn't much substance to it, to the relationship. There really isn't, and that's just, like I can't, our conversations are almost always about Violet, like we said, and if not then they're generally very, very superficial. She's not a friend, because if we were to say goodbye tomorrow, would we ever speak to her again? No, but our baby loves her, and she loves our baby.

This lack of definition left him at a loss, not knowing how he should interact with Lupe: "You know, I feel moments of discomfort a lot when Lupe's around, um, just because of little things like that, like that, or like the class thing. . . . Every day I feel uncomfortable when she leaves, because I don't know how to say goodbye to her. I don't know if she's a friend of mine or, you know. I don't know, [to Jessie] do you feel weird when she leaves? I feel weird no matter what. *I don't know how to say goodbye to her.*"

Much of the distress employers experience, then, is played out in daily interactions, in the everyday exchanges that both reflect and constitute social relationships of inequality. Noah assumed that learning about Lupe would help to level the playing field, since she knew so much about him and Jessie and their daughter. He sought to counter this unidirectional flow of information, which re-creates relations of power by foregrounding who is required to learn about the other person and who does not have to be bothered. However, Lupe wouldn't comply; for her, the lines were clearly drawn, and she did not want to, did not know how to, or did not feel comfortable being Noah and Jessie's "friend." Thus, Noah could not figure out how to define the relationship in any way but the one he most wanted to avoid, and he was reminded of this every day when it was time to say goodbye to Lupe.

Noah knew that these difficulties stemmed from the inequality of the relationship but didn't know exactly how to talk about it: "it might have something to do with racism, it might have something to do with class. Whatever it is, she plays into it; we play into it, but she still hasn't become an equal." In fact, "I just somehow imagine that this is about class and money and it's not about, you know, I don't know. When we're in the position of being in the higher class, it's easy to state, you know, we want the other person to just not think of class. It's very easy for me to say that, but obviously it's a lot more hard to actually do that." Noah and Jessie did not like having to accept this difference, as it did not fit their politically liberal orientation. It was also disconcerting because it made them recognize their own, more powerful position. As graduate students, their privilege was more invisible than most employers'; they earned little and felt poor. Lupe's presence, however, made Noah recognize that "you're not really poor, and then when someone comes in who really is poor *and* is of a different class, it's just, you know, it's in your face every day." Jessie agreed; when they first hired Lupe this had become glaringly obvious, making them feel guilty and anxious about who they were. She remembered "feeling suddenly like we were in this other class . . . and *what in the world?*"

As graduate students, Jessie and Noah perhaps seem atypical employers, economically on the margins of the middle class and too easily aware of power and the workings of inequality. However, many employers expressed similar unease around domestic service, relating stories of unfamiliar, often sticky, situations, moments that forced them to (re)consider their own privilege.

While many employers expressed ambivalence and disquiet about domestic service, others denied any such feelings. They were reluctant to acknowledge any differences between themselves and their domestic employees, emphatically rejecting any suggestion of inequality. These denials were usually unsolicited, revealing employers' own discomfort or preemptively responding to popular expectations of exploitation.

Christine and Paul, for instance, lavished praise on Teresa, thankful for everything she did and how well she took care of their daughter. They admired and appreciated her, especially because she was a "self-starter" who did not wait for direction but saw to everything that needed to be done. Teresa had taken charge of both Debbie and the house from the start. She was highly responsible, and she was an enterprising person, always looking to improve herself and to be better at her job. Without any word to them, for example, Teresa had learned to drive and bought a car so that when Debbie started kindergarten, Teresa was ready to take her. Now that Debbie was in first grade, Teresa had started cleaning additional houses during the day. They did not mind. Teresa always made sure that Debbie and their house came first. They trusted her completely, because she was a self-starter. As such, they had never invoked a status differential. Paul asserted that

> we never tried to have a status thing, with like we're the boss and you work for us, so, uh, you know. We told her, you know, "Hey, bring your friends on over, bring your daughter over, yeah sure, you know, wherever you're going." So, you know, we've had that kind of relationship, and we think that has also allowed her to stretch out and feel comfortable, and, uh, she's a very, very strong person in so many ways. I don't know her own story, you know, what things she suffered through, but she's very humble; but we know she's also this strong person, physically and, you know, mentally strong person.

Christine and Paul respected Teresa's hard work and internal drive. They proudly informed me that she was doing well economically, having recently purchased a new car. In a way, then, Teresa's ambition and work ethic revealed a middle-class sensibility. Paul and Christine had given Teresa free reign precisely because they had recognized this, and as a result, she had "blossomed." According to Paul, she sees herself in a different light, in a different way, and that she deserves the finer and better things in life and she's got her a nice new, uh, new minivan . . . and I see that personal growth in her, so I think, because of the, uh, and so we don't do a lot of questioning of her, because we know she's a self-starter since day one, and I don't know how it was with the, with the other people [she worked for], whether she felt that she had the kind of autonomy that we give her, and I think giving her that autonomy has allowed her just to stretch out and really blossom and just do the, you know, do what she needed to do. She doesn't seem to feel the kind of pressure or, you know, to have to be anxious about anything with us, and I think it's just allowed her to be relaxed and, you know, come into her own as an individual. . . . I've really seen that in her, and other people have said that too, as a matter of fact, [to Christine] your sister said "since Teresa's been with you guys, she has really, really blossomed," and I think, I think so. You know, it's been really good for both parties.

Paul and Christine projected middle-class aspirations onto Teresa, reading her desire for "finer and better things" as a sign of her (desire for) upward mobility. If Teresa shared their middle-class aspirations and values, she was not really different from her employers. In turn, their relationship was not marked by difference or categorical inequalities. Rather, it was a simple business exchange, one from which both parties profited. Teaching her that she deserved more, Paul and Christine had in fact coached Teresa to achieve the American Dream. And, of course, the income they provided enabled her pursuit of this Dream. Emphasizing their "help" allowed Paul and Christine to neutralize any suspicion of mistreatment or claims of unequal power relationships.

The Limits of "Americanness"

Paul and Christine rejected the implication of privilege by assimilating Teresa into their own class—into the American Dream—thereby foreclosing the possibility of inequality, even as their earnings varied significantly. Other employers also refused their own positions of power through the language of nationality, but rather than implying incorporation, their denials foregrounded difference and exclusion.

Take Carla: forty-seven, white, and mother of two, she had employed three different nannies over the years: a Filipina woman, a Salvadoran woman, and one who was "the blonde, blue-eyed all-American girl." What was amazing, she told me, was that the Salvadoran and the Filipina nannies did whatever she asked. Rosa, her current nanny, would "do everything—nothing is beneath her, literally, not that I would demean her." Conversely, the American had had an attitude problem: "it was a little bit the air she gave, you know." The difference, Carla concluded, was that "when they're immigrants, they have an expectation of what they think that they can accomplish when they get here."

Carla did not consider her demands excessive but reasoned that the "blonde, blue-eyed all-American girl" was selfish. For her, this difference turned on the distinction between "immigrant," or Salvadoran or Filipina, and "American" nannies. Drawing this boundary, Carla sidestepped her own privilege, displacing it onto the American nanny's impertinence. Yet what made her experiences with the American unpleasant was not just the nanny's reluctance to do what she was asked, but what this refusal highlighted: as an American, the nanny had the same rights as Carla. By contrast, if she hired an immigrant woman, Carla would not have to worry about infringing on another's prerogatives. What Carla never mentioned was whether Rosa or the other nanny were on the path to becoming American citizens. It made no difference: to her, "American" clearly meant "blonde and blue-eyed." This is a common conception, permanently denying immigrant workers access to the benefits of "Americanness."[5]

Cheryl, thirty-five, African American and expecting her second child, similarly shifted class anxiety onto national, ultimately racialized, terms. She had hired the Sparkle and Shine Co-op to clean for her but was less interested in this group's ideals than in good service. Cheryl found that the Co-op was effective, weeding out the women who did not clean well or had negative attitudes. She had tried other cleaning services, but they had had a different manner, more "white bread." They were very expensive and acted as though they were doing you a favor, she told me. Cheryl did not want to be one of those people who treated their "cleaning people like servants," but she certainly took note of unwarranted surliness: "I think, you know what though, I think I'm just weird with that. I'm weird with help, because I never want to make it seem like, you know, 'go do that,' or, *you know what I mean?*" She explained: "I don't know what it is, I mean, I grew up like in boarding schools and stuff, and so I had friends who had servants, and I just never really liked the way, you know, it just all came across. *You know what I'm saying?* It just, you know, all came across, really, *you know,* but I just, it was never really my thing."

Co-op members, on the other hand, cleaned well and had a cheerful demeanor. Still, her husband was convinced that they hated him, and he always left the house while they were there. She said, "I mean, it's that whole thing, between, you know, the Hispanic working population, feeling like the *gringos,* and you know, whatever, whatever. "Oh hi, hi, hi," and as soon as they turn around their backs, they're like *you know.* Or just like when you walk into an Asian nail salon . . . *that same mentality* . . . and he swears, I mean, he's half joking, but he's like *don't fool yourself."*

Cheryl could not name the problem. Lacking a vocabulary to talk about privilege, she resorted to phrases like "you know what I mean?" or "you know what I'm saying?" Certainly we know what she was saying; we all know about class but have trouble speaking it. Instead, we shift it onto idioms of nationality and race, both of which "function as sites of displacements of class, and as crypto-class discourses" (Ortner 2003: 51). These slippages confirm the abiding overlap among categories of race, class, and nation. In the U.S. example, "middle class" is inextricable from ideas of whiteness and "Americanness"—together they form the unmarked norm, the privileged subject against whom everyone else's deviance is measured. Significantly, while racial, ethnic, and national *difference* are more easily acknowledged, whiteness, as the norm, remains unsayable.[6] The illusion, or delusion, of color blindness functions in much the same way as the denial of class difference—both fictions naturalize and erase inequality through the language of merit (e.g., Brown et al. 2003; Doane and Bonilla-Silva 2003; Bonilla-Silva 2006). Foreignness, on the other hand, remains utterly marked and unproblematically singled out, particularly in a context of increased political polarization over immigration.

Not surprisingly, then, Cheryl found a way to express difference through national categories. Referring to other cleaning services as "white bread," she highlighted both their whiteness and their "Americanness." Phrases such as "white bread" critique whiteness as empty and insipid, while at the same time confirming it as unmarked norm. Used as a synonym for boring, bland, and normal, "white bread" verifies the inherent correspondence between whiteness and "Americanness."

Cheryl also drew a meaningful equivalence between the "Hispanic" women who cleaned her house and the "Asian" women who work in nail salons, for in both cases, she could not understand what the women were saying. This verified her suspicion that their foreignness was immutable, an unbridgeable chasm. Referencing nationality, Cheryl explained away any suggestion of exploitation or unfairness on her part. The Co-op's members had a "good" attitude, she declared. They wanted to be there; as immigrants, they could not really ask for more. They knew that, and Cheryl knew that, and thus both parties understood how the relationship should work.

Conclusion

Thus, taking on a domestic employee does more than secure the material grounds of "Americanness"; it actively reconstructs and redefines the very possibility of membership in the nation. Through the quotidian exchanges of domestic service, employers generate a logic of exclusion that reaffirms not only their position on the inside but also domestic workers' place on the outside. Characterizing domestic workers as forever foreign, intrinsically unassimilable, employers categorically excluded domestic workers from the benefits of membership. More than rhetorical sleight of hand, this particular constellation of equality, access, and "Americanness" reveals the limitations of the American Dream. It also has real, material repercussions, reproducing the inequalities that underpin a middle-class lifestyle. Invisible to employers, these disparities are illuminated through domestic service, precisely because of its location in the home. As they collide, unwillingly, with these realizations, employers begin to articulate what was once perhaps practical knowledge, re-creating—and deepening—the naturalized difference of immigrant women. They essentially render these women invisible, for as outsiders they do not, they cannot, count. In so doing, employers elucidate how the global and the foreign remain indispensable to the construction of "Americanness" and the American Dream.

CHAPTER 3

Making Mothers Count

If reproducing immigrants' invisibility makes it easier for employers to contend with the differences and inequalities so essential to pursuing their American Dreams, it also envelops and erases the labor of the middle-class women who deploy this strategy. As the previous chapter points out, each generation must reproduce its own Dream, thus making parents' success reliant on the achievements of their children. Reproductive labor, then, is as crucial to middle-class success as the productive labor that underwrites it. However, reproductive labor remains unrecognized and uncounted, and since women continue to be responsible for the majority of this work,[1] they bear the brunt of those erasures. That is, motherhood, for the middle-class mother, remains embattled and uncertain, at times crushing individuals' very sense of personhood, of social membership and individual worth.

In this chapter, I explore not just the sense of insufficiency that suffuses contemporary middle-class experiences of motherhood but also the ways in which one particular mothers' group sought to redefine the value and importance of care work. Obviously self-selected, these women's feelings and words were nevertheless echoed by almost every middle-class mother I met in Los Angeles. Their stories crystallize the ways in which motherhood produces a sense of estrangement. More importantly, their struggle to rethink the social worth of mothering foregrounds how a particular understanding of value, based on the erasure of reproductive labor, constricts their access to full social membership.[2]

Generation X, Motherhood, and Stereotypes

A 2003 *USA Today* article (Peterson 2003) characterized Generation X mothers as "entitled." The author interviewed several women who expressed a desire to work part-time or stay at home with their children and concluded that these mothers sought a return to pre-feminist ideals, stressing "family values" and dismissing the gains of second-wave feminism: "Their own moms pioneered greater access to the workplace while juggling family demands. The younger moms often take for granted the options their moms helped win" (Peterson 2003: 1D). The article continues: "Gen X women are postponing marriage, having children later, are more fearful of divorce and doing their darndest to prioritize family, Howe says. He sees them at the 'cutting edge' of a generation that is 'very protective of family life'" (Peterson 2003: 1D). And, finally: "Among more affluent Gen X moms, not working outside the home is 'the new status symbol,' Howe says. 'Working used to be high status. Now that same working mom is considered a wage slave'" (Peterson 2003: 1D).

I cite this article because it fed on and perpetuated the same stereotypes I originally held about stay-at-home mothers. It recycled a mixture of curiosity and contempt that has come to characterize representations of Generation X mothers, specifically those who stay at home full-time. At the turn of the millennium, newspapers, magazines, and self-help books, for instance, highlighted an increase in the number of middle-class women leaving the workforce.[3] Their explanations rang familiar, reproducing the same framework that limits discussion to begin with: this must be some return to tradition, a rejection of their mothers' generation, an increasingly conservative generation in an increasingly conservative country.

I also refer to this article because it elicited frustration from many members of my mothers' group; more than a few mentioned it to me. Catherine, for instance, complained that the article completely missed the point:

Well, the headline was basically, the title was something like "Mothers Have It Their Way," but the first paragraph was mothers are deciding more and more to go back to the way it was, you know? They want to be at home with their kids, and it was very much a feel-good fifties kind of thing, and it was like, oh good, everybody wants to be back in the fifties. It was not a sense of they want something different from what we've ever had. . . . It very much took away the, you know, the *revolutionary* aspect of it, which is we're not asking just to be at home, we could have done that. We've done that. Been there. We're asking to be home but also have flexible work options and that kind of stuff, you know? We want family friendly economic policies and they didn't talk about that at all.

Catherine's remarks emphasize how this type of framing narrows the scope of the conversation. This chapter considers Catherine's use of "revolutionary," exploring how one mothers' group sought to redefine the issue, to challenge the usual conversations we have about women, work, and motherhood.[4]

This group, a local affiliate of a national organization, was located in an affluent area of Los Angeles and consisted primarily of white, middle-class, Generation X[5] mothers with young children. Most of them were married, and they were all heterosexual. Some stayed at home to care for their kids, while others worked[6] part-time, and still others engaged in full-time paid employment. Despite their individual positions, or perhaps because of them, members did not engage the questions I had anticipated: The difficulties of juggling work and family life in contemporary American society are well known. The media, politicians, pundits, and scholars have addressed the topic, debating the consequences of women's work outside the home and wondering about the fate of the nuclear family. So when I joined the group, I expected similar discussions, along with a healthy dose of theorizing about bonding with children and how to be a good mother. To my surprise, I found a group of articulate, thoughtful women with divergent and complex ideas about motherhood.

For these women, motherhood had become a predicament, characterized by ever-present feelings of exhaustion, deficiency, and guilt. Theirs is a generational story; it is also a story about race, class, and social privilege. Although they held differing views about household work, childcare, and paid employment, the group's members belonged to the same generational cohort and shared the experience of starting a family at a time when global transformations had altered the nature of the workforce. Most of these women belonged to the "top-level professional and managerial workforce" (Sassen 2000: 509), whose jobs demanded increased time and intensity. These growing work pressures led to a steep rise in working hours: in 2000, Americans worked thirty-six more hours than they did in 1990, almost a full workweek (Webb 2001).[7]

These changes in work patterns coincided with the coming of age of a particular generation of women, women whose ideas about family and paid employment were formed in the wake of second-wave feminism. Gen X women never doubted that they *could* and *would* enter the workforce, excel in whatever they chose, and compete on an equal footing with men. Even the wage gap, a last vestige of unequal treatment in the workplace, was shrinking for them: in 2002, the Bureau of Labor Statistics found that women aged twenty-seven to thirty-three who had never had a child, earned 98 percent of men's wages (Venable 2002: 1).[8]

As such, the urgencies of feminism seemed to fall away for many of this cohort. Indeed, scholars explain the shape of third-wave feminism[9] through its intersection with Generation X; they maintain that a sense of entitlement and focus on individualism in the third wave stem from Gen Xers' overall attitude, taking for granted the gains of the previous feminist waves. Women of this generation grew up thinking they could do whatever they wanted—their gender never posed an impediment, and as white women,[10] they were not aware of racial barriers or of their own (invisible) privilege. Thus, Gen Xers seemingly faced no limits.

For members of the mothers' group, race and class privilege certainly worked together, the one concealing the other.[11] Most were white and most belonged to the "professional middle class" (Ehrenreich and Ehrenreich 1979), whose status is based on social capital—education and white-collar jobs, for example—rather than income levels. This class includes "such diverse types as school-teachers, anchorpersons, engineers, professors, government bureaucrats, corporate executives . . . scientists, advertising people, therapists, financial managers, architects" (Ehrenreich 1989: 12).

Significantly, Gen X women learned to construct their own subjectivities through their careers. As Ortner points out, Generation X "has always been, first and foremost, about identity through work: jobs, money, and careers" (1998a: 421). Members of the mothers' group defined themselves through the kinds of work they performed and also through economic independence—both of these marked them as adults and as valuable members of society. As such, social status rested on economic well-being, producing a slippage between social and economic capital.

Like other women of their generation, members of the mothers' group grew up with the expectation that they would have professional careers, because they could—because work provided validation and financial independence, because they defined themselves through it, and finally, because they needed it to stave off an always-looming economic disaster. Sexism, race, and class fell away as obstructions to workplace success, concealed through privilege. Encouraged to do anything they wanted, they were never told that they would have to make a choice between work and motherhood. Therefore, for all of them, whether they expected to work or to stay home full-time, motherhood came as an abrupt change, once invisible impediments suddenly rendered indelibly clear.

Having children made it difficult to continue down a career path at the same pace, particularly at a time when work encroached further and further into people's lives. In turn, workplace demands made it impossible to be a "good" mother. To make matters worse, mothers had to gauge their suitability against popular representations of proper motherhood, an unachievable standard even for those women who did not work outside the home. All of a sudden, members of a generation that was promised everything experienced betrayal; they were forced to recognize that they could not have it all and were compelled to make choices that were insufficient—to stay at home, to engage in full-time paid employment, or to work part-time?

Decisions about Work and Home, or the Myth of "Choice"

This betrayal was initially felt as a lack of workable choices. Gen X women were raised to expect a full range of options, but instead found limited, always unsatisfactory, alternatives. The contradictions between home and work are well rehearsed in American public culture as in academia. For the members of the mothers' group, this opposition remained theoretical until they became mothers. Once they had children, everything changed, and all at once, the "choices" available to them seemed completely inadequate. They scoffed at the idea of "choice," arguing that although previous generations had struggled to open up possibilities for women, they had not gone far enough.

Working Full-Time

Popular representations of working mothers often portray these women as selfish, placing their personal aspirations above the needs of their families. However, decisions to work outside the home are not necessarily based on a desire to work full-time. Some families rely on a second income to stay afloat economically or to maintain a certain standard of living. Jessica, for instance, worked full-time as an elementary school teacher. In her late thirties, Jessica wanted to be a stay-at-home mother to her two children, but she could not afford to do so. Although she suspected that they could figure out a way to manage, her husband insisted that they wouldn't make it on his salary alone. Jessica's mother had stayed at home for many years, and Jessica always expected that she would do the same. Having to work full-time made her unhappy and left her with a deep sense of inadequacy. Despite all the time she spent with her children after school, on the weekends, and all day during the summer, she continued to feel that she was somehow failing them.

Yet Jessica's story was not as straightforward as it might at first appear. On the one hand, she wanted to be a full-time mother, but on the other, she enjoyed her job and liked "feeling like I'm using my brain." She would probably miss working if she gave it up altogether. Furthermore, she knew that her income helped with her family's day-to-day needs, and it also allowed her children an array of opportunities they might not otherwise have. She thought it crucial for her sons to be exposed to as many different things as possible and spent much of her free time ferrying them around to chess, swimming, soccer, art, piano, or karate classes. Finally, she knew that having an income was important in terms of planning her future. As a child, she had seen her parents suffer after her father lost his job. To this day, her mother continued to work, even though she had some health problems. Jessica did not want to end up in the same place: "And that's why, you know, I feel like I have to keep working, too, for that retirement, 'cause I hear all these, you know, moms talk about retirement and how they're worried about it, and I think that that's a very real concern."

Jessica once told me that she was one of the most unhappy members of the group—that everyone else seemed to have "it" more or less figured it out. However, the difference was not that other working mothers were completely at peace with their choices, but that their frustrations had other sources. Unlike Jessica, who felt pressed into a full-time job against her will, other members explained that their careers allowed them to stay "sane" or "healthy." Of course, most of these full-time working mothers also relied on their income.

For many full-time workers, career expectations loomed large. After dedicating a lot of time and effort to a particular occupation, these women were reluctant to "give it all up," and they knew that taking time off or working fewer hours could effectively derail their careers. Anne, a physician, told me that certain medical specialists find it impossible to cut back their hours. Surgeons, for example, have almost no leeway, for they must maintain their skills through constant practice. As an internist, Anne had more room to maneuver, but she confessed that she was lucky—she had chosen her specialty not for its practicality but because she liked it. As a student, she pursued a career that interested her, thinking that she could figure out the "family stuff" later. Looking back, she realized that she had been "naïve."

Catherine, a Ph.D. student in her late twenties, was reconsidering her commitment to academia. Although she had always known that she wanted to be a full-time mother, she attended an elite university and also planned to pursue a professional career. She was ambitious, and her twin aspirations—motherhood and a career—didn't necessarily feel contradictory before she had her son:

> When you're thinking about these things, you're not totally coherent, right? Sometimes I really thought about them together but other times I really didn't . . . and, when I made the decision to go to graduate school I was much more in the mode of, this is what I really love. I'm really great at this, I really want to do this. And I was kinda thinking about how this fit into having kids, but not as much, you know. That really wasn't the priority in choosing that career, and lo and behold, now I have the issue.

When I met Catherine, she was trying to figure out what to do next: finish her dissertation or try to find another career. She calculated that a tenure-track job, like "most really rewarding work out there," would demand sixty-hour workweeks, and she wasn't willing to teach part-time. Part-time positions, she explained, were "crap—it's not rewarding. You're not part of the department." She would jump at the opportunity to work part-time: "If I had the option to work really twenty hours a week . . . *if* I could really work twenty hours a week, on a long-term tenure track, like a career, not just part-time pay and no status and not teaching the classes I want and blah, blah, blah. *If* it were a real long-term career, yeah. There's no question. I would be all over that." Her stress on the word "if" underscores the near impossibility of Catherine's ideal. She was angry that this was not a real choice. Most professions do not allow any flexibility for mothers, but she refused to believe that it had to be that way: "We need a total revamping of the way most professions work. I mean that's my take on it. . . . I don't buy it. To me it's baloney that it has to be that way. It has been that way, because traditionally it's been men who've done it, and it doesn't hurt them to do it that way, and it's more efficient even economically for them to get it all out of the way up front, the low pay years, and then get more money more quickly. I think it's all about what's efficient for men's life lines." Catherine's comments also presented a biting critique of workplace "culture," disputing the supposed "rationality" and economic exigencies that require people to spend more and more time at the office:

> I've talked to several doctors who think that that's absolutely the case, and in fact that the twenty-four-hour and the forty-eight-hour and the seventy-two-hour shifts are all about I did it, so you have to do it too. It's all about pulling your weight, and it's almost like hazing. And there's a lot of stuff in workplaces that's like hazing. . . . And I think it's about suffering. There's a real culture of I have to be here til nine and suffer. It doesn't matter if I'm playing computer games at my desk or not, but I'm here. I'm not with my family. I'm suffering and somehow that makes you worthy of promotion or whatever job advancement, you know? And that is a real male thing, I think, that culture of suffering and hazing, and that whole thing. So I think a lot could change.

All the working mothers related similar complaints. Unfortunately, they lamented, the demands of the corporate world are out of control. A "martyr" culture pervades the workplace, where the more hours you spend working and the less you have a life, the better worker you are. It does not matter how much, or how efficiently, you produce, as long as you're there. Louise, an architect, explained how it worked in her office: "The partners that don't have kids can go in every Saturday, that's kind of like their thing. And even before I had [my daughter] I realized, cause I was going in on Saturdays too, I realized, a partner, all he wanted to do was just shoot the breeze for an hour, a couple hours. I'm like 'this is Saturday.' "

Kelly had a similar story. After her children were born, she continued her full-time job as a financial analyst but insisted on leaving at 7 PM every day. Knowing that she would be going home at seven, she worked more intensely and did not take breaks. Although her coworkers remained at the office for hours after she left, they were not nearly as efficient, wasting time on personal phone calls, gossiping, or surfing the Internet. Nonetheless, she felt chastised and was often derided for leaving work so early.

As the mothers argued, corporate culture values only time spent at the office, time devoted to earning money. Rather than focus on long-term goals such as employee retention and satisfaction, or broad social aims such as raising children, the corporate world emphasizes short-term gains such as improved quarterly reports.[12] It is clear, then, that providing family leave, flex-time, or on-site childcare would detract from rational, economic corporate ends.

At the same time, however, this system seems to thrive on "suffering," "hazing," and "martyrdom," disregarding efficiency. This model of the workplace gauges contributions in terms of time, not productivity, and contradicts basic assumptions about economic rationality. Why would a rational economic model penalize Kelly when she was more efficient than anyone else in her office? From the mothers' descriptions, it is clear that long workdays also have a social end; these workplace practices (re)produce a specific type of worker. As rituals, hazing, suffering, and the like, create a work identity that is in large part defined through devotion and group solidarity. The limitations of this system, its lack of rationality, only became clear when these women became mothers—when they could no longer conform to its standards.[13] Once they were on the outside, they realized that workplaces did not have to function in this manner, and they wanted to redefine the ideal worker to allow for flexibility and to prioritize productivity over time.

Within the existing system, women who enjoyed their careers, relied on their income, and wanted to have a family felt cornered, trapped between unsatisfactory alternatives. Barbara, for example, had her first child in her late thirties. In her early forties, she was thinking about having another but was not willing to sacrifice her job. It took her a long time to get back into the swing of things at work after her daughter was born, and she feared that it might be impossible to do so while taking care of two children, even though she employed a full-time nanny. Whereas Barbara felt that she had a choice, limited as it was, Jenny couldn't even entertain the idea of having a second child. She needed to work and couldn't afford care for another child.

Anxieties about childcare not only influenced decisions about having additional children; at times they pushed women into full-time work.[14] Childcare was increasingly unaffordable, even though the availability of cheap domestic labor in the LA area made hiring a nanny less expensive than center-based care. Nevertheless, women who worked part-time often labored just to cover childcare costs. Thus, mothers had to choose between working full-time or staying home full-time, and anyone who needed an income was forced into a full-time job.

Decisions about full-time work, therefore, were complex, requiring careful calculation about a range of concerns. These decisions were always lacking, asking individuals to make impossible choices. They had to give up a career they wanted to pursue or forgo income they needed; they had to stop working at a job they enjoyed or feel that they never spent enough time with their children.

Staying at Home

Ostensibly at the opposite end of the spectrum, stay-at-home mothers made decisions based on similar constraints, and, perhaps surprisingly, economic considerations were also key to these decisions. Contrary to the USA Today article, these women did not base their choice purely on ideological grounds. They did not necessarily believe that staying home made them better mothers or was crucial to raising healthy children. Rather, many framed their decisions in economic terms. Before her daughter was born, Ellen rose through the ranks at a well-known Internet company. Ellen had always defined herself as ambitious, and she enjoyed her work a great deal. In her early thirties, she felt that she had hit the glass ceiling at her job, and she and her husband decided to start a family. While she was pregnant, she worked part-time at an Internet startup, but after her daughter was born, she realized that childcare costs would offset her earnings:

Even though I was making half of the director's salary, on top of what my husband was making, you know, we would have to pay for childcare if I was gonna do that. I was netting forty cents to a dollar. We even talked to our financial planner. We were talking to our financial planner at that point, doing our financial plan, and all that kind of stuff. So we knew enough to do the math and know what's it gonna be, to know that it might not be worth the hassle. The money that I might end up netting might not be worth the hassle.

Ellen would have preferred to work, but her husband was a junior associate at a law firm, and if they both worked full-time, neither of them would see their daughter. So Ellen reluctantly decided to stay home, and she resented that she had been pushed into this position by tax policies and the costs of childcare. She explained that her husband could not stay home, because he was at a critical point in his career; she, on the other hand, had arrived at a crossroads, trying to figure out what to do next. Although it made sense in this context, this kind of explanation masks the fact that it is the women who most often end up staying home. Framing the decision in terms of career trajectories does not explain why it is almost always men's careers that cannot be interrupted.

For women, timing and careers were also primary considerations in opting for full-time motherhood. Many stay-at-home moms who felt that they had ultimately made the right decision for their families did not arrive at this choice by following ideological imperatives. Rather, their decisions often coincided with turning points in their careers. At thirty-five, Diane had experienced a long career in public relations. Quite by chance, she was laid off a month into her pregnancy and found herself at a loss. Who would hire a pregnant woman? At the time, Diane had not decided whether she would continue working after she had the baby, but she thought that she might. There was a day care center at her job, and this made it feasible; "I wasn't entirely sure . . . but I wanted the option." Getting pregnant when she did, however, narrowed her possibilities. She was sure that no one would give her a job and came to the conclusion that she would stay at home. This decision was also influenced by her upbringing—her mother had stayed at home and encouraged Diane to do the same.

After a few years at home, Diane had seemingly experienced an ideological shift. She told me that she had put off having a family because she was raised to think that she should have a career. Now, however, she was starting to rethink this philosophy: "I don't know if that was all so great. For families, you know? Pushing women to feel like they had to go out and put family aside, so my views kind of changed." I was intrigued by this comment and inquired further, asking why it wasn't so great. She explained that she had come to the conclusion that women couldn't do it all, and they had to make a choice. She had always privileged work over family life and realized that if she had not been pregnant when she got laid off, she would have taken another job. Then she would have felt that she could not have a family right away, because she had just taken on a new position, and in turn, she would have put off starting a family. But she also admitted that she had made this choice at a time when she was reconsidering her career. It had been the right decision for her "because I figured out that PR wasn't the career for me, and that's what kind of changed my mind." The idea that she could have indefinitely put off having a family for a job she was starting to rethink made Diane wonder about her own unquestioning adherence to workplace protocol. On the other hand, she knew that she would eventually go back to work and was taking this time to explore what she wanted to do. She had met with a career counselor more than once.

While Diane had made peace with her decisions, Meg was more conflicted about being a full-time mom. A specialist in nonprofit management, Meg had quit her job after her three-month maternity leave ended. At that point, she had been trying to decide between a new job and going back to the old one, but she didn't think that either was a good fit. Along with career indecision, the high costs of childcare influenced her final choice. She based this decision

> partly by the influence of my husband's opinions about who was the best childcare provider for our daughter being me. And some health problems I was going through at the time and didn't feel like I could manage working, the health problems, and my daughter, and so I kind of . . . forget it, I don't want anything to do with work. . . . [The decision] was made much more out of fear than anything else. Fear that I couldn't handle the stresses, and also I'd done enough research into the childcare field, you know . . . to know that it was very difficult to get good quality childcare that we could afford. That if I did want to work part-time, then we were gonna have a very hard

time finding that, you know that match that worked out. While I was comfortable with the idea of hiring a childcare provider that was in our home, [my husband] was not at all interested in that. He would rather her going to a more formal childcare setting, you know, like a setting. . . . I think I was a little bit more relaxed about the idea of her going into childcare. . . . I'd like to think I didn't have some of the hang ups other people did, because I had sort of this idea that as long as she had solid relationships with the caregiver, you know, with a steady person. . . . [My husband] would have done it himself if he hadn't been taking the bar exam.

Childcare, career uncertainties, her husband's own career path, and financial concerns all played a hand in Meg's decision. Fear was also a crucial consideration for Meg, as it was for the other mothers. They often expressed this fear, the recognition that it was impossible to be both an ideal worker and an ideal mother. Something always had to give. Lauren reminded me of this, mourning her one-time career:

I can't be both . . . personally, I *cannot* do both. I can't work a stressful job. I mean, oh, I can go get some job where I'm making, you know, whatever, where you're not taking it home with you. You know, any job where you're making good money, you're gonna have to work late once in a while, go on a business trip, something like that. But I could get a nine-to-five job, where you walk out the door at five o'clock, I could maybe do that. The only thing is that you need to be available for your kids, school and things like that. Like when they get sick.

Lauren's decision was also based on fear, on the realization that she could not do both jobs adequately. Taking care of her children meant being available at all times, especially since her husband was a busy physician and could not be interrupted at work. Lauren, who had worked as a banker for many years, knew that she would never be able to take care of her kids while working at a high-powered job.

We see then how economic constraints, social expectations, career concerns, and workplace demands shaped mothers' choices. Ideology took a back seat to pragmatic decision making; in all of these examples, economic calculation trumped personal desires and beliefs. Thus, Jessica worked even though she preferred to stay at home; Ellen wanted to work, but she was a full-time mother; career uncertainties played a part in Diane's and Meg's decisions; and Catherine was contemplating switching to a career that would allow more flexibility, despite the fact that she loved what she did. Through their narratives, it becomes clear that the language of choice is obfuscating and that it pits mothers against one another, blaming individuals for their imperfect choices rather than focusing on the lack of suitable alternatives. As Meg explained: "What really bugs me a lot is the idea almost all women that I've met really feel that it was their choice . . . wherever they are, that it was their choice. And we have a certain amount of control. But the choices are so constrained, and that's where, that's where I have a lot of differences about it. Yeah, I know that it was my choice . . . but if you look at the options that were presented. . . . Why make a judgment about what I do and what you do?"

"Losing One's Place"

What most of these mothers wanted—yet few seemed to find—was the opportunity to work as well as to spend time with their children. This choice was the least available, and most women wound up having to choose all or nothing. Neither of these choices was perfect, each creating a set of difficulties; everyone felt inadequate for her decisions. Jenny summed up their predicament: "I mean everything about being a mother is fraught with guilt. If I put my kid in day care, I'm guilty, if I have a nanny, I'm guilty, if I stay at home—guilty, if I work—guilty. And that's BS, because nine times out of ten our kids are going to grow up to be these functioning, healthy, productive . . ."

In both cases, mothers could no longer engage the working world on its own terms, and they felt that this made them invisible. Work was central to their definition of self, positioning them in the world and providing the economic independence that marked them as full, adult members of society. No longer able to define themselves through this, they felt their own subjectivity erased, that they disappeared as socially meaningful, valuable persons. Individuals who had once identified with their work now had to find a new source of identity. Unfortunately, despite a deeply held stake in their children's futures, motherhood was hardly a satisfying replacement, as it remained socially invisible, undervalued labor and thus conferred little social status.

As mothers, these women became invisible, precisely because our society defines value and success through achievement in the workplace and obscures the necessity and importance of reproductive labor. These underlying assumptions place home and work in opposition to each other, and make it increasingly difficult to reconcile the two. They also limit individuals' choices, through concrete economic constraints—unaffordable childcare, tax policies, and a lack of maternity leave—as well as through the popular understandings of success, defined through achievement in the workplace, that shape these mothers' senses of self.

This focus on the economic was crucial, for the sense of betrayal that these mothers felt came from a loss of economic, class-based privilege. When they became mothers, barriers arose as if from nowhere, barriers that not only prevented further advancement but seemingly took away their existing achievements. In some ways, they experienced motherhood as a "falling from grace" (Newman 1988), as downward mobility. As Newman explains, downward mobility applies to both income and status loss, especially in a context where professional employment and personal identity are isomorphic.

Both working moms and stay-at-home mothers suffered this fall from grace, or "fall off a cliff" as Ellen put it. Motherhood precipitated a loss of self; their mothering work and their concerns as mothers remained invisible, making them less than full members of society and pushing them out of a system of privilege they had once enjoyed. For working mothers, this manifested in the give-and-take between home and work. The demands of each and their putative opposition made mothers feel inadequate in both arenas. They did not have enough time for their kids but were reluctant to ask for flexibility at the office, as this would only serve to confirm that motherhood and flourishing careers are incompatible. Instead, they had to prove that they could still perform, and often this meant having to erase all visible traces of their families. They did not line their desks with pictures of their families or decorate their walls with their children's artwork.

When they could not bend to all the demands of the workplace, their pay and their job status suffered. Louise, for instance, reduced her work schedule to 80 percent when her daughter was born. She thought that a thirty-two-hour week would ease her stress, and her employers were amenable to this change. Despite taking a pay cut, she was still working forty hours a week. She also recognized that if she hadn't rolled back her schedule, she would be putting in fifty hours. Louise was satisfied with this compromise, feeling that she had achieved the best of both worlds. Still, her story points to a new type of wage gap, one that begins to widen as soon as a woman becomes a mother. Members of the mothers' group knew this statistic well: whereas women without children have achieved virtual pay equity, mothers earn only 70 percent of men's wages (Rivers and Barnett 2000; cf. Budig and England 2001; Correll et al. 2007; Gough and Noonan 2013; Pew 2013). Working mothers, then, were always scrambling at both ends, feeling that they couldn't keep up, and increasingly vulnerable in terms of their jobs.

Mothers who stayed home experienced this fall from grace acutely, for they had effectively ceded the part of themselves that defined them as valuable members of society. They once had successful careers and earned respect through their jobs; now they were invisible, and their mothering was neither valued nor recognized as work. For instance, Lisa was incensed by an incident at her husband's workplace. Her husband told a female coworker that he could not stay late one evening, as his wife had to attend a meeting of her mothers' group. A few days later, the coworker informed him that she had to get home early, since her dog-owners' group was getting together. Lisa was furious, feeling abased, as though her mothering work was meaningless. She was also upset for her husband; he was very supportive of her choice to stay home, and she didn't want him to feel put down by his coworker's comments.

Social scorn was hard to take, and it was effective precisely because it hit a nerve. Women who had learned to define their identities through their occupations and through financial independence experienced a major loss when they exited the workforce. The idea that only paid employment confers full personhood was so ingrained that many had not respected their own stay-at-home mothers. Lisa, for example, remembered thinking "mom this is it, for you . . . I was like, you've gotta be kidding, staying at home and raising your children." In a similar vein, Ellen told me that she had always been perplexed by her mother's choice:

> I was just like, well, wait a minute, something doesn't jive here. So the expectations that were put, they were putting out for me, were so different than what she was doing. I think that was sort of a discon-

nect. And I remember distinctly thinking, well, that's never gonna be my life. I have other things I want to do, and I just can't even imagine, you know, being at home with my kids sort of as my primary activity kind of thing. . . . I struggled with this—wait a minute, I know in my mind you're a very intelligent, very articulate woman. Why aren't you doing *anything*?

Such strongly entrenched prejudices were hard to shake off, and even now the mothers continued to define themselves through their previous jobs. Lisa admitted that at the group's meetings, she still introduced herself as a writer, even though she was no longer working as one.

Members recognized, and sought to emphasize, the significance of their work as mothers, yet they often hesitated to identify "only" as mothers. Ellen's experience highlights this:

I think visibility and social status are about that, in our culture about paid work. When [my daughter] was three months old I went to our insurance agent, and it was my first time that I would have a real mission, you know. Something I knew I had to do. . . . So I hauled her in the carrier into the insurance agent's office, and I'm sort of in my element. . . . I'm like, okay, I haven't lost my mind. This is a useful thing that I'm doing, and I'm giving him all my information, until it gets to the part where he asks me what my occupation is, and I just simply froze. . . . I knew at that point that I was not working, but he asked me for my occupation, I was just like, I mean, I was like, I didn't even know what to say, and I thought about it, and so then he throws in a little list and says well, we have "homemaker." And I'm like, I didn't know what to say, and all I could say at that point was sort of "yeah, that's fine." And I still remember coming home that night and just bawling my eyes out to my husband, like "Oh my God . . . my idea of what that is, so does not describe me, that I'm just, I don't know what to do. . . ." You know that that's the way the world would classify me, and even though I know what seriousness I put on that term, I don't know, I don't know who the heck I am anymore, because everybody else thinks I'm X now, because I have this label, and it so doesn't match with who I think I am, or who I've been for the past thirty years of my life.

Ellen's comments capture the sensation of falling from grace—from one day to the next, she no longer knew who she was and was horrified to think that others were classifying her as something/someone she did not want to be. She had lost her social position. Always vocal about her frustrations, she spoke about the rage she felt at the beginning. When her daughter was a few months old, she took on more active involvement in the mothers' group and started reading about motherhood:

> At that point it was because I was pissed. In fact, my little sister made a comment. We went to see my parents . . . when [my daughter] was about five months old. . . . I had a talk with my parents and my sister. And my sister was just like, "Ellen had a baby and got pissed." And I was, I was pissed. I read Ann's [Crittenden] book, and I almost couldn't make it through chapters, because I was so angry, because I could relate, and because I was like, oh my God, she is articulating why I feel the way I feel. And it isn't me; it is systemic; I am being screwed. You know? And so it's not, it's not a normal. She was just really able to articulate why I felt so lousy.

Ann Crittenden's (2001) *The Price of Motherhood* emphasizes the economic constraints on and costs incurred by mothers in American society. Ellen's reference to this volume underscores economic anxieties, a primary concern for mothers who have given up paid employment. For these women, the loss of a professional identity was exacerbated by a newly found economic dependence. Exiting the paid workforce meant giving up their income and relying on their husbands' earnings. As a result, many explained that they no longer felt like equals in their marriages. Diane informed me that she felt bad for her husband, because he had married a peer and she no longer was; in addition, she now felt that she had to rein in her spending in a way she had never had to before. Her husband never said anything, nor did she think he cared, but she was always aware that she was "spending someone else's money." Money became an increasingly uneasy subject of negotiation between spouses. Furthermore, its power to signify—and take away—adulthood, independence, and equality constantly reminded full-time mothers that they had lost something valuable. Meg explained:

> You feel like you don't have any sort of entitlement or control over certain kinds of decisions. You get to decide over very small, insig-

nificant things, but not some of the larger stuff, and so. . . . I think all of that kind of creates, creates a thing, and there's this, sort of, idea that, yeah, it's all household money, but the fact of the matter is, is it's that it's not . . . you become acutely aware of that. I don't know that the men become aware of it. I think you feel it much more as a woman.

For women who were accustomed to working and were members of a generation who defined themselves through work, equality, and independence, financial dependence was a hard pill to swallow. Not only did this require reworking a sense of an independent adult self, but it also placed these mothers in a potentially perilous position (cf. Gerson 2010). The years spent at home do not allow mothers to accrue Social Security credits or contribute to a pension fund. Part-time workers face similar difficulties, since they earn reduced salaries and receive no benefits. Thus with motherhood, the future became uncertain, particularly when they imagined the possibility of divorce or widowhood, both leading causes of poverty among women.

A lack of income could also leave women prostrate, trapping them in bad relationships. Meg explained that she needed to make money. She had recently found out that her mother was in an abusive relationship but couldn't leave because she had no income: "And I can see even in my own marriage how much of the power dynamic changes between the husband and wife . . . into that, into those sort of stereotypical, I'm trying not to call them traditional, those stereotypical roles—main breadwinner, primary caregiver, you know? And I find it even though I don't feel any danger in my own marriage, I can see just how insidious that . . ." Similarly, Lauren warned that before I decided to marry anyone, I should make sure we had a conversation about children. She definitely recommended having children but told me to be careful, because the partner earning higher income has the power to make decisions. So even though she was not thrilled with life in Los Angeles—she felt isolated and did not have family close by to help her with her two children—she had to live wherever her husband's job took them.

What unified all of these women, both stay-at-home and working moms, was the loss of self that accompanied the transition to motherhood. Regardless of their "choice," all of them sustained a loss of social status, a fall from full social persons to devalued, invisible mothers.

This became clear as they realized that they had few choices, and this realization transformed frustrations into anger and anger into a sense of betrayal.

Reframing the Problem

These vexations led individuals to the mothers' group, in search of support and some way to make sense of their experiences. The group provided an alternative explanation, a different perspective on their current predicament.

That this mothers' group was approaching the problem in a different way hit me as I was driving home from my very first meeting. This particular meeting had started off in a predictable manner, addressing topics that meshed with my preconceived notions. When I arrived, five or six mothers were wrapping up a premeeting session on plans for the chapter's upcoming open house. Everyone turned around and stared as I walked through the door, and I introduced myself, saying I had been exchanging emails with someone named Molly. They welcomed me, and Ellen told me that the chapter had been active for a year and a half and now had about thirty members. The group met twice a month and also sponsored play groups, a book club, and scattered social activities, such as the occasional potluck dinner or tea for new members.

The meetings were held in the library of a private school. While we waited for everyone to trickle in, the mothers chatted about their children, their husbands, and what they had been up to since the last meeting. At 7:30, Ellen, who founded the chapter and was now president of the national organization, opened with a few announcements. She brought us up to date on plans for the open house. She also wanted everyone to know that she was working on the formation of a national coalition around issues that affect mothers, and in that capacity, she would be traveling to New York in a few weeks for meetings with women from different organizations.

Introductions followed, and we went around the room and said our names; everyone (but me) mentioned how many children she had and how old they were, as well as her current work situation. I noticed that many of them introduced this last part with "in my previous life, I was . . . ," and it also struck me that most of them had, or used to have, fairly successful professional careers. When I introduced myself and my project, all of them seemed genuinely interested and said they were happy that people wanted to learn about the issues they face.

As there was no predetermined topic for that meeting—an unusual state of affairs, I later found out—Ellen suggested an "open forum," where members could talk about whatever was on their minds. She tossed out a number of subjects, but they settled on, or rather began with, relationships. At first the conversation stayed on the personal. Although as an anthropologist I was interested in the personal details of everyone's lives, this discussion topic seemed to confirm my assumptions about who these women were and what they were doing. Molly, a former television producer who was taking some time off from work, worried that her husband resented the time she spent with her daughter and that they never had any time alone. Linda, who took frequent business trips, suggested that maybe Molly's husband wasn't comfortable with his daughter, and suggested that Molly figure out a way to leave him alone with the kid. She explained that when she started traveling for work, her husband, who stayed at home with their daughter, began to understand Linda's exhaustion. Moreover, taking care of the baby strengthened their father–daughter bond. A few more members weighed in on the idea of making husbands "less scared" of their children, and then the conversation segued to maintaining healthy relationships with their husbands. They all agreed that spouses needed to make time for each other. Another member explained that she and her husband had a "date night" once a week; even if they didn't go out, because hiring a sitter was expensive, they would set aside time to spend together. Ellen added that she was lucky that her in-laws lived nearby, so that she and her husband could get away for the "occasional overnight."

Linda reflected that parenting young children was hard on a relationship, and someone questioned whether the divorce rate for couples with children was higher than average. No one knew the answer; they started talking about the causes of these strains, and Stephanie brought up the division of household labor. She felt that she did most of the work at home, and everyone sympathized. They were all dismayed over this state of affairs, because they didn't particularly like household work, because they resented that their husbands didn't notice how much work they actually did, and because they felt that they had reverted to stereotypical gender roles. Anne said she realized that her husband did do his fair share of things, although she did not always remember this. But Ellen countered that "male" tasks, like taking out the garbage or mowing the lawn or paying the bills, could always be put off. On the other hand, "female" responsibilities, like the laundry, could not. She sometimes wondered how many days in a row she would have to leave her husband without underwear before he would think to wash the clothes. He would do it if she reminded him, but she found this offensive. Anne said she didn't know how this had happened. She was brought up to think she could do anything, and now she and her husband were locked in stereotypical gender roles.

Liz suggested that the tax structure might have something to do with it, and this precipitated a discussion about being the secondary wage earner. They all found it demoralizing that the secondary wage earner bias often wound up negating their income. For instance, Lynn was angry that her husband told a friend that Lynn's earnings went mostly to pay the nanny. Not only was it untrue, she felt that it nullified her contribution to the household. Ellen said that being the secondary wage earner and no longer engaging in paid employment scared her; it made her feel vulnerable and less than equal in a relationship to which she had always contributed. She and her husband had had some hard and frank discussions about divorce, because she feared what could happen to her if they ever broke up. Therefore, even now, when she wasn't working for pay, she was preparing herself for the future. The work that she was doing for the mothers' group was part-time and unpaid, but it would allow her to reenter the job market on the same terms as those on which she had left. Money is power, she asserted, and leaving the workforce definitely changes the dynamic in a marriage.

The meeting ended on this discussion of jobs, the division of household labor, and the tax structure—a point that left me intrigued. I knew little about the tax code, and I also found it interesting that a conversation that began with marriage and relationships had worked its way to this particular endpoint. The conversational flow made sense: it's hard to manage relationships with young children because they require a lot of care; the primary caretaker is exhausted, while the other parent may not understand this experience; little time together adds to this tension, as does housework, which is annoying, invisible, and unrewarding; and finally, not earning an income affects not only who performs most of the housework but also the dynamics between husbands and wives. They began at the individual level, examining relationships, and even though they continued to talk in personal terms, the focus moved to broader social structures. Talking about taxes underscored how even the most personal relationships and private interactions are shaped and experienced through broader social institutions.

After attending a few more meetings, I realized that economic considerations such as taxes came up in almost every discussion. These were central to members' views on motherhood, shaping mothers' subjectivities as well as their choices. A cut in economic privilege had set off a chain reaction, in which women lost not only their income but also their identity and their sense of value, while putting their future at risk. Because they experienced this in economic terms, they voiced their criticisms of the system through these terms, challenging concrete economic policies and questioning a notion of value premised on the workplace.

Furthermore, stressing economic constraints redefined the source of their difficulties. These mothers refused to take full blame for their difficulties, arguing instead that their problems stemmed from the erasure of care work in American society. They maintained that mothers' troubles would not be resolved as long as social and economic value remained attached to the workplace. Viewed in this light, mothers' predicaments underscored systemic, not individual, failures. This perspective reveals an analytical shift, moving attention away from individuals and toward the social system that defined their choices.

A New Basis for Subjectivity

Members came to the group after experiencing a rupture not just in their perceived life paths but also in their sense of self. They had lost their place, and through their involvement with the group, they found a way to make sense of it all. This is clearly seen in the ways that they told their stories, taking up the language of constraints, loss, and economic anxieties; furthermore, their individual narratives all turned on having made an impossible, imperfect decision between work and home (e.g., Ginsburg 1989).[15] This served to make sense of their fall from grace, allowing them to fit this breach into a coherent sense of self. That is, it provided a way to understand and organize seemingly disparate events into a continuous narrative—to make sense of an unexpected turn of events. By ordering events, biographical narratives allow individuals to interpret and attach meaning to their lives (e.g., Myerhoff 1978; Ginsburg 1989; Brodkin 2007; Landsman 2009). They explain how individuals got to the here and now, highlighting both pivotal events and underlying ideologies.

The mothers' group, then, taught members to understand their experiences in a specific way and allowed them to construct a new sense of self. As members learned to reframe the issues, the conversation shifted away from individual choice and toward systemic failures. They altered the meaning of motherhood, shifting their own perceptions that motherhood is an individual relationship—a tie between mother and child—to a recognition that motherhood is a social relationship. Thus, it is not caregiving itself that lends shape to their experience of motherhood; rather, it is the social and economic status of caregivers that defines what it means to be a mother.

This redefinition of experience served as a critical intervention. It changed the story from one where mothers were inadequate, unproductive, and unrecognized to one where mothers heroically carried on invisible but critical work in a deeply flawed system. This analytic reversal allowed mothers to see themselves as full persons again, reminding them that their work was both vital and valuable.

In meetings and in informal conversations, through face-to-face interaction with women who shared their frustrations, individual mothers gained validation for themselves, their work, and their plight. As Catherine explained, this was necessary, even urgent, for mothers:

> No question I envisioned being a mother as a big source of pride and self-esteem. I guess what I didn't realize is you get so much outside validation through work, and you don't through the childrearing. I mean you can sit there and say to yourself "Wow—I'm so glad that I've been there for my son. He's so happy. I'm so glad . . . and this is really great." I know I'm a really good mother. but it's different. It's different to have someone else tell you, either through grades or pay or whatever, "Wow—you're doing a really great job." You know. You're really important, and it's really different. And I guess what I really realized is that I miss that outside validation. I really miss it. And so I'm trying to train my husband to give it to me more, as a mother, because it is, it's a real issue for me.

Whereas Catherine had to "train" her husband to do this, the mothers' group automatically provided that service. Just being in the presence of other mothers would grant her a social identity, conferring a new sense of self.

At its most basic level, the local group provided members the opportunity to interact with like-minded individuals. Certainly membership was self-selective. Participation in the group revealed an interest beyond the concerns of childrearing and a willingness to engage the idea that mothers' problems were social constructions. As many members told me, this group was different from other mothers' groups *because* it dealt with such issues. Catherine, for example, said she couldn't stand going to play groups where mothers stood around and talked about things like diapers. Similarly, Erica enjoyed the group because it allowed her to feel that she had an identity beyond being a mother to her daughter. All of her friends were having children at the same time, and it was sometimes hard to move past that "least common denominator" in their conversations. She liked the book club and the meetings because they allowed for "intellectual" discussions.

Nevertheless, members did not necessarily want the same things from the group. Some expressed a keen interest in the group's advocacy agenda, and they had all read one or two popular books about motherhood in American society.[16] Others became more engaged in this after attending meetings, and still others said that this "political" aspect did not concern them. What brought them together, then, was a similar experience of losing their place. And, in coming together, they were able to reformulate a sense of identity through a newfound sense of community.[17]

Addressing the Problem

Members approached the problem on two different, yet inseparable, levels. The most important, most difficult, task at hand was to alter social norms: making reproductive labor valuable and valued, and ensuring that mothers and their work counted. The second, more practical and perhaps more feasible, approach required transforming the tax structure and advocating for things like paid maternity leave and flexible workplaces. The first step toward both of these was educating members themselves, helping individual women to regain a sense of self and to cope with their day-to-day realities. The mothers sought to transform not just their own circumstances but the broader social failures that make motherhood a vexed position in American society.

Education was central to the group's mission; as seen above, this interest began with attempts to inform members about the economic and social roots of their problems. In a perfect world, members could have concentrated on changing these social structures, but they knew that while they were waiting for social change, they would have to deal with existing constraints. Thus, they chose meeting topics that would give members the tools to make the best out of their current situations.

In one year, I attended meetings on estate planning, caring for elderly parents, the tax system, career planning, financial planning, women's health, and current events. Professionals spoke at all of these meetings, and they outlined the issues at hand, giving members the resources to follow up should they wish to do so. All of these speakers stressed preparation, warning that a failure to plan could be catastrophic. For example, having uncomfortable conversations with parents about long-term care and looking into long-term care insurance would ease future economic—and care—burdens. They should deal with this issue now to avoid the difficulties of the "sandwich generation," or women who found themselves caring for elderly parents soon after their own children grew up.

Similarly, understanding the tax system would help members formulate their financial plans. It would also serve to clarify how fiscal policy affected not only their decisions to work, but the shape of their families. At Ellen's behest, Meg and her former coworker Tanya put together a session on taxes. Ellen explained that the national group was trying to decide how best to approach mothers' issues, and taxes were a central concern. The question remained: Would members find these issues compelling and engaging? Ellen was convinced that every member would be interested if she realized its relevancy, and so Ellen asked Meg to organize a meeting around it.

Meg and Tanya began the meeting on fiscal policy by talking about "economics as values," rather than as a preexisting, objective, and external category; after all, she said, "the economy is really a product of people, and a product of our decisions." She then presented a snapshot of income distribution in the United States by running through the ten-chair exercise (see introduction). This exercise would reveal how tax structures and fiscal policies squeezed individuals in the middle; it would also highlight the need for income redistribution. Meg explained that taxes provided one way to effect that kind of change. Current tax policies, however, benefit only the wealthiest and squeeze people in the middle and bottom income brackets. Tanya then demonstrated how progressive, regressive, and flat taxes would affect the three different sections of the population, emphasizing, once again, the inequalities of the current system.

Tanya also discussed the secondary wage earner bias and the marriage penalty, arguing that both penalize working mothers and uphold specific family structures. The marriage penalty effectively deters poor people from getting married, encourages middle-class couples to file taxes separately, and does not really affect the wealthiest. The secondary wage earner bias lowers the tax burden for single wage earner families, and this is unlikely to change, because the government wants to encourage a traditional family structure.

Meg and Tanya's presentation emphasized middle-class concerns, driving home the point that current tax structures unnecessarily, and unfairly, burden those in the middle. They spoke to a specific audience, who could only respond from their own experiences. Thus, we never talked about the two women who were left standing, but we spent a few minutes discussing the top rate, the income level that defines the wealthiest. This top rate was set in the 1940s and continues to stand at $250,000. The mothers were surprised that this was the cutoff, for it seemed low and unfair. How do you compare Bill Gates to someone who makes $250,000 a year? This arbitrary number created a lot of problems for the middle class. Summing up, Meg stressed:

> If you feel like, and that's because the scarcity that they feel around their economic situation is real. It's real, right? I mean, you've got seven people fighting over three chairs; there's a lot of competition for these chairs here, and then you've got two more people waiting in the wings who need these chairs. And so, I kind of just, I wanna emphasize. . . . Just real quickly to wrap up. I just want to say. . . . Here folks are experiencing *very real, real scarcity*, but if you look at the entire picture, there's enough. It's just whether or not you feel you can lay claim to these other chairs. So if we want to change this picture, what do we do? There are three different strategies we could

use. . . . One we like to call, you can grow your own chair. . . . Another way you can do it is to prevent chairs from accumulating at the top. . . . But at this point, there's so many chairs over here, that what we're pretty much left with here is redistributing, and that is tax policy, um, what we do is we can, we can levy the taxes on the wealthy and corporations and redistribute it back to these folks [points to the seven women sharing three chairs] in the forms of childcare, health care, you know, programs, you name it, in ways that help to alleviate the pressures that these families experience. In that sense, we can redistribute the chairs.

This session was interactive and engaging. Members found it interesting and useful. Ellen asked how they would pitch a session like this—how would they get people there? Linda suggested that they talk about it as a session on "the economy" not "economics," as a way to make it seem less theoretical, less out of reach. "Economics" reminded too many people of a required college course. I was surprised at Linda's comments, since the members always talked about economic concerns, always in concrete ways. This highlighted, however, how the group reframed mothers' predicaments by rendering intimidating subjects, like "economics," personal and accessible. Members, therefore, learned to understand their problems through the language of economics and fiscal policies—lending authority to their claims.

Advocacy

Following the national organization's lead, the local chapter was beginning to pay more attention to advocacy. At the local level, advocacy consisted of consciousness raising within the group and small-scale attempts to engage the community. Much of what the group did in terms of education—for instance, the meeting on taxes—doubled as advocacy, since it also functioned to raise awareness.

In 2003, as part of the national organization's Mother's Day campaign, Ellen hosted a local meeting on motherhood and invisibility. The goal of the meeting, and indeed of the campaign, was "Making Mothers Count." As the meeting began, Ellen split us into two groups and asked us to talk about the invisibility of caregiving. She wanted members to think about their roles as mothers in four different arenas, "social/emotional," "professional," "economic," and "in the family," suggesting that they consider which aspects of their work were in/visible. We broke up into smaller groups for twenty minutes and then reported back on our conversations. Both groups discussed a familiar range of topics: husbands, work, exhaustion. For instance, we spoke about the expectations put on women, and how these make it even more difficult for women to quit their jobs. Someone asserted that mothers are not respected because they have no economic power; she suggested that mothers need to learn to speak the "male" language of money to be able to wield power.

Next, Ellen brought up the notion of economic value and care work. She emphasized that the United Nations recommends that gross domestic product take unpaid care work into consideration. In the United States, however, GDP ignores unpaid care work, even as it takes the drug trade into account. This only reinforces the belief that care work is not work.[18] To make her point, Ellen told us a "joke": If a man marries his nanny the GDP goes down, because he's no longer paying her to do the same job. On the other hand, if a man puts his sick mother in a nursing home the GDP goes up, because now he's paying someone to do the job of caring that he or someone in his family was doing.

The meeting proceeded, covering many of the topics I had been hearing about for a year, such as the lack of paid parental leave and how the Social Security system doesn't provide credits for care work. Ellen then reviewed the national organization's plan for advocacy, which included raising awareness, education, and political activism. All these activities would take place at the grassroots level, as well as through lobbying local, state, and federal governments.

Because I was familiar with most of these issues and topics, I found this meeting a little tedious. Later, looking at the Mother's Day pins and cards, it occurred to me that the point of the meeting was not to raise awareness among members but to give them a way to talk about these issues that would resonate with people outside the group. Wearing the pins and handing out these cards represented this campaign's most concrete intervention. The pins said: "I'm a mother. I care. I work. I count." Thus they instantiated the message of the campaign, literally making mothers visible by making them easily identifiable. Asserting their identity and value as mothers, these women would no longer fade into the background.

The cards were meant to accompany the pins; members could pass these out to family and friends, and they could hand one out to anyone who asked about their pins. The cards detailed "mom metrics," a series of facts about mothers:

81 percent of American women will become mothers.
69 percent of mothers work for pay in addition to providing two-thirds of all unpaid family care.
Unpaid caregiving is not counted as work in the gross domestic product.
Women spend an average of 11.5 years out of the workforce caring for children or elderly parents.
For each year out of the workforce, a mother receives 0 credit toward Social Security benefits.
Among young women and men without children, women now make 98 percent of men's wages. Yet mothers make 73 percent or less of the wages of all others in the workforce.
Of the world's wealthiest nations, only two—the United States and Australia—do not provide paid parental leave for full-time employees.

I had heard some of these numbers before, but now they came together, packaged in an attempt to define motherhood through numbers. This was significant, because many members experienced loss as economic, as driven by numbers. Moreover, the language of numbers, commonly understood as scientific and indisputable, granted this campaign an aura of legitimacy; to be taken seriously, members were taking up the language of authority.

This information, then, was not meant for members but for the public at large, an attempt to circulate this group's take on motherhood. Ellen reported that wearing her pin had led to a number of interesting conversations. The previous week, she had spent twenty minutes in a parking lot talking to a woman who asked about her pin. The woman was so impressed with everything Ellen told her that she pulled out a checkbook right then and there to make a donation to the organization. This only confirmed Ellen's suspicions that the group was addressing important, widely felt issues and that many women would join the mothers' "revolution," if only they knew about it.

Ellen's use of the word "revolution" brings us full circle. At the start of this chapter, I asked if Catherine's assertions were true for this group of mothers: Were they in fact proposing "revolutionary" changes? Rather than taking on this notion of "revolution"—an impossible question to answer—I focus on this group's difference. The connection between subjectivity, motherhood, and economic status is central to this distinction.

Work identity and social status—which were mutually defined—joined to construct members' subjectivities. When they became mothers, their worlds were upended; they no longer fit into the model of a good worker, or even a worker. They felt erased as persons, losing an identity defined through occupation and economic independence, and therefore their social position. The mothers' group provided them with the language through which to understand and talk about this loss and gave them a new perspective on their problems. It also provided a new version of themselves as workers by expanding this concept to incorporate what it had previously erased—motherhood. As a result, group membership allowed them to regain a sense of self.

It is this reframing that distinguishes the group's engagement with motherhood. First, members redefined the problem as systemic—and economic—based on a narrow understanding of value. Dealing with this problem required two separate tasks. The first would work to remove concrete economic constraints; ideally, mothers would band together to influence legislation that would change the tax system, mandate paid leave, and reward companies that allowed flex- and part-time arrangements. The second centered on advocacy, a direct attempt to make motherhood valued, to *count* the work that mothers do. Although this latter component required resignifying "value," members were not trying to undermine the system that once produced them as privileged. Rather, they sought to regain their position of privilege by showing that care work is also (economically) valuable. They self-consciously took up the language of numbers to insist that the system accommodate them, that it *see* and recognize their labor.

In all of these efforts, members spoke from the subject position of "mother," yet their relationships with their children were not featured in these discussions. Motherhood was instead presented as a social and economic location—a position of disadvantage. For them, motherhood was not defined merely through the quality of the relationship they had with their children. It was no longer understood as a personal relationship, separable from broader social structures, but through the social and economic position of the (white, middle-class) caregiver.

This version of motherhood, characterized by estrangement, contrasted with the experiences of domestic workers. Certainly, domestic workers engaged in socially and economically devalued work, and their own reproductive tasks were deemed unimportant; yet they defined success through the ability to provide for their children rather than through the type of jobs they held. In the next chapter, I analyze two groups that sought to organize domestic workers and discuss how (domestic) work, motherhood, and invisibility combined in different forms for Mexican and Central American women.

CHAPTER 4

Organizing, Motherhood, and
the Meanings of (Domestic) Work

One afternoon, Josefina and I dropped in on Alicia, a woman Josefina knew from Mexico. Alicia took in alterations, and Josefina wanted to see about getting a skirt hemmed. We arrived at Alicia's, called out her name from the street, and a young girl appeared on the other side of the gate with a set of keys. Inside, we found Alicia clearing the lunch table. Josefina related the reason for our visit, and they discussed the skirt for a few minutes. Business completed, Alicia inquired about Josefina's family, asking where Josefina and her sisters were living and working. Josefina explained that her two sisters were still employed at the same restaurants but that she was now at the Domestic Workers Group—working in an office. In the time since the two had last met, Josefina had left her live-in job, moved in with her cousins, worked as a telemarketer, sold tamales on the street, looked for another live-in position, and finally become a staff member at the DWG.

In turn, Alicia brought us up to speed on her own family: her son worked on the UCLA grounds, her daughter had just started a new job at a factory, and she stayed at home to watch her two granddaughters. Alicia had recently quit domestic work but continued to take in sewing to supplement the family's income. They were able to sustain this arrangement because their rent was relatively low, just five hundred dollars a month for a one-bedroom apartment. The place was dirty and rundown, she said, but the price was right. According to Alicia, landlords used to clean and paint apartments before new tenants moved in, but since rents were sky high now, landlords could do as they pleased. They knew people would take anything that was remotely affordable, regardless of its problems.

Driving back to the office, I started thinking about our conversation—how people shifted from one type of job to another, the limited employment opportunities open to immigrants, and how families pooled their income together to be able to afford miniscule, poorly kept apartments. I asked Josefina what the difference was between factory and household work (the two types of jobs that are most available for Mexican and Central American immigrant women). Without missing a beat, she replied "nothing"—except that working in a house is better than in a factory, because domestic workers do not have to pay taxes. A factory worker's already low income decreases even more when you factor in taxes, she said, and promised to show me old check stubs from her brief stint in a factory. She went on: domestic employment allows you more freedom. In a factory, you are constrained by fixed schedules, and are constantly monitored. Although domestic work is hard and poorly remunerated, it is better paid than factory work, which is also physically exhausting. Overall, then, domestic service is the more favorable option.

This response, this exchange, took me aback. Although I knew that individual women moved back and forth through various types of work, often holding more than one job at a time, I never expected Josefina to tell me that domestic service was not entirely special and different in itself. Josefina worked as an organizer at the Domestic Workers Group, and I had often heard her expound on the evils of this occupation. Moreover, she had told me numerous times that she continued to identify as a domestic worker, even though she was no longer employed in that capacity. How, then, could she claim that it was not very different from the other types of work available to immigrant women?

In conceiving a project about immigrant domestic workers, I had assumed that there was something fundamentally different about this occupation, that it would somehow define the women who take it up. Yet comments like Josefina's persistently pointed me in another direction. If immigrant women did not identify with their jobs, how did they understand themselves, their lives, and their struggles? And what role did paid employment play in all of this? Beginning from domestic service as identity, I found instead that this job was inseparable from the broader experience of immigrant life, specifically the female version of this experience. Defining themselves as mothers first, immigrant women focused on providing for their children. Working allowed them to support their families, and was therefore essential to their self-definitions—the type of work they performed, less so.

This chapter considers how paid employment, motherhood, and identity combine for Mexican and Central American immigrant women; it does so by exploring domestic service as occupation, specifically by looking at two organizations devoted to improving the lot of domestic workers in Los Angeles, the Domestic Workers Group (DWG) and the Sparkle and Shine Cooperative (the Co-op). The DWG and the Co-op sought to rectify the more injurious aspects of paid domestic employment, but neither ran as its organizers and members would have liked. Both faced financial and logistical difficulties, and both lacked a devoted, or even sizable, membership. When studying activists, it is important to note that they are necessarily self-selected—their dedication and advocacy reveal a self-conscious engagement, perhaps a higher stake in the issue than those who do not take up direct action. But what can we learn when individuals who join these causes appear almost indifferent to them? Why were members so disconnected from the primary goals of the DWG and the Co-op? And what does this reveal about immigrant women's experiences?

In this chapter, I show how the daily struggle to make ends meet, to be good mothers and provide for their children, as well as desire for recognition of these endeavors, led individuals to the Co-op or DWG. Analyzing how and why individuals came to both associations, along with their ambivalent commitment to these, allows me to explore how immigrant women configured their identities as workers, mothers, and successful selves.

Work, Motherhood, and the Self

Chapter 3 discusses how individuals in the mothers' group experienced a loss of self with motherhood. No longer able to identify with or define themselves through their professional careers joined with a newfound financial dependence to erase their sense of self as independent adults. As such, they sought, literally, to revalue motherhood, to underline its importance by foregrounding its economic worth. Their attempts to classify motherhood as "work" reveal the centrality of paid employment to members' sense of self. This perspective not only defines a full adult person through financial independence; it also conflates occupation with identity.

This specific way of understanding oneself reveals a particular set of assumptions about the relationship among paid employment, motherhood, and personhood. Taking for granted that an individual's profession underpins her social value, this point of view inevitably posits a conflict among the three. It also obscures alternative ways of conceptualizing personhood, especially the possibility that identity does not necessarily overlap with occupation. By contrast, for the Mexican and Central American immigrant women I met in LA, the constellation of motherhood, self, and work was differently arranged. Individual identities developed not through (financial) independence, self-fulfillment through work, or even a specific occupation, but instead through particular social relationships—their sense of self rested on their roles as mothers. Central to this was the ability to support their families, and thus having an income was critical to their self-definition. They explained their labor in terms of their kids, often narrating their struggles through the idea of "sacrifices" made for their children's futures. As Estela, a sixty-five-year-old Salvadoran immigrant, responded when I asked how she had managed to work so many hours for so many years, "When you love someone, not to say your children who are the most sacred thing you have, you make the time."[1] Work therefore served as a tool; it was not a goal in itself.[2]

Cecilia's experiences illuminate this alternate way of connecting paid employment, motherhood, and self. Arriving from Mexico in her early twenties, Cecilia had worked hard to support her three children by herself, taking jobs in factories, houses, and restaurants. When I met Cecilia, she spent the better part of an afternoon lamenting that her children had left her. She told me that she had literally worked night and day to put them through school and to make sure they did not lack for anything. They all went to Catholic school, and the two younger ones had both attended college. Even more, while they were in high school, she had purchased a house, which she was still paying off. A single mother, she had been so busy managing multiple jobs that she had had little time for friends or even herself. Despite her tremendous efforts, her kids had gone off to college, leaving her alone in that big empty house. Now in her early fifties, she felt abandoned, her hard work unappreciated and invisible. She did not regret the sacrifices she had made, since all she had ever wanted was to have children, and she was proud that she had been able to provide for them. What she resented was their lack of appreciation. In this country, she insisted, mothers are not respected or valued; in Mexico, by contrast, mothers are celebrated. May 10 (Mother's Day) is a big holiday in Mexico, while here, she always had to work: "I am always depressed on May 10th. First of all, because it's not, they don't see it as important as, like they do there . . . and because in Mexico, on May 10th nothing is open. People don't go to work. I always have to work on May 10th."[3]

On one level, then, Cecilia was a "successful" mother (and immigrant), buying a house, providing for her children, and even sending them to college. At the same time, however, she was indignant that her children did not acknowledge this and so did not allow her to feel secure in her sense of self. When they moved out of her house, Cecilia felt like a failed mother—why else would they leave? They also made her look bad in front of her family, who wondered where Cecilia had gone wrong. Cecilia's story illustrates how women define themselves through their roles as mothers, and how paid employment and the ability to support their children influence this; her experiences also highlight a need for acknowledgment and appreciation for these tremendous efforts. Unlike the middle-class, native-born mothers, immigrant women such as Cecilia did not feel that motherhood erased them as valued and valuable persons; rather, they defined themselves through, and sought recognition for, their work as mothers.

Down and Out in Beverly Hills

Unfortunately, most found that making a better life for their children was harder than they imagined before arriving in the United States.[4] Here they had to combat social and economic invisibility, supporting family in both the United States and their countries of origin.[5] The need to earn money, then, became ever more frenzied, taking on a "hyperreality" (Parreñas 2001: 224)[6] as individuals fought to ensure their families' survival.

These pressures rendered immigrant mothers exceedingly vulnerable to exploitation and abuse at work. The injustices of paid domestic employment are legion, as is the literature detailing these. Scholars have foregrounded how this occupation reproduces hierarchies of race/ethnicity, class, gender, and citizenship across contexts (e.g., Rollins 1985; Chaney and Castro 1989; Palmer 1989; Romero 1992; Gill 1994; Colen 1995; Momsen 1999; Anderson 2000; Chang 2000; Hondagneu-Sotelo 2001; Parreñas 2001; Regt 2009; Brown 2011; Macdonald 2011). Through spatial arrangements, the expectation of deferential treatment, and constraints on moving about the house, domestic workers' difference and lower status is constantly marked (e.g., Sanjek and Colen 1990; Gill 1994; Constable 1997; Stephenson 1999; Dickey 2000; Lan 2006; Casanova 2013). In addition, domestic workers are subject to surveillance; sexual, physical, and verbal abuse; meager pay; and at times, insufficient food. Finally, the putative separation between home and work, combined with the sense that a domestic worker is just like "one of the family" (e.g., Childress 1986; Young 1987; Bakan and Stasiulis 1997) allows employers to disregard both the domestic worker and her labor.

In the day-to-day, these indignities manifest in personal stories of mistreatment and degradation (cf. Burnham and Theodore 2012). The domestic workers I knew all had difficult jobs, and they had all experienced humiliation at some point. The difficulties for freshly arrived immigrants, or anyone who needs work, begin as individuals look for work, often at an employment agency, and continue through the daily ins and outs of the job itself. It all starts with the arduous, often frantic, search for work. Many women explained that they had found jobs through referrals from friends and/or employer recommendations. This seemed the least painful route, as it obviated the need for domestic employment agencies. These agencies, at times the only recourse for finding employment, were notoriously abusive, taking advantage of people's desperate need to earn money and undocumented immigrants' fears of being deported. Tagging along with Josefina, I learned a lot about one particular agency in the San Fernando Valley, run by a woman named Sarah. We would often wait near this agency and hand out information to women coming in and out, and despite the many complaints about its owner, everyone seemed to agree that this particular agency was not very different from others. Sarah would charge individuals ten dollars to apply—ten dollars that jobless women could ill afford to pay—and then keep them there for days on end without finding them work. When she finally found a house for someone, she would send more than one woman to the same employer, charging each a forty-dollar finder's fee, and then letting the destitute would-be domestic workers battle it out themselves.

The first time I accompanied Josefina to this agency, we ran into two women who had stormed out in a rage. María, the first one, was thrown out after confronting the owner. María insisted that she had paid her ten-dollar application fee two months earlier, but Sarah claimed not to have it and wanted her to fill out another form. She tears them up, María told us. All of the women knew that Sarah routinely threw out applications, thereby erasing any record of their payment. In fact, Sarah would not even write down the locations of the houses to which she sent her customers, telling each woman to take down the address herself.

María, however, knew better. The last time Sarah had found her a job, she made Sarah write down the address, and she kept the slip of paper at home in case she ever needed it. This morning, María had shown up looking for work and took issue with Sarah, who told her that she had to fill out an application. They argued, and Sarah called building security to kick María out. María was furious; she had every intention of making a stink and said that she would certainly show up at the DWG's next meeting.

That morning, I found the stories outrageous, but Josefina didn't seem particularly surprised. And, after a few more agency trips, I grew almost as nonchalant as Josefina, sadly accustomed to all of these grievances. Clearly, agencies and agency owners could get away with these antics because there were too many women willing to endure the indignities and corruption. They were desperate for work and too afraid of losing any opportunity and/or of being deported. Josefina's own story exemplifies the process: When she first arrived in the United States, she spent many months depressed and searching for a job. A former schoolteacher and union activist, she didn't want to take just anything. However, after six months of not working, she went to a domestic employment agency ready to do just about anything. She was tired of not having money to send to her son in Mexico, of feeling degraded for relying on her cousins to support her, and of putting up with circulating rumors that she was just plain *floja* (lazy).

At the employment agency, she waited for many days until someone finally picked her out and hired her:

I went to the agency, and that was where . . . they practically put me on sale, no? And that's where I stayed, because I said this is where I'm staying, it's not so much out of love [for the job]. . . . Yes, at the agency, they, they, they sold me into work, they sold it to the *señora*, and the *señora* felt responsible for me, *as though she had bought me* and not my services, but *me*. So I felt very, I felt very humiliated, but what to do. . . . It's the agency, the agency that really holds the function of selling slaves. They practically raise your lips to check your teeth, really.[7]

Her employer chose Josefina for the way she looked: "She chose me because of my color. She chose me because I was strong, and because . . . maybe I was strong, because, she saw I was, well, a good age, no? Like with experience and everything and said, 'I'm taking her.' "[8] As Josefina points out, agencies do more than just exploit individuals' poverty and fear of joblessness and deportation; they objectify women, selling them along with their labor. They also create racial preferences, disciplining migrant women, and placing them within racial hierarchies.[9]

Still, landing a job was just the beginning of the problem: Josefina found herself working six days a week, taking care of a sick infant and two other children, while cleaning a three-bedroom house and cooking for a family of five. Her employers, particularly the *patrona*, were fickle, okay with something one day and angry about it the next. She was not allowed to speak to anyone, not even the gardeners, and rarely had enough time, even on her day off, to go out and see her sisters. Nevertheless, she put up with all of this for three years until the exhaustion became too much, and she finally resigned.

Stories like Josefina's were not uncommon. Every time Josefina and I went out, we would hear complaints about long hours, poor pay, and unsympathetic, sometimes abusive, employers. Volunteering at a legal clinic for day laborers and household workers, I met Judith, a former secretary from Peru. Judith had been working for the same family for three years, at first sleeping there five nights a week, but now she stayed over only on Fridays and Saturdays. She worked from 6:30 AM to 8 PM, earning a mere sixty-seven dollars a day. The family had three children, a four-year-old and two eight-year-old twins. She arrived every morning at 6:30 AM, woke up the kids and helped them get ready for school, serving them breakfast and making their lunch. During the day, she would clean, wash, iron, and prepare dinner. She used to iron in her room but the señora accused her of sitting around and watching novelas (soap operas), so now, even though she still stored the ironing board in her room, she brought it out to the kitchen and ironed there. Things had calmed down since the youngest started preschool, as she no longer had to watch him all day. In general, she was so busy that she rarely had a chance to sit down and have lunch. She didn't eat dinner at work either, waiting until she returned home, usually after 9 PM. In fact, every night before dinner, the señora would come in and check the pots to ensure that Judith had served the family everything.

Some employers, some jobs, however, were better than others. Living out and cleaning by the day usually pay more; live-ins suffer the worst abuses, because their time is never theirs. Like Judith, who stayed at her employer's until 9 AM on Sunday morning, making and serving breakfast but not getting paid for the day, women who live in find that every second of their day is squeezed, turned into a work task. They are always at work: there is always something that they could be doing, and their employers always expect them to be doing it.

What makes individual women endure such conditions is a distinct lack of choices, in terms of employers as well as occupations. Paid domestic work, whether cleaning or taking care of children, by the day or as a live-in, is tiring physical labor that is often unrecognized as work, poorly remunerated, isolating, and invisible. It is, however, one of the few available options open to Central American and Mexican immigrant women, whose "choices" for making a living include any or a combination of domestic service, factory work, street vending, and selling beauty or health products from direct sales companies such as Avon, Mary Kay, or Shaklee Vitamins.[10] Most of the Mexican and Central American immigrant women I encountered in Los Angeles engaged in more than one job at the same time, shifting back and forth from factory to household work and supplementing those earnings through sales of health and beauty products or street vending. Almost everyone assured me that domestic service was the best available possibility, as it paid more and allowed more flexibility than any factory job. Nevertheless, the women I knew would often work weekends or late nights, patching together income from a variety of sources to scrape up enough money to pay their (shared) rent and their bills, send money to their families back home, and still have enough left over to buy bus passes and food.

It's a vicious cycle: a desperate need to work, along with fierce competition, makes individuals put up with degrading, poorly paid jobs. And the fact that so many people are willing to do this work allows employers to pay almost nothing. The most desirable positions pay individuals fifteen dollars an hour to care for children and/or clean in LA's wealthiest neighborhoods. At worst, domestic workers survive on less than minimum wage, at times toiling as live-ins, as Judith and Josefina did, for less than four hundred dollars a week. Alma, a woman I met on the bus one morning, summed it up for me: people put up with everything out of "*miedo y necesidad*" (fear and need). Everyone comes to the United States with need, and once here, this need only intensifies; few have any financial cushion, life in this country is more expensive than they had expected, and they have the added burden of making enough money to send some back home. Fear refers to undocumented immigrants' constant worries about being found out and potentially deported, which makes them too afraid to complain about their work; but fear also characterizes the experience of immigrants who have legal papers, as everyone worries about losing her job, or not being able to pay the rent, or not having enough money for food. Poverty, social invisibility, narrow employment options, and ignorance of one's rights—these are the predicaments of immigrant life, driving women into domestic work and keeping them from leaving or advocating for change.

If individuals could not make a dent in the system, could not or did not want to stir things up for fear of losing their jobs or being deported, the idea of joining together held more promise. In a group, domestic workers could potentially make their voice heard, fight against unjust employers, and promote change. This is where the Domestic Workers Group and the Sparkle and Shine Cooperative came in. These two organizations sought to alleviate the abuses and affronts endemic to this occupation, but neither was entirely successful. I was puzzled by this, as both seemed to offer what many individual domestic workers wanted or said they wanted. Josefina and I always found people eager to talk about their jobs and the problems they faced, and many women appeared genuinely excited when they found out about the Domestic Workers Group. On the other hand, few of these women ever showed up at meetings. Similarly, the Co-op received daily calls from women looking for work, but numbers remained low, from five to eight women at any given point; moreover, when the group did hire someone, new members, like the old ones, frequently expressed dissatisfaction.

Certainly, many of the problems these organizations faced stemmed from the very nature of their task. Domestic service is isolating and atomizing: most women who engage in this occupation work alone and for one employer at a time. In addition, domestic work is highly informal and, at least in Los Angeles, quite fluid as an occupation. It is impossible to pinpoint just what and whom it includes; for instance, does it count as domestic work if an immigrant woman cleans her neighbor's refrigerator for ten dollars or watches a friend's child while her friend is at work? Competition is also steep; the glut of immigrant women desperately looking for any kind of work drives wages down and keeps individuals tied to their less-than-satisfactory jobs; they know that if they quit or threaten to quit, someone else will willingly take their positions. Finally, individuals are busy, overwhelmed with multiple jobs and responsibilities at home, so they do not have much time for other commitments.

Despite these types of complications, there is a rich legacy of domestic workers organizing, both historically and across national contexts.[11] In the United States, since 2007, a collection of groups around the country have participated in the National Domestic Workers Alliance (NDWA) (Poo et al. 2013); this coalition has effectively lobbied a number of states, including California,[12] Connecticut, Hawaii, Massachusetts, New York, and Oregon, to institute a version of the Domestic Workers' Bill of Rights (cf. Goldberg 2015). That its director, Ai-jen Poo, was named a 2014 MacArthur Genius indicates increased attention to the plight of women who labor in private homes, and at the same time, has raised the public profile of the organization and its struggle. Indeed, in August 2015 an appeals court restored overtime pay and minimum wage standards to home care workers, a campaign in which the NDWA actively engaged (Scheiber 2015).

The accomplishments and disappointments of different activist efforts are rooted in particular historical circumstances. In the rest of this chapter, then, I consider why attempts to mobilize immigrant domestic workers in turn-of-the-millennium Los Angeles faced an uphill battle. I examine the Co-op and DWG, homing in on the gaps between member expectations and what each group could offer, to emphasize the relative ordering of occupation, income, and motherhood in shaping individuals' sense of self. Beginning from Josefina's assertion that there is little difference between domestic and factory work, I argue that it is not one particular job that defines Mexican and Central American women's day-to-day life in this country. Rather, it is migration, learning to survive in a new place, access to a limited number of jobs, poverty, and social erasure—and how all of these intertwine with motherhood—that lend shape to their experiences.

This discussion is not intended as a critique of these organizations; rather, it presents an attempt to grapple with the ways immigrant women define themselves and their lives in the United States. This analysis coincides with my resolute support for all efforts to improve the lives of domestic workers, and more broadly of immigrant women, as I believe that the ethnographic perspective can only enhance these undertakings. The strength of ethnography is its ability to present a more complicated and nuanced terrain, in this case urging us to consider how certain activist categories may obscure particular experiences.[13] Rather than assume this is politically problematic, we might ask how ethnography can clarify alternate ways of proceeding, or at least prompt us to pose a different set of questions. As Valentine so aptly points out:

> effective advocacy and ethnography must engage in precisely the kinds of deconstructive methodologies that so many critics have condemned as apolitical. That is, in order to understand and act on local manifestations of violence or to engage in a politics of social change, all those features of contemporary social analysis often gathered under the umbrella of "postmodernism"—the focus on multiple, shifting identities; the borderless nature of political discourses and practices; the investigation of what power is—are as vital to committed, ethical, and effective advocacy as they are to ethnography. (2007: 252)

What I am concerned with is the same question I posed in the introduction: What is left out of the discussion when we focus solely on occupational category? How might other angles of entry, additional approaches, help in our fight against the economic and social marginality immigrant women all too often inhabit? To get at these, we must first investigate how they frame their own struggles.

Cooperative Endeavors

The Sparkle and Shine Cooperative was established in the late 1990s through the efforts of a local social justice organization, which wanted to provide jobs at fair wages for domestic workers. The group originally operated out of a worksite for day laborers, and had changed its practices, membership, location, and coordinators various times by the time I arrived in the fall of 2002. When I first started spending time at the Co-op, it had recently become independent of the organization that spawned it, changed locations, and was now housed in the offices of a different social justice organization. In 2002, the group boasted four members and two trainees.[14] Over the course of my fieldwork, these numbers shifted various times: two members left, a few trainees came and went, and three new women joined the group. I constantly heard about how many more members they used to have, but it seemed that for the previous two to three years, membership had held steady between five and ten women at any particular time.

The Co-op's aim was to systematize the most informal aspects of domestic work. Membership in a larger group would provide individual women with an extra layer of protection; no longer working alone, they would be less vulnerable to fickle or exploitative employers. This process of coming together and learning to stand for one's rights would help and empower the members as it allowed them to earn a living wage, affording increased job security and flexibility. Further, since members considered themselves to be self-employed, they referred to "employers" (*patrones*) as "customers" or "clients" (*clientes*), shifting the terms of the relationship through this change in vocabulary. Envisioning this Co-op as a first step, its founders and organizers hoped to be able to expand the cooperative model, thereby eventually mitigating the status of domestic workers across the Los Angeles metropolitan area.

Regularizing relationships with employers was crucial to the Co-op's mission. The Co-op had a contract for each house, an estimate sheet that members had filled out, detailing the tasks to be completed and the agreed-upon pay. This would avoid future problems, stating clearly what the customer requested, and could be used internally by Co-op members going to a house they had never cleaned before; it would also serve as evidence if a customer complained or tried to renege on a deal. If there were any issues—if customers had complaints, tried to pay less, or in any way abused or humiliated the members—customers would have to deal with "the office." The existence of an "official" center rendered the job less informal and less subject to employer whims. As well, members often cleaned together, which also gave them added strength vis-à-vis the customer. More importantly, since the Co-op had more than one house, members would have a cushion on which to fall back if they needed to quit a particular job. The idea, then, was that participating in a group would allow individuals to be pickier in their choice of customers and to insist on just treatment and a fair price for each house.

Cleaning together also allowed them flexibility, to take on different types of jobs, to take time off in case of illness or other personal emergencies, and to switch customers around in case one of the members didn't get along with a particular client. Each member had a cell phone that would allow communication with one another, with the office, and with customers. As most of them relied on the public transportation system, a cell phone came in handy in case of delay; it was also useful when there was a problem at a particular house, or when they had forgotten something, or just wanted to set up meeting times. Further, the Co-op encouraged the use of natural cleaning agents, avoiding as much and as often as possible the toxic chemicals found in most homes.

Significantly, the Co-op's goals extended beyond dealing with customers and exacting a fairer price for each house. Through membership, individual women would also gain awareness, education, and a measure of economic security. For example, higher earnings along with health insurance would allow members to go to the doctor, a luxury that many immigrants forgo for lack of insurance and/or money. Additionally, the group had been set up to instill a cooperative spirit, to produce a sense of community. Members cleaned together, earned the same wage (twelve dollars an hour), and sought to create income parity. Every week, they would spend at least an hour arranging the schedule and ensuring that everyone made roughly the same amount.

Ownership was also central to the Co-op's mission—an opportunity to build something for the future and to learn valuable skills. Like many of the immigrant women I met in LA, a number of the Co-op's members had trouble reading, and most of them had tremendous difficulties with numbers. Needless to say, reading bank statements and working with daily averages, bank balances, and cash flow was new to most of them, and participation in the Co-op taught them basic financial literacy. Cristina, who volunteered her services as coordinator, and the office assistant took care of most of the accounting, but the members were supposed to supervise, and only members could write checks or handle cash. Moreover, Cristina helped all of them file their taxes as foreign investors. A record of paying taxes would serve them if the opportunity to file for legal documents ever presented itself.

Ownership, however, also entailed added responsibility: members returned 20 percent of their earnings to the Co-op to finance the assistant's pay, their insurance premium, and cell phone bills. During weeks when they did not have enough money in the bank, members had to make sure that all of the bills were covered and the assistant paid before they could write out their own checks. Even with pooled earnings, the Co-op did not earn enough to be self-sufficient. There were not enough houses, customers came and went, and sometimes members would mess up and have to pay for something they broke. Thus the group relied on grants from foundations—money that also had to be managed, and the members had to agree on how to spend it.

All of this required extra time, and indeed, each woman invested a lot of hours in the Co-op. Every Monday afternoon, the group was supposed to meet from 2 to 5 PM, but these sessions generally lasted much longer, sometimes until 7 or 8 PM. During the meetings, they would set up the week's schedule, discuss issues, and make plans. Cristina, who ran the meetings, would sometimes add an "educational" component, talking about such things as women's rights, recruiting new members and/or customers, or cleaning with natural products.

Despite these well-meaning goals, the Co-op did not function as envisioned. Often there was not enough work, and many members did not make enough to live on; everyone was stressed about money, especially those who could not rely on a husband or boyfriend to supplement their earnings. The group was also quite fractious; members did not entirely trust one another, and most disliked Cristina, always suspicious that she had an "agenda." They complained, constantly, about how little they were earning, about the meetings, about Cristina, and about one another. These conflicts point up the competition so characteristic to the state of "hyperreality" (Parreñas 2001; cf. Mahler 1995).[15]

Sacrificing for Your Family, or Why Join?

I arrived at the Co-op during a moment of transition, just as members were switching workplaces and broader institutional affiliation, and, as Cristina explained, after a year of much dissent and unhappiness within the group. To that end, she had asked Irma, the wife of a former coworker, to conduct a ten-week "seminar" to strengthen the group's unity and to set up more concrete governing rules. Cristina and Irma had agreed that Irma would earn five thousand dollars for this effort, a subject of constant protest from members, who were furious that they had to pay anyone such a large sum. They just did not see the point of this seminar, and they really hated having to sit through those long meetings, always quick to point out that no one was paying them for this time. They were not interested in these sessions or the work to be accomplished. During these long sessions, they hardly seemed to be paying attention, shifting around in their seats, staring into space, doodling if they had paper in front of them, fidgeting, and playing with their phones. When Irma asked a question, they would answer by rote, providing the "right" answer—yes, they wanted to be business owners; yes, this required responsibility and tough decisions; yes, they wanted to learn—but these responses were always delivered in a monotone and disengaged manner.

Reactions to Irma's presence and general disinterest in the matters discussed highlight the fact that members found this aspect of the Co-op a needless burden. For as much as they could provide Irma with the "right" answers, owning a business and improving the state of domestic service were not their primary concerns. As much as they wanted better pay and fair treatment, they were more preoccupied with earning money than with these abstract, long-term goals. They needed income *now*—an urgency that overwhelmed every other consideration.

How individuals came to join the Co-op and their manifold grievances indicate their comparative disinterest in long-term business goals or domestic service as occupation. Aída, for example, had been trafficked from Mexico into the United States in her late teens. At fourteen, she had been raped by a neighborhood boy and forced to marry him after her family found out that she was pregnant. A few years later, two men showed up in her town and asked if she wanted to go to the United States. Deeply unhappy at home, she jumped at this opportunity. Once she arrived here, she was forced to work in a brothel just south of Los Angeles for several months, until the authorities raided the house where she was held. She was sent to jail but quickly released into the custody of an organization that helps women who have been trafficked. This organization gave her a choice, to stay here or go home. She opted to return to Mexico, where she found only scorn, as her family and friends shunned her for what she had done. She then decided to leave her town and moved to another city with her daughter. There she worked two jobs but still couldn't make ends meet. She felt uncomfortable living in Mexico after everything that had happened and was increasingly desperate about her economic situation. So she contacted the organization that had helped her and asked to return to Los Angeles. This organization inquired whether she would like to clean houses, and when she responded yes, they set her up with the Co-op.

Aída joined the Co-op three years prior to my arrival, and her tenure had seen a number of ups and downs. At first she refused to participate in meetings, often missed work, and drank too much. Recently, however, she had started getting her act together, taking more interest in the business, only to be disappointed by the Co-op's financial state. This upward swing began when she found out that she was eligible to apply for a green card under a T visa,[16] and that she could bring her daughter here once her papers were straightened out. At twenty-four, all she wanted from life was to help her parents and to make a better life for her seven-year-old daughter. She was not crazy about living in the United States. She didn't think she would ever get completely used to it, but at least being here allowed her to support her family: "It is more better here, because there, a lot of work, little money . . . and here, well, maybe I'm not, not such a big deal, I don't have the things that I would want to have, no? But at least I'm not working as much as I did there, where I worked from 7 AM to 6 PM, 7 PM, and to live in misery."[17] Earning a living and getting her daughter ahead ("*sacar adelante a mija*") were the reasons she had left Mexico, and they continued to be her priorities, shaping every aspect of her life, including her involvement with the Co-op.

Even as Aída's increased interest in the business was guided by the desire to bring her daughter here, her commitment to the Co-op wavered. She was disillusioned; while she appreciated that customers treated them well, the group had too many internal problems. They did not have enough money coming in, and every month she worried about making the rent. Moreover, meetings were too long and accomplished nothing; and, to add insult to injury, they earned no money for all the hours squandered at those get-togethers. Like all of the women, she complained about infighting and about Cristina. She suspected that the organizations that helped them out were using the group to get money from private foundations. She explained that all of the members shared these doubts, but they were too afraid to say anything. They did not trust Cristina, and they did not believe in her plans for improvement or expansion.

Listening to this litany of misgivings, I asked why she stayed. She responded that she needed steady proof of employment to get her daughter here, and importantly, she had to make a living. She explained, "everybody sacrifices to get her family ahead."[18] For her, the Co-op was "like the bad husband who is humiliating me, but why don't we want to leave him? Because then what are we going to do? We're going to die of hunger."[19]

This statement condenses Aída's engagement with the Co-op: how it helped with several concrete goals, earning an income and bringing her daughter to the United States. She was willing to sacrifice for these goals, to fulfill her role as mother, a crucial element of her identity. Trafficked into prostitution and rejected by her parents, extended family, and native community, Aída's sense of self had been completely demolished by her initial experiences in the United States. The only thing that made her feel good about herself was sending money home, the ability to support not only her daughter but also the parents who had abandoned and repudiated her. Stripped of any other way to sustain relationships with her family, subsidizing her parents became even more important than usual. Additionally, bringing her daughter to the United States would not only get her away from people who would censure and disparage Aída, but would also provide her with a better life and ample opportunities for the future. The sacrifice was worth it— that is why Aída stayed at the Co-op. The business's long-term prospects easily took a back seat to these more immediate considerations.

Eva's reasons for enlisting in the Co-op also revolved around her relationship with her children. Eva left El Salvador in the late 1980s after breaking up with her husband, and single-handedly supported her four children, while also helping her parents. She put her two sons and one of her daughters through school, sending her younger son to medical school. She was extremely proud of this accomplishment, always reminding people that her son was a doctor. All of this, however, had required and continued to call for hard work and sacrifice; she put up with a job she did not like and made do without certain necessities. For two months after I first met her, she walked around without glasses. She could not see very well and suffered from constant headaches, but she had broken her previous pair and could not afford new ones. She was sending all of her extra money to El Salvador to help her older son, who had been out of work for a year. She informed me: "Here, I only work, and only work for my children"[20]

When I met Eva, she had been at the Co-op for almost four years. Previously, she had worked in factories, stopping only when she could no longer get enough hours. Her income falling, she decided that she would devote herself full-time to Mary Kay sales, a job that she enjoyed tremendously. She dedicated herself to Mary Kay for a few years until she found that she could no longer support herself that way. She began looking for other work and, quite by chance, came across a flyer for the Co-op. She saw the word *negocio* (business), and this piqued her interest.

Eva had never cleaned houses before, but she liked the idea of a *negocio*; she had learned all about *negocios* from Mary Kay and knew that she would earn well. So she called the Co-op, became a trainee, and learned to clean. To her surprise, cleaning was easier on her body than factory work. She also appreciated the Co-op's insurance benefits and the fact that she didn't have to spend eight hours at work every day. At the Co-op, she had more free time and a cell phone, both of which also helped with her Mary Kay sales. This job, then, was a pragmatic choice for Eva; she was fixed on sending money to her children, and since the Co-op also gave her time to pursue her Mary Kay business, it was a convenient arrangement.

Still, Eva was less than happy with her job. It was tiring, there was too much infighting, and all of this internal strife left her embittered. She did not trust Cristina, who favored other members and needlessly took up too much of their time. She hated the weekly meetings, finding them useless, and resented that they interfered with other income-generating activities. If they did not have these Monday sessions, members could clean houses and earn more money during that time, or she could visit her Mary Kay customers, or perhaps even both.

After seventeen years in Los Angeles, Eva knew her way around, what she needed to do to make ends meet. She talked about leaving the Co-op but stayed because of its benefits. She also knew that life in this country required sacrifices, but that these eventually paid off. In fact, "I am thankful to this country, because I have been able to get ahead, to get my children ahead. I can also help my parents. I have felt very thankful. I have liked it, because here I've been able to help my family, even if I don't have money for extras. I have a house I can retire to someday . . . in El Salvador . . . and so I say, what else can I ask for? God gave me a house, he gave me children that I love so much, my mother who is still alive, my father."[21] Putting up with the Co-op, then, was not all that different from her other sacrifices. And, on the whole, they had been worth it.

Aída and Eva, and each of the other members, came to the Co-op under different circumstances and for seemingly diverse reasons. In the end, however, they were all drawn in by the immediate, tangible benefits—the promise of steady income, health insurance, and a cell phone. Like Aída and Eva, the others were displeased with the state of the Co-op, arguing that they did not make enough money, meetings were interminable, and Cristina treated them unfairly. Yet they all remained. The three women who left during my stay were all kicked out. All three left reluctantly but later reported to me that they were better off now, that they had been unhappy and were glad to be rid of the Co-op. Nevertheless, no one left until she had to, and all three cried when they were asked to leave. Disgruntled though they were, they knew it was more important to have a reliable source of income.

Cooperation, Competition, and the Imperative to Make a Living

This need to make money often came into conflict with the ideals of collectivity and unity. Because there were never sufficient jobs and members did not earn enough to live comfortably, there was always a not-so-subtle undercurrent of suspicion and competition within the organization. As poor immigrants accustomed to struggling for meager earnings, compounded by the fact that the Co-op never managed to break even, members operated on the assumption that income was scarce and that if they did not take it someone else would. They were extremely suspicious of one another, certain that whoever seemed to be doing a little better at any particular point in time was somehow taking advantage of the others.

Thus, competition and resentment over jobs were central impediments to smooth functioning. Even though income parity was central to their mission, members did not always feel that job allotment was entirely fair. They all worked on and decided the schedule weekly; yet whenever they spoke about particular jobs, they would say "*me mandaron a . . .*" (they sent me to . . .) or "*no me dan horas*" (they won't give me hours), always divorcing themselves from the process. This kind of statement underscores not just their feelings of powerlessness in terms of making decisions, but also each person's sense that everyone else was somehow doing better or had an unfair advantage.

The cooperative spirit and the idea of income parity did work to a certain extent. Mercedes, forty-four and from Mexico, often labored seven days a week to support herself and her two teenage daughters; even so, she could barely manage to scrape by on her paycheck of eight hundred dollars or so a month. She never earned enough, even though she always volunteered for additional jobs. The other members were acutely aware of her needs, and whenever there were extra hours to be had, they usually asked her first if she wanted them. Still, they all held onto the better customers as tightly as they could; they all really needed the money, after all.

For instance, one Monday afternoon, Mercedes got very upset when Cristina suggested that she take a trainee to the Zuckers'. Never one for public argument, she insisted that she didn't need anyone's help with that house and, after much acrimonious discussion, managed to have the schedule rearranged so that she could go there alone. Later, as I drove her home, she confided that she wanted to go to the Zuckers' by herself because it was the only house where she felt that she got a break, "*la única que está a mi favor*" (the only one that works to my advantage). It was a small house, and she earned eighty dollars there. Plus, the customers were extremely nice. They didn't want her to arrive before twelve; the wife always brought her coffee and a snack in the middle of the afternoon; and by four, they kicked her out. Working for the Zuckers felt like an afternoon off, and she earned eighty dollars for her troubles. It was worth it, then, to insist on it at the meeting, even though she generally tried to keep the peace. If she had to bring someone along, she would have to split the eighty dollars, taking only forty dollars home at the end of the day.

This understandable reluctance to share earnings not just with one another but also with trainees worked against the Co-op's long-term interests. There were not enough members to sustain a larger clientele, and as long as they did not have enough jobs, the group would never become self-sufficient. Yet taking on trainees meant having to share their current income, as there would be more members vying for the same number of hours. The Co-op would only be able to acquire new customers once the trainees were full members and trusted to clean by themselves. The problem was that members could not afford a further reduction in their earnings in the present, even if it would bring them more in the future.

Further, even as the Co-op aimed to provide a living wage as well as a buffer against abuse and disrespect, the vagaries of the market were such that the women struggled to land and hold onto any job that was available. They held fast to all their customers, even the most challenging or low-paying ones. For instance, Mercedes had a customer who paid her thirty-six dollars every other week. One week, Mercedes reported that this woman had asked her to help scrub the kitchen floor with a toothbrush, this on top of cleaning the whole house—and all for thirty-six dollars. Mercedes refused to let this customer go despite Cristina's urging. She counted on that money and worried that she might not easily find another house to offset its loss.

In that vein, the group would take almost every job that came its way. When trainees complained about customers that required too much travel time or too much effort, members would respond that they would do whatever work was available. Eva put it best one day when she pointedly informed a potential recruit that "*aquí nos volamos cualquier trabajo*" (here we do any job). She'd had it with the trainees who were always whining, she said. Everyone hustled and sweated to make the Co-op successful, but the trainees seemed to expect "*una mesa servida*" (literally, a served table).

Members, then, were willing to put up with low-paying customers and would not sacrifice income for the future growth of the business. Long-term gains were dimmed by current necessity, and individuals who lived from paycheck to paycheck couldn't forgo paying the rent, eating dinner, or buying a bus pass for the promise of future profits. Their assessment of the situation made perfect sense within their range of experience. There were not enough jobs, and like all of the immigrant women I met in LA, Co-op members were accustomed to the barest forms of survival.

Organizational Goals: The Domestic Workers Group

The Domestic Workers Group took a different approach to the ills of domestic service, seeking to create a visible political presence for domestic workers through education and organization. When I first encountered the group in November 2002, it was undergoing yet another leadership change. A project of a broader immigrant rights organization, the DWG had undergone several upheavals in the preceding years, changing leaders a number of times.[22]

In 2002, the DWG was in a rebuilding stage; membership had dwindled after a few years of internal disorder. The lack of stable leadership meant that for the past few years the DWG had been in a constant state of reinvention. As such, it was hard to define just what the group's mission was, although when I arrived, organizers' attention centered on recruiting new members and disseminating information about the rights of domestic workers. As part of these efforts, organizers actively courted media attention. In addition, Josefina would go out regularly, riding the buses and hitting coffee shops or donut stores where domestic workers gathered, to speak to individuals, tell them about their rights, and try to recruit them.

This focus on distributing information perhaps detracted from planning activities to draw in new members or keep current ones engaged. Aside from helping to hand out information and going to meetings, I attended just two DWG events while I was in Los Angeles—a yard sale to benefit the home organization's Day Laborers' project and a Christmas party. There were no other planned events, and even meetings were not held with any regularity, happening perhaps every month or two.

Intangible Benefits

Much like the Co-op, the DWG's goals and the desires and engagements of individual members did not always correspond. As a result, the group had a hard time attracting and keeping members. According to Josefina, the rolls included at least fifty women, but the largest number I ever saw was perhaps twenty women who attended the annual Christmas party. As a rule, ten or fewer would gather for meetings. Despite Josefina's efforts, it was always the same women who attended, and try as we might, we rarely inspired any of the women we met on the bus to join the DWG or even come to a meeting. The women we were trying to recruit often worked six or seven days a week, spending what little free time they had at home with their families or taking care of things they could not see to while at work. On top of that, many lived far from the DWG's offices and did not want to dedicate an entire morning or afternoon to attending a one- or two-hour meeting. And, charismatic as she was, Josefina had little to offer these women aside from the promise of a brighter future if they joined a long-term struggle. The DWG did not provide jobs and could not attend to individual complaints. When we handed someone a sheet detailing her rights, we could not tell her that the DWG would mediate with her employers. Rather, we gave her the information, hoping that she would take it up by herself, something not too many women would do for fear of losing their jobs.

Certainly, the women we spoke with were well aware of the abuses that this occupation entailed, and they were always happy to discuss these. Still, infrequently held meetings that centered on domestic work or other issues surrounding the DWG's continually changing leadership did not pull in too many people. Individuals needed concrete incentives to join or even attend one of the DWG's gatherings. This became clear when Rosario was leader, as she arranged for the DWG to hand out bags of food after every meeting. The free food proved incredibly popular, prompting the women we met on our rounds to express interest in joining, perhaps even to come to a meeting. Also, it drew many members, even the most delinquent, to monthly gatherings, as they eagerly anticipated their packages of mashed potatoes, canned ham, fruits, bread, and the like. After a few months, however, the practice was canceled, and attendance dropped sharply at subsequent gatherings.

Without food, potential job contacts, or the promise of assistance with job difficulties, the DWG did not have anything tangible to entice potential new members, or even to draw the existing ones to regular meetings. So just what was it that attracted the few loyal members?

Recognition and Rights

Like the Co-op's members, individual women came to the DWG for reasons not directly linked to the DWG's goals; they sought to ease some of the hardships of immigrant life, but not exactly to dedicate themselves to a struggle for future rights. The promise of a vague future reward did not keep them there. Since the DWG did not find people jobs, they did not come for work. Moreover, the identity of domestic worker did not necessarily serve as a mobilizing point, at least not divorced from other aspects of their experience as immigrants. Rather, the need for community, to be seen and heard and to forge bonds with others, seemed a key motivating factor in decisions to join. The erasures of immigrant life can be crushing. Through migration, individuals are torn from the communities that originally provided a built-in audience and easily definable sense of self. Arriving in LA, where they have no *place*, they suddenly find themselves invisible. Here they must carve out new social worlds, vying for status and respect within these. They thus scramble to be seen, hustling to find accurate "reflecting surfaces," looking for "opportunities to appear in the world, thus assuring themselves that indeed they exist" (Myerhoff 1978: 32). The DWG provided one such occasion, supplying a group of ready "witnesses."

But this type of recognition was itself a luxury. For recently arrived immigrants or those with children to support, the urgency of making money overshadowed other concerns. Women who worked six or seven days a week, often at more than one job, had little time for other endeavors. And, in fact, DWG members were at a different point in their lives than the women at the Co-op. While they continued to work hard and stretched every cent they earned, they didn't have to devote all of their time to earning money. They'd been in the United States longer, had adult children, and had experienced considerable improvements in their standards of living.

Patricia, a Salvadoran immigrant in her fifties, was one of the earliest members; she joined the DWG after many of years of living in the

United States and after working in a house, a diner, a factory, and as a home care aide. She arrived only after her son became an adult and began to support himself, and after many years' experience had led her to a better-paying job. Initially, she was reluctant to join the group: "I didn't, I didn't take such an interest in the domestic workers at first, well, because I was already at that time, I was legal. I already had everything, and I said, well, why would I fight. But then I started to think that I should orient the other women, how, how they should live."[23]

At first, Patricia didn't see how the DWG could help her; since she had a green card, she "already had everything." The biggest obstacle facing domestic workers, she asserted, was a lack of legal status. Further, she explained that she joined because she liked the idea of helping other women. Of course, this desire carried with it the assumption of reciprocal recognition. Lacking other sources of validation, Patricia yearned for appreciation of her successes. She'd made something of herself here, raising a son, obtaining a green card, and learning to drive, among other accomplishments. Yet neither her son nor her friends paid her the respect she craved, and so she continued to search for a willing audience.

The original coordinators had nurtured Patricia, but a change of leadership put an abrupt end to her love affair with the DWG; Patricia felt that the new organizer purposely sidelined her, and she exited in a huff. After leaving, she poured her energies into her church; she began volunteering at the hospital and visiting prisoners—once again gaining respect through her ability and willingness to help those less fortunate. When I met Patricia many years later, she had just come back to the DWG. She was selling Mary Kay, dreamed of selling enough to earn a company car, and thought the DWG would be a good place to recruit customers. Her return, like her original membership, then, was spurred by her longing for recognition—in this case, a brand new car would serve as proof of having made it.

This desire for respect and recognition also propelled Doña Flor's involvement at the DWG. Doña Flor, who left El Salvador for Los Angeles in the late 1980s, first came across the DWG in the late 1990s in her quest to straighten out her legal status. Although she had been looking for legal advice, she joined the DWG because she enjoyed interacting with the other members. When I met her, three years later, she continued to attend almost all activities. At seventy-nine, Doña Flor had more free time to dedicate to the DWG than a lot of the other members did. In her fifteen years in LA, she had been employed in both factories and homes, serving as nanny, house cleaner, and home health care aide. Now she only worked four or five hours a day, taking care of a "*viejito*" (old man). She would have liked to work more, but because of her age many people would not hire her. She didn't explain her participation in the DWG in terms of free time, however, but rather as a commitment to younger generations. She repeatedly declared that she was fighting to help younger women, since it was too late to do anything for herself. Underlining her dedication, she often reminded us that she had to take three different buses just to get to the DWG. Echoing Patricia, then, Doña Flor characterized her involvement with the group as selfless; she was there to "help," participating not just in the practical dimensions of the struggle but also providing guidance from her more experienced position.

Interestingly, Doña Flor garnered more recognition and respect from other members than anyone else. Although they sometimes resented each other's efforts to steal the spotlight, members were willing to appreciate Doña Flor's endeavors because of her age. This special position afforded Doña Flor the attention and deference she desired. In large part, this drove her willingness to attend functions or help out. Her devotion to the group, however, ended after she returned from a conference in New York. The DWG wanted to send a representative to an international conference on domestic service, and Josefina could not go because she lacked legal documents. Unable to fly, Josefina suggested that Doña Flor, who had taken advantage of the temporary protected status extended to Salvadorans in 2001,[24] go in her stead. Doña Flor had a great time in New York, but she forgot her wallet and a medallion that her grandson had given her in the hotel. She was devastated by this loss, and asked Josefina and Jenny, the group's acting leader, to call the hotel and inquire about her things. She called Josefina and Jenny every day for over a week, but Josefina was upset that she had not been able to go to New York herself, and it took her a while to get back to Doña Flor. By the time someone from the DWG phoned the hotel in New York, Doña Flor's things had vanished. Doña Flor was furious, convinced that they waited too long, or worse yet, that they had not even bothered to place the call. She blamed Josefina and Jenny and vowed that she would not return to the DWG as long as they were in charge. It was their responsibility, she affirmed, *to pay attention to their members*—an assertion that summarized many people's engagement with the group.

Asserting One's Rights or Making a Living?

For most members, then, the DWG furnished the possibility of respect and appreciation, fighting against the erasures of immigrant life. Although the devaluation of domestic service and domestic workers compounded their marginality, for these women it existed regardless of occupational status; they all experienced it even as they moved back and forth through different types of work. Moreover, their experiences at the DWG did not necessarily change their perspectives on or approaches to work and/or employers. At the DWG, they had learned about their rights—that they indeed had rights—but they were not always willing to assert these. Like Co-op members, they needed an income in whatever form was available.

Carmen, for example, continued to put up with less-than-ideal employers. Even though she knew her rights, had even written a play reprising them, she remained at jobs with disrespectful employers and houses where she was asked to perform highly distasteful work. One day she informed me that Melissa, a longtime employer, had told her not to come back. I asked what happened, and she responded that Melissa had left her a note asking her to wash some bloody underwear by hand. Carmen put the underwear in a lingerie bag, added bleach, and stuck it in the washer. Apparently, however, Melissa noticed that something was amiss and fired her. Carmen's replaying of the story, her casual tone of voice, and the lack of outrage or anger over Melissa's request suggested to me that this wasn't the first time Melissa had made such an offensive request. Carmen was upset, not so much at the idea of this task as at the fact that she would now have to make do without eighty dollars a week or figure out a way to replace this income. Despite everything she had learned at the DWG, economic survival remained Carmen's abiding concern. It was one thing to know about your rights and quite another to give up steady income, or any income at all, on behalf of them.

Domestic Workers' Rights as Women's and Immigrants' Rights

Over the course of my fieldwork, I encountered only two women, Norma and Josefina, who defined themselves as "domestic workers." Not surprisingly, perhaps, both had served as organizers at the Domestic Workers Group and both were enthusiastic about and committed to strengthening the rights of domestic workers. Even so, Josefina and Norma, like the other women I met, did not see domestic service as its own problem; instead, both understood the difficulties of this occupation as part and parcel of immigrant life, specifically the experiences of immigrant women.

As an organizer for the DWG, Josefina's primary role was recruiting members and disseminating information, and she generously allowed me to tag along with her. I spent countless hours with Josefina, listening to her appeals to other domestic workers, describing the slavery of the job and all of its attendant indignities. She was committed to the fight, not just on behalf of domestic workers but for all immigrants. As such, she participated in the campaign to get licenses for undocumented immigrants, traveling to Sacramento more than once. She also attended demonstrations on behalf of factory workers, was a member of a joint Korean-Latino immigrant organization, and took part in the 2003 cross-country ride for the undocumented.[25]

For her, all of these causes were part of a single struggle for immigrants' rights. She believed that improving domestic service was a key component of this battle, because it was the desperation and poverty of immigrant life, of having children to support at any cost, that drove women into this kind of work and kept them at miserable jobs without complaint. It was important, therefore, to educate women and inform them of their rights. This would allow them to defend themselves against employers:

> I want the women to learn to defend themselves. That is their tool. I want the women to learn, to take the CPR course, because it is a tool of their trade, right? Because that document will help them. I would like for the women to have what I do not, without jealousy: to learn to speak English, to use the computer, so that *they are no longer just a woman, just an object. I do not want that. Just a maid—I do not want that. I*

want more and more, but education is what I want. Because with education, we will end ignorance. Ending ignorance will open doors.[26]

Here, Josefina relates her hopes for the DWG as well as a plan for ameliorating the conditions of domestic work. Her comments also stress that the fight is a much larger one—it is about improving the lives of women. Josefina did not want the DWG's members to be "just a woman, just an object."

According to Josefina, her work was not just about immigrants' rights but specifically about women. Female immigrants were relegated to domestic work and other poorly paid jobs because they were women. And, because they were mothers concerned with feeding their children, they took these jobs. It was a predicament particular to women, but unfortunately, women were too often left out of the picture in broader battles over immigration. Thus, Josefina believed that domestic workers—and other immigrant women—had to make their concerns public and fight for inclusion in the agenda. She told me:

> The women have to be seen; they have to advertise. They have to make themselves known, that exploitation exists, that we have needs, that we need to move the family. That we need to take a job that's far away, but since we have no car, we have no license, we don't want to risk what little we have to buy a, a car and have it taken away just around the corner, and we have no option to get it back. It's lost money. So why risk it, and we take the poorest job, less work, poorly paid, because it is closer, reachable by bus, and close to a lot of movement, because there is no other choice. So we get stuck there. So the women have to, have to realize what the need is, and that is how I take up the theme of the licenses, the theme of legalization.[27]

All immigrants potentially suffered from lack of legal status, dependence on public transportation, and poverty, but women experienced these differently, often ending up in domestic work. Domestic service was inextricable from immigrant life, from the female version of this experience, and this was Josefina's fight.

Norma also characterized her endeavors to improve domestic service as an effort on behalf of women, of mothers. I originally met Norma during a brief trip to Los Angeles in 2000, when she was head of the DWG. However, by the time I returned to begin fieldwork in 2002,

Norma was long gone. I didn't see her again until the summer of 2003, when she joined the Co-op at Cristina's behest. Like Josefina, Norma worked in domestic service when she first arrived from Mexico in the early 1990s. She crossed the border with her husband and two young children, only to find hunger, homelessness, and desperation on this side. Her husband abandoned her a few months after their arrival, leaving Norma with no money, no home, and two children to feed. She wound up taking a live-in job with an employer who allowed her to bring her children. The job, however, was miserable; she worked long hours for little pay and was assaulted more than once by the *patrona*'s suitors.

Norma was still working in a house when she came across the DWG. She immediately felt at home with the group, and she became a member. She subsequently went to work as a paid recruiter and eventually became the coordinator. She reported that under her rule, the DWG had flourished, with hundreds of members, its own newspaper, and an active theater group. She was only let go, she explained, because of internal politics within the DWG's sponsoring organization.

After she lost her position at the DWG, she went back to cleaning houses here and there, and took on whatever other jobs she could find. However, her attitude had changed; informed of her rights, Norma decided that she would never again put up with employer abuse:

> There's a lot of need; and with my children, I went through a lot, and a lot of things happened to us, you see. I, I, I started to become empowered, and there was a moment when I said no—why do I have to put up with things? I can support myself in some other way, selling gum, but no one is going to humiliate me. No one is going to offend me. Selling gum is very dignified work. I started thinking in another way. I started to clean houses, right, but I started cleaning them in another way. I would go there and say, this is what I can do for you. . . . Does that work for you? If not, I'm leaving. Like that, see. . . . I decided that, see. If you don't like something, you tell me, I will try to fix it if I can. If I can't, then you should find someone else to come.[28]

Norma knew that other women endured miseries to be able to feed their children, but she would rather live under a bridge than forgo her rights. She could not withstand any more injuries to her dignity and was willing to live with the consequences.

Norma's refusal to put up with poor treatment or be further humiliated led her to continue working against the indignities of domestic service even after she left the DWG. Although she had to take other jobs and did not always have time, she sought to create another organization for domestic workers. Her goal in life was to end the abuses of this occupation. However, she believed that these difficulties stemmed from much larger causes, from the poverty and desperation that kept many women in bad situations. For Norma, this was an impossible predicament: having to choose between feeding your children and humiliation.

Like Josefina, Norma defined the troubles of domestic service as part of the larger problems women face. She told me that domestic service was a last remnant of slavery, and the reason that no one noticed this was that even in contemporary society, women were trained to serve men. She explained:

> The *doméstica* didn't stop being a slave. The *doméstica*, then, um, still they continued to consider her part of that, because the man. . . . On the one hand, your family would tell you that you have to prepare yourself to be your husband's slave. They wouldn't tell you that, but you have to learn to serve your husband. So they taught us to serve. In church, they also teach us to serve. In church, they teach us to serve. Everywhere they teach us to serve. The penitent woman is submissive. I don't agree with that; yes, I belong to the church, but I'm very liberal. I teach women to be liberal. I've gotten into trouble, no, but well, that's part of life, isn't it? All, all those many women in, in those times were women who had never had an option to study anything. They had only been prepared to be homemakers, in Mexico. Here, not so much anymore because now there's another way of life, but the people who come here to work as *domésticas* are from our countries . . . raised for that, right?[29]

Norma wanted to alleviate the unsolvable decisions that immigrant women face, to free them from enslavement. The answer was education, empowering women so that they did not have to put up with (men's) abuse:

Part of my goals is to have power, you know, and for women to have power, you know. . . . And I will do everything possible so that women do not spend seven years like me, under the power of one man. I will do everything possible so that women do not have to be under the power of male employers . . . and who are the ones who need this the most? Domestic workers, right? For me, it ceased to be the domestic worker as a worker but rather a struggle *as* women . . . and then I started to recognize that there was more to do than to inform workers about their rights.[30]

Ultimately, then, Norma's conception of domestic work was indivisible from the condition of being a woman. Domestic service both reflected and perpetuated the difficulties with which (immigrant) women contended. For her, as for Josefina, combatting the most problematic aspects of this occupation was not an isolated goal but part of a broader social struggle.

Conclusion

Poverty, a narrow labor market, and individuals' need to provide for their families weave themselves through the above discussion. In a context of limited possibilities, where they often moved from one kind of work to another and back again, immigrant women worried about making a living much more than about how they made this living. That domestic service was not the most relevant category of experience for members of the DWG and the Co-op was clearly seen in the frustrations each organization faced. This point was further affirmed by Josefina and Norma, the only two women I met who wholeheartedly adopted the identity of "domestic worker." Indeed, Norma's remarks bear repetition: "For me, it ceased to be the domestic worker as a worker but rather a struggle *as* women." And as women, they struggled to provide for their families, to create opportunities for their children. They engaged in productive labor in service of their reproductive endeavors, rendering these visible and valuable. Beginning from this relative ranking of motherhood and occupation in defining the self, the next chapter explores how immigrant women frame and understand their lives in the United States, how they gauge their successes as immigrants, as mothers, and as valuable social members.

CHAPTER 5

Dreaming American

The morning of Carmen's sixty-fifth birthday was windy, rainy, and with temperatures in the fifties, freezing by LA standards. We had decided to spend the day together, but when I arrived, she didn't want to go out. She'd been watching TV and informed me that a big storm was coming. We had coffee and caught up on a few days' gossip while we tried to decide what to do. Suddenly standing up, Carmen declared that even though the weather was horrible, we had to go to Social Security. We could postpone our other plans but not this one. She'd been looking forward to this visit for weeks, telling me repeatedly that the only thing she really had to do on her birthday was to sign up for her Social Security benefits. Braving the rain, we drove to Social Security, where she learned that she would soon start receiving $360 per month. While thankful and excited to get this extra money, Carmen also felt let down. Afterward, in the car and over lunch at Denny's, she mentioned that her friend Ana received an $800 check from the government every month, but then, sighing, added that Ana had always held higher-paying jobs.

Carmen's simultaneous excitement, gratitude, and disappointment that morning foreground the multiple and contradictory ways in which immigrant domestic workers experienced and thought about success and the American Dream. For Carmen and other immigrant women, the American Dream remained both reality and unachievable end; although its promise was bright, the Dream was constantly deferred. The lifestyles they had pictured before coming, continued to imagine through television, and saw firsthand in employer homes remained out of reach. If Carmen envisioned opulence—a monthly check for $800 and a free government apartment when she got "old"—she got instead $360 a month.[1] Yet immigrant women earned better here, and even though they labored to make ends meet, putting up with poorly paid, backbreaking jobs, many believed that their only hope for a viable, or any kind of, future lay in this country.

After thirty years of struggle, of exhausting, low-paid work, Carmen still saw the United States as a land of opportunity. Claiming monthly benefits and the possibility of having health insurance through Medicare seemed a bounty, for in Guatemala she would have worked harder for less money and could never have expected any help or reward for her efforts. Our visit to Social Security that morning was an important rite of passage for her, the first time she would receive (financial) recognition for her contributions to this country. Although she had anticipated an extra $800 a month, a sum that would make her feel wealthy, a $360 check was not insignificant: the previous year, she had earned $10,000.

In previous chapters, we saw how employers marked off the borders of "Americanness," but also how they felt unable to fulfill many of its requirements. Grappling with a system that measures worth through occupation and earnings, middle-class women felt unable to reconcile the ideological and material demands of motherhood. This put a dent in their capacity to become independent adults, valuable persons, worthwhile Americans. In this chapter, I turn to the immigrant women who worked in their homes. These women also subscribed to the American Dream, defined success as economic mobility, and tied individual value and national belonging to motherhood. Yet, as chapter 4 discusses, the immigrant perspective rested on an alternative arrangement of self, occupation, and motherhood—elevating reproductive over productive labor and engaging in paid employment in service of the former. Therefore, I argue, despite the economic hardships, patent structural exclusions, and social erasures that accompany immigrant life, this version of the Dream was characterized by possibility rather than failure, amplifying rather than contracting the parameters of "Americanness."

Of course, the American Dream is made possible only through exclusion; indeed, racial, gender, class, and national distinctions materialize the boundaries between those entitled to the good life and those who merely work to enable others' Dreams. These increasingly impermeable lines are necessary and necessarily invisible, for the

Dream will only function if we are all committed to its pursuit. I return, then, to the question I posed in the Introduction: Are these women dupes, seduced by the promise of material gain to provide the labor that subsidizes others' successes? Is this merely an/other example of "cruel optimism," which "exists when something you desire is actually an obstacle to your flourishing" (Berlant 2011: 1)? As Berlant asks: "Why do people stay attached to conventional good life fantasies—say of enduring reciprocity in couples, families, political systems, institutions, markets, and at work—when the evidence of their instability, fragility, and dear cost abounds" (2011: 2)?

This chapter plumbs the experiences of Mexican and Central American women in Los Angeles to complicate to these questions. It explores how financial advancement coupled with self-transformation to make individuals successful, and therefore, from their own perspectives, "American," worthy of belonging. Immigrant women simultaneously acknowledged—indeed, many criticized and even organized to change—the difficulties of life in the United States, while at the same time subscribing to the American Dream. Juxtaposing these apparently paradoxical certainties, I analyze immigrant women's affective attachments to this country, how these related to economic mobility for themselves and for their children, and the time frames in which these operated.

A Note on Terminology: "Americanness," Success, Belonging

De Genova maintains that "Americanness" is inherently racialized, inextricable from whiteness, and thus advocates "the specific antiracist necessity of repudiating 'American'-ness" (2005: 209). Without denying the widely assumed connections between whiteness and "Americanness," I take up the term in an alternate manner, referring not to legal categories or mainstream perceptions of immigrants, but to a particular way-of-being arising in the United States. Immigrants did in fact become "American," changing into different kinds of persons through their experiences in LA. This was a distinctly immigrant version of American, a fusion of practices and dispositions brought from home, learned from other immigrants, and gleaned from contact with nonimmigrants. While this take on "Americanness" might not have resonated with employers, it was nonetheless American, produced only in the specificity of the U.S. context. And this new way-of-being held tremendous value for immigrant women, a process of transformation through which they came to understand themselves. At times they referred to it as becoming American, at times opting for terms like personal transformation or self-improvement. I use "American" deliberately, to disrupt a strict separation between American and immigrant, a putative distinction that conceals and reproduces social inequalities by maintaining immigrants outside the frame of the nation.[2]

Further, I do not use "American" and "Americanness" to refer to legal categories, for the experience of citizenship remains vexed, variable, and for many immigrants completely inaccessible. Beyond question, possession of legal papers alleviates a fundamental source of concern for immigrant women, especially as intensified regimes of "crimmigration" (Stumpf 2006) and deportation have rendered undocumented immigrants increasingly visible and vulnerable.[3] Indeed, in the wake of 2006 immigrant rights protests across the nation, several stalled attempts at federal immigration reform, intensifying rates of deportation, the growing visibility and activism of undocumented youth, and the virulent anti-immigrant tone of the 2016 election and its aftermath, "illegality"[4] and citizenship have progressively penetrated the public imagination. Nevertheless, in turn-of-the-millennium LA, I found that issues of legality did not necessarily play a central role in the day-to-day, arising instead in particular moments and social contexts (e.g., Corcoran 1993; Coutin 2000, 2013). Even more, legal status—whether in the form of a work permit, temporary protected status, legal residency, or citizenship—did not allay the other, defining difficulties of immigrant life (cf. Preston 2013). Official documents, after all, could not counteract a tight job market, little to no schooling, and/or a lack of English.[5]

For instance, Eva had a work permit, but still she labored, and earned, alongside women with no papers; she didn't speak English and had little formal education, so legal documents or no, she didn't have access to better jobs. On the other hand, Julia, also a member of the Co-op, was undocumented, but she earned more than her colleagues. She had been in the United States for nearly twenty years and had managed to get a driver's license and Social Security number long before an official ID was required for these documents. Julia had a higher standard of living than any other Co-op member, primarily because she had a husband who also contributed to the household. Pooling their income, they were able to support three sons and maintain two cars. Julia wasn't wealthy, but she was better off than her peers. Similarly, Carmen's friend Margarita arrived in LA in the early 1970s but was unable to arrange her papers until the late 1980s, and only became a citizen in 2003. Even so, Margarita had always done better than Carmen; she had been working for the same family, an affluent family, for over thirty years. That particular job, found by chance, paid her more than Carmen had ever earned, thus affording her a more comfortable lifestyle. In fact, when I asked Carmen how life had changed after she got her papers, she responded:

> The important thing was that I had my papers, that I could go to Guatemala, go visit the family. The only thing at the beginning was that I had my papers to come in and out [of the country] but I didn't have any money. . . . That is, sometimes, you have one thing but not the other. But the important thing is that I was no longer scared, no longer, actually, I was never scared. . . . But I was, I was always careful not to cause any problems so as not to have problems with immigration or anything like that. I was living correctly, very, I never caused any kind of problems.[6]

Legal status, therefore, was not a surefire guarantee of economic security. By itself, it could not ensure upward mobility, nor did it render immigrants less "foreign" in the eyes of the native-born. Accordingly, I use "Americanness" as an index of belonging, as marker of success, not of official citizenship. To be sure, success is neither a transparent concept nor an idiosyncratic goal; it is an ideal that both results from and abets a relentlessly advancing neoliberalism (Pazderic 2004). As such, it makes possible "a supposed true self, that is both under the illusion of freedom yet caught up in the imperative to succeed" (Pazderic 2004: 198). In other words, supposed freedom of choice does not liberate us; rather, by making us believe that we are acting in line with our own wants, it obscures the compulsory nature of neoliberal aims (e.g., Hage 2003; Ahmed 2010; Berlant 2011; Halberstam 2011).

At first glance, Mexican and Central American women's enthusiastic embrace of the American Dream appears to affirm hegemonic conceptions—the Dream as transcribed for and by a new generation of immigrants. Still, as the following sections punctuate, against the backdrop of the poverty, immobility, and desperation these women fled, it makes sense. From their vantage point, striving for more, working to belong, was more than mindless replication of capitalism. For many of these women, success in the United States literally represented freedom from want—the difference between eating regularly and going hungry, between certain exclusion and the possibility, faint though it might be, of belonging. Their continued linking of hard work, economic mobility, and social membership called on seemingly hegemonic notions, upending these to expand the framework of "Americanness."

American Nightmare

Inhabiting the social and economic margins, the Mexican and Central American women I met in LA nevertheless expressed admiration for and desire to belong to this country, a land of opportunity. This seems counterintuitive, for poverty unquestionably remains the first and most pervasive experience of migration, prompting individuals to leave their home countries and shaping every aspect of their lives in LA. They flee destitution only to arrive in a place where jobs are not always dependable, earnings never sufficient, and livelihoods continuously at risk.

Carmen, for example, left Guatemala in the early 1970s. She had three young sons, whom she could barely afford to feed, despite working seven days a week. She herself often went hungry:

> Even if I was dying of hunger, but what I did—see what one does, what I did. When I worked in restaurants, I didn't have time to eat, but when I cleared the tables, you know many people don't eat all of their food. They cut a piece of meat and leave that . . . *ay niña*, I would take the pieces of meat, and eat them, there by the sink. I was completely malnourished. I didn't have, I ate what we call the leftovers, what was left on the plates. But I said, this food is clean.[7]

She was desperate, and when her friend Jimena offered her the opportunity to come to the United States, she snapped it up. She would have to leave her three young sons behind, but this was the only way she could imagine long-term survival. Jimena, a former coworker who had gone to LA two years earlier, called to find out if Carmen had any problems with children: "I told her no: children don't bother me. What

I want is to leave, because you know the life I have here—a life of suffering, a life of hunger. It was, it was constant torment for me. So I told her that I wanted to leave, and she said that that was fine, that I should get ready."[8]

Jimena hooked Carmen up with a family of seven who needed a live-in nanny. Her new employers advanced her the money for a plane ticket, and after borrowing cash from a few friends and convincing a bank clerk to predate a statement for a newly opened savings account, Carmen was able to obtain a tourist visa. She intended to go to the United States for two years, save up money, and return to Guatemala.

Things did not go exactly as planned. In LA, Carmen worked six days a week as a live-in, earning $150 a month for taking care of seven children and maintaining the house. Worse yet, she had to pay off the price of her plane ticket. The rest of her income went directly to her children, so on Sundays she cleaned another house, earning twelve dollars to cover her own needs. She certainly could not afford extras or frivolities, barely scraping by on twelve dollars a week. She never had enough money to save, living paycheck to paycheck.

She continued at this hectic pace for many years. As her children grew up, her life became increasingly expensive; now she had to provide school fees, uniforms, and the like. At one point, the father of her two younger sons stole the funds she had sent to her kids. When she found out that her children hadn't paid for their room and were buying food on credit, Carmen had to borrow money from a friend. A few years later, Marta, a neighbor whom she had asked to look out for her sons, phoned Carmen to tell her that her youngest son was in the hospital. This turned out to be a lie, but Carmen didn't realize that until she had forwarded Marta a sizable sum. Irate, Carmen bought a phone card and called to rebuke Marta: "You, señora, you would think, I said, Marta that being in the United States, I said, is being in heaven. You're wrong, I told her. The United States, if you don't work, you don't eat. You don't know, I said, what it cost me, and this money that I sent to you, I said, I owe it. I borrowed it, because what I earn here is nothing. I didn't have that money."[9] Such unforeseen circumstances with her sons, low wages, and the high cost of living in LA prevented Carmen from accruing any savings. She worked and worked just to cover the basics.

Even so, things were better here than in Guatemala, and she stayed rather than return to the misery she'd left behind. And eventually, things got easier. After fifteen years of live-in work, she started to clean by the day, earning more and enjoying increased freedom and flexibility. Also around this time, her sons began to fend for themselves, and this further relieved her stresses. By the time I met her, thirty years later, Carmen's economic situation had vastly improved, although she was far from wealthy. She watched every penny, sharing a one-bedroom apartment with two of her sons, whom she had brought to the United States in the mid-1990s. Carmen regularly complained about living with her sons: she had to clean, do their laundry, and cook for them. She also continued to help them out financially, even though the youngest was thirty-eight. Every few weeks, she would tell me that she was going to leave them and find her own apartment, where she could enjoy privacy and peace of mind. But she never had enough money to make the move, for housing was prohibitively expensive. She paid four hundred dollars a month in rent, which was a lot, but not nearly as much as a new apartment would cost.

Carmen's is one of numerous tales of poverty and privation. Viewed from the edges, life in LA was almost entirely toil and struggle. Individuals worked long hours at multiple jobs, scrambled to pay rent, and at the end of interminable days, returned home to cramped quarters in run-down buildings—all of this in the hopes of a brighter someday. Not only did they work nonstop, but they had to do so in a strange city where they did not know the language and had limited social support.[10]

For instance, Consuelo, Mexican and in her late thirties, lived in a two-bedroom apartment, sharing one of the rooms with two of her cousins, while a third cousin slept in the living room, and another family—a husband, wife, and his cousin—lived in the second bedroom. The building they lived in was old, dingy, and dilapidated; the elevator was often broken and the entrance always dirty. Women hung their laundry in a courtyard in the center, which, as there was no available green space nearby, was always filled with children playing. Walking into Consuelo's apartment, the kitchen was directly on the right. It was small, with a half-size refrigerator, a dishwasher that they used for storage, a sink, a stove, and some overhead cabinets. Next to the kitchen, right in front of the door, was a narrow dining area with just enough room for a table and four chairs. This small alcove opened into the living room: a couch and two plants set against one wall, two desks with boxes piled on them on the adjacent side, and a twin-sized mattress propped on the third wall. The room Consuelo shared with her cousins was tight, with barely any space between the queen-sized bed where her cousins, a married couple, slept and Consuelo's twin bed. The room also had its own bathroom, which the four of them used. Both this room and the other bedroom, which I never saw, had locks on their doors. Despite being crowded, the apartment was always spotless; in both the kitchen and bathroom, there was a list of who had cleaned what and the date of the cleaning.

Although she shared this space, Consuelo struggled to come up with her portion of the rent. She had no children, which made her life easier, but she'd had trouble finding steady work that paid adequately. The year she arrived, she'd worked in a factory during the day and as part of a building cleaning crew at nights. This arrangement, however, proved exhausting, and after a year she gave up her part-time job. She continued at the factory for a long time but was eventually laid off. Then she worked for a florist for a month, earning only forty dollars a day. She couldn't subsist on this income, so she quit and found a cleaning job. Unfortunately, the pay was too little for too much effort, and she never returned after the first day. Through a friend from church, she landed another cleaning position, working every Friday while looking for full-time employment. A few weeks later, Eva, a friend from church, told her that the Co-op wanted new members, and Consuelo decided to give it a try. Her stay at the Co-op was not an easy one, however; members complained that she was slow and inefficient and that she didn't clean well. When her membership came up for discussion, she was passed over. The next time I saw her, she was working at a factory three days a week and cleaning a house on Fridays.

A trained secretary in Mexico, Consuelo complained about the poverty and desperation of this country. Life here revolved around *renta y biles* (rent and bills): "The truth, the truth, we all have need. . . . We all come to this country out of necessity. I'm not going to say no, because I had need in the moment that I no longer had money, but, well, and also with people outside the cooperative, who say that here you suffer a lot, that here you cry, you cry tears of blood, because of what happens to you. And, it's the truth, because sometimes, there's no job that is easy to find."[11] And because everyone's need was so pressing, no one really helped you out:

People who are already earning money become, they become a little prouder. . . . Yes, because sometimes when you arrive, those who are already here, already have work, don't try to help. They feel that, that they are better than those who come and don't know, who don't know how to manage here. And those who are already here know. They already have experience, they already know how life is here, how to look for work, how to work. . . . And so people, well, no, instead of helping they kind of laugh at you or like that.[12]

Consuelo had had to learn everything for herself; neither her brother nor her friends provided assistance (cf. Parreñas 2001).

To make matters worse, the lifestyles of the native-born seemed to mock immigrant hardships. Employers, especially, were decadent and ungenerous. Cleaning one afternoon, Eva and Aída found almost an entire pizza in the trash; the customer had ordered lunch and rather than offer Eva and Aída something to eat, he had tossed what he couldn't consume. Typical, they observed; his wife always bought expensive clothes and threw them out while still in good condition. On a different occasion, Eva pointed out that Aída was sporting new sneakers, practically brand-new and very expensive, discovered in another customer's garbage.

Employers' wastefulness and careless opulence were a constant shock, always accentuating the fantastical nature of employers' worlds and the incommensurability of their experiences. One afternoon, Carmen called to report that Melissa, a woman for whom she cleaned once a week, had recently bought hundred-dollar tennis shoes. Carmen had found Melissa's old sneakers, which were still in mint condition, in the garbage, along with a receipt for the new ones. She was sorry that she didn't fit into the old ones, as they were in perfectly good shape, and she wanted to know if I wore a size 9. A size 5 herself, Carmen couldn't bear to let these go to waste. Her tone of surprise and admiration said it all: she would have liked to have that much money, to shell out a hundred dollars in such a casual manner, but at the same time, she found this an outrageous indulgence. For Carmen, spending twenty-five dollars on shoes was a big splurge, and Melissa's receipt reminded Carmen of everything she didn't have and would probably never attain. It was easier to compare her own standard of living with that of other immigrants, as thinking about employers only underscored her own marginality. In employers' terms, Carmen's successes remained negligible, since she earned far too little to be able to approximate their way of life.

American Fantasy?

Carmen's accomplishments only made sense vis-à-vis other immigrants—and the life she had left in Guatemala. It was this perspective that gave meaning to her successes and defined the immigrant version of the American Dream. Immigrant women asserted that as difficult as their lives might be in LA, things would be worse in their home countries. The United States afforded more opportunities to get ahead, for both themselves and their children.

Norma, an ardent advocate for the rights of domestic workers, explained that from the moment she had set foot in LA, she dreamed of returning to Mexico. She wound up going back after a few years, but found it too hard to survive. When she first returned to her hometown, she earned well for six months, but then stopped making money altogether, as there was no work. She soon remembered that this was a seasonal cycle, that everyone had to stretch six months of income to cover an entire year. Frustrated and stressed, Norma decided to cross back into the United States. Arriving in LA for the second time, she knew that she would never go back to Mexico. Things were easier here; at the very least, making a living was possible.

Doña Flor took it even further, exclaiming: "Here, there are many, many, many, many possibilities. This country has opportunities for anyone who appreciates it and bad luck for those who do not. Because there are people who are in this country and don't appreciate the opportunity that the country provides. Because, to be honest with you, the country provides good opportunities, many opportunities, even benefits. Here, the person who doesn't succeed, it's because she doesn't want to."[13] Even Consuelo acknowledged this, explaining why she remained in LA: "I stay because I want to, well, study here, and then see what, what I can achieve later on."[14] She also appreciated the material possibilities the United States had to offer: "Like everyone, like all women, I like clothes, I like entertainment, visiting places."[15]

Through time and hard work, you could do better here. Carmen, as we saw, had experienced an enormous increase in her own standard of living over her thirty years in the United States. Her friend Claudia had been even more prosperous. Claudia was in the employ of a famous musician, and she had done quite well for herself: she and her husband, who didn't work, had purchased their own home in Northridge. This house had a separate bedroom for each of their three children as well as a two-bedroom apartment above the garage, which they rented out to white college students. In addition, Claudia, her husband, and all three of their kids had their own cars. Most importantly, Claudia was able to prepare her children for the future; her daughters worked part-time, but they also attended the local university, and her son, who was still in high school, was looking forward to college.

Claudia's resounding success, earned through persistence and considerable sweat, stood as an example of what could be achieved in LA. And it was this sense of possibility that defined the American Dream for immigrant women. In the United States, the potential for a better future remained open in ways that were foreclosed in other countries. Josefina, who was undocumented, often criticized employers, government policies, and immigration law. Yet, she professed, "Just now, I started loving this country. I started loving it like you have no idea, and, and for that reason, because the country is not to blame for my situation. I like that in this country there are many opportunities, just that we don't know how to channel them, but that's why I say, because it's given me a lot, the liberty to be born again, because I came to be born again, because here, I was born again. I suffered. I lifted myself up, but everything, but I don't blame the country."[16] She especially appreciated the freedom of expression. In Mexico, she explained, they didn't allow you to enter the *cámara de diputados* (the Congress). They wouldn't even let you approach the building, which is always surrounded by police authorized to use force. By contrast, she had joined several protests in Sacramento and had encountered no difficulties:

I don't feel persecuted [for voicing opinions/speaking out]. I feel good. I feel as though I were in my house. That is what I like about here: freedom of expression, right? I like the liberty, the law of this country, because the laws are just. And if they apply them to you, it's because you've really violated them. And what I like here is that there is no bribery. You can't purchase the law. The law is law. That is what I like here. That is what I like here. That's what I like about this country. . . . I've had the luxury of sitting in the capitol and listening to the politicians debate a law and more for immigrants. It's very nice to be there, and that's what I like, that they let us walk in their house, that they let us in.[17]

What Josefina valued was that she would be taken into consideration, that she had the potential to improve her situation, not just financially but politically. In both economic and legal ways, the United States allowed for some movement. Here, if you worked hard, you could change your station in life; other countries made no such assurances.

This belief in widespread opportunity underwrote immigrant women's faith in the American Dream and, in turn, served to define the moral borders of Americanness. Echoing their native-born, middle-class counterparts, they held that anyone who put in the effort could get ahead in this country. Failure, by corollary, signaled individual inadequacy. Raquel, Guatemalan and in her mid-thirties, explained that it was possible to do anything here *if*:

> I think that that, that has helped me *a* lot, being an open-minded person, and being able to learn, and especially to have friends, women I've met, and from them I've learned, they give me courage to say okay, it can be done. That is, if many, many can, why can't I? Yes it's difficult; *yes it's difficult*, because, well, you don't know what, what complications will arise, right, but in your mind, as long as you focus on that [goal], and as long as you wholeheartedly want to reach it, come what may, well that will, that will teach you to value what you want. . . . To learn that if you want something, well, you have to, you are the only one who can do it. . . . Yes, with sacrifice . . . because no movies, no television, nothing. . . . You can sacrifice a lot as an immigrant and make your, as they say, your dreams come true but you have to know how. And especially with your friends . . . to know with whom to go here and there . . . learn how to spend your time on the things that really matter.[18]

As she had discovered, pursuing (and fulfilling) these aspirations meant forgoing sleep. For eleven years, she worked seven days a week. In her first position, she began her day at 5 AM, commuting for over two hours on the bus and cleaning a house while taking care of a five-year-old boy all day, sometimes even Friday and Saturday nights when her employers went out. On a good day, she would leave her employers around 6 PM, and then go to her ESL classes at night school, returning to her apartment around midnight. After a few years, she switched to another job as a teacher's assistant at a nursery school where she worked five mornings a week. In the afternoons and on weekends, she would clean houses or take care of children, and at night she went to school. Then she began working at the school full-time, as a teacher's assistant, attending first community college and then Cal State LA at night and working as a weekend nanny in Brentwood. In 2008, she finally earned her BA, was completing her student teaching requirements, and was looking forward to graduate school—all of this made possible only through "*sacrificio y consistencia*" (sacrifice and consistency), for what she most missed was sleep.

If hard work provided the only way up, its opposite, idleness, was the ultimate offense. As Doña Flor admonished: "Work is an honor, the law of everything Christian. Idle people without work, who like to be kept, that is the worst."[19] One of her grandchildren, Miguel, would never amount to anything. At twenty, he was all indolence; having dropped out of high school years earlier, he had no job, wasn't even looking for work. He preferred to watch TV or play video games all day. By contrast, she couldn't praise Diego, her other grandson, highly enough. During an eight-year detour in prison, Diego had become a U.S. resident, studied English, and earned his high school equivalency. Now he worked with computers and had recently purchased a two-bedroom house in Alhambra. Only twenty-eight years old, he had more than proven his determination, and Doña Flor was confident that he would continue making something of himself: "That's a sacrifice that anyone who wants to succeed will make. Because everything, everything won't come to you happily."[20]

In the United States, success was conceivable, but it required ambition, hard work, self-discipline, and tenacity. Necessary for material mobility as well as instantiations of moral worth, these attributes converged to produce a deserving national subject. Immigrant workers and their native-born employers, therefore, were engaged in the *same* pursuit, a moral struggle that simultaneously required, produced, and confirmed an individual's ability to be properly American.

Despite its slipperiness, then, the American Dream retained its promise—an opportunity for future success. For women who had little hope of financial stability in their home countries, even this (constantly deferred) possibility held enormous appeal. In their definition, success was a dual concept, encompassing both economic and personal advancement; they sought to *salir adelante* (get ahead) and to *superarse* (literally, to surpass or outdo oneself). Of a piece, these processes entangle past, present, and future to produce the self in the now. They are simultaneously individual and collective, aiming for the future but experienced in the present and understood through the past.

Salir adelante (getting ahead) implies both increased economic stability and the idea of advancement. Added wealth will move individuals out of poverty, releasing them from constant anxiety and allowing greater material comforts; moreover, this will furnish a range of other opportunities, such as going to school, that help to create a better future. Importantly, this concept entails both oneself and one's children, for most women made the decision to migrate, and they continue to understand their efforts in this country through their kids. Securing their children's futures, getting them ahead (*sacarlos adelante*), is thus integral to success.

Like *salir adelante*, *superarse* also emphasizes this notion of progress, pushing it beyond the material. The verb *superar* has several meanings, including: (1) to overcome or get through a situation, and (2) to exceed, to beat. Both senses capture the needs and desires of immigrant life, and they are intimately linked. Immigrant women define success as prevailing in difficult circumstances and also through personal improvement; in fact, the latter is necessary to and results from the former. Yet, unlike *salir adelante*, which applies to both oneself and one's children, *superarse* refers specifically to the self: the added -*se* makes the verb reflexive. *Superarse* therefore signals a personal transformation, exceeding or bettering oneself.

Salir adelante and *superarse* crystallize immigrant understandings of success, defined as economic mobility and self-transformation. These seemingly separate feats are in fact imbricated, for economic mobility requires navigating life in LA, learning who and how to be here, or as Coll puts it, "learning the ropes" (2010: 74). Making it in the

United States requires change—you have to become a different kind of person, an "American" with "American" habits, practices, and desires. Becoming American not only facilitates material advancement—it is itself proof of success. Everything individuals learn and become here functions as cultural capital, gaining weight within a symbolic economy that characterizes the United States as more sophisticated and advanced, an object of desire and a place of imagined wealth for women living on the margins in both LA and Latin America.

Past, Present, Future

Accounting for material mobility necessarily implies temporal difference—fixing a point in the past from which to measure how far you have come. For immigrant women, it also, importantly, required an eye to the future, considering not just where you came from but where you will go. In reckoning their successes, they assessed not only what had been but what would be, as well as what would have been had they stayed in their countries of origin.

Lucía, for instance, came to the United States to get away from the poverty that had plagued her in Mexico. Growing up in Oaxaca, she lived in a small house that didn't even have a stove, much less a television. The youngest of seven children, she was eleven when her mother passed away. Her siblings were all working elsewhere, so she had to assume responsibility for the household, left to take care of her father. Cooking, cleaning, and working the fields, she had no time for school, and besides, her father did not believe in education for girls. At seventeen, as soon as she could, she left home to join her sister in northern Mexico, where both worked as live-in maids. They couldn't earn enough, however, and after moving to Tijuana and back again, they decided to try the United States, "simply thinking of a better life one day, or not going back to the same."[21] She wasn't after "comodidad" (material comfort) so much as "una vida mejor en todo" (a better life in every way).

In LA, she worked as live-in maid for about five years and was able to procure legal papers through one of her employers. From there, she got married, had three children, and switched to working by the day. She joined the Co-op, and when I met her in 2002, she was both cleaning houses and working in the office, organizing the schedule and attending to phone calls with customers. Lucía cleaned two houses a day and attended school at night, while her husband held two separate jobs. While in Mexico this strenuous grind would go unrewarded, in LA it made a difference. She and her husband owned two cars and were able to move into a larger one-bedroom apartment. Most importantly, her children did not want. Even better, she could provide possibilities: the clothes, toys, tutoring sessions, and after-school activities that would ready them for a brighter future.

Thinking about her life in Mexico, she explained that there was no reason to go back. What would she do there? What would happen to her kids? There was no benefit to living in Mexico. Her sons would have to suffer the way she had, living "*en esa pobreza*" (in that poverty). "*Yo no veo futuro allá*" (I don't see a future there), she explained. Life here was better. She affirmed, "that's why I'm sacrificing, really, so, so that they can one day be someone."[22]

Ten years later, Lucía had switched to tenant organizing, a move facilitated through the efforts of the Co-op's coordinator in tandem with one of the group's most loyal customers. Her job required long hours, and did not pay much more than her previous occupation, but she was pleased to be out of domestic employment. In addition, one of her sons had graduated from high school and enrolled in community college, another was completing high school, and the last one was finishing the eighth grade. Dealing with the pains of adolescence was not easy, and she had to make sure she kept them on the straight and narrow. Still, she would have had a very different experience had she stayed in Mexico—more importantly, her sons would have had considerably fewer options, a decidedly different future. This knowledge animated her endeavors, confirmation that she was doing the right thing, that she was and would be successful.

At seventy-five, Carmen's perspective on the American Dream varied significantly. In her early sixties, she had suffered a significant fracture in her arm, one that required surgery and more than two years of physical therapy—all (fortunately?) financed by her employer's insurance, because she fell at work. Insurance, however, could not make up for lost wages, and so she continued to work throughout all of this. She cleaned houses until 2010, when, in the aftermath of the financial crisis, she lost her few remaining customers. At seventy-two, she was tired of cleaning, had few possibilities for new clients, and decided she could live comfortably, if sparingly, on her Social Security earnings, Avon and Shaklee Vitamin sales, and one hundred dollars a month she received from a previous employer. In addition, she signed up for food stamps. Determined to learn English, she started going to school again, and she remained an active member of the Bus Riders Union; she also babysat for her young grandson, while his mother cleaned houses. She was enjoying her "retirement," even though her economic situation remained less than ideal.

This precarious balance collapsed in 2012, when the state decided that the one hundred dollars a month she had been receiving from employers who had moved away counted as income and that she was not, in fact, eligible for food stamps. Worse yet, they retroactively disqualified her from the program, rendering her liable for the cash value of the food stamps she had already collected—about fifteen hundred dollars in all. Unable to straighten out the situation, she found herself having to make do with even less, once again tightening her belt as the state began to discount what she owed from her monthly Social Security checks.

Having arrived at a much different, much more ambivalent future than she had imagined, Carmen nonetheless maintained her trust in the American Dream and knew herself to be successful. Above all, she had transcended the crushing poverty she'd lived in Guatemala:

> Here we are poor, but we are better off than when we were dying of hunger in Guatemala, because here, thankfully, there is food. . . . You see the 99-Cent stores and everything. You can eat from cans or eat whatever, but there is food in this country, and if you throw out food or you don't eat anymore, it's because you don't want it, but there's food. It's not like the situation I had, eating dry bread, stale, hard bread for three days . . . and that I tried to make one piece last as long as possible, so that I wouldn't run out. That is hard. That's why I say that I know what poverty is. I know what misery is, and I know what it's like to be hungry.[23]

The misery she left behind loomed large, coloring her every experience in Los Angeles and marking a sharp before and after.

The prosperity she had enjoyed in the United States was made palpable when we visited her family in Guatemala. Carmen's father, her brother, and his wife resided in the village where Carmen was born, a small community near the tourist town of Antigua. They lived on a plot with three small huts made of wood, aluminum sheets, and cardboard. The lot was filled with overgrown plants, and a narrow dirt path separated the huts. Carmen's brother and his wife shared one hut, her father slept in another, and the third served as a kitchen. The kitchen had a free-standing stove, a table, a place to fix food, and a grill over a fire pit. Outside, there was a *pila* (water basin, washing sink) to wash clothes and dishes.

Upon arrival, Carmen introduced me to her family and took me on a quick tour of the property. Then, while she met with her brother to discuss financial arrangements for their father, I sat in the kitchen and watched her sister-in-law Florencia prepare lunch. As she fanned the fire, Florencia began to ask about life in the United States—ever since September 11, she'd been hearing about its dangers on the radio and told me that she worried about Carmen. But, she continued, sighing, she'd once had the chance to go to the United States and was still sorry that she had not taken it.

Florencia began her career as a maid at age seven, when she started working for a local family; she stayed in the same house for eleven years, when she left her Guatemalan employers for an American couple who paid her better and treated her well. They loved her, and when they decided to return to the United States, they asked her to come along. Florencia was excited to go and prepared herself for her new life; her mother, however, put a stop to these plans. Florencia was not yet married, and her mother refused to care for Florencia's one-year-old son while she went off to the United States.

Florencia was forced to stay, and she still remembered the final dinner she served her employers. She recalled: something was wrong at home, and her brother had come to get her just as she was preparing the soup. Florencia refused to leave, telling him she'd be there later; she wanted to be there for this last meal. The following morning, her employers departed. When they returned to Guatemala a few years later, they tracked her down to see if she was ready to go with them, but they found her with two children, a husband, and a house—more immobile than ever. Florencia sighed again: her American Dream had ended long before it could even begin.

Rather than go to the United States, earn a better living, and learn to read, she stayed in her town. Eventually, she married Carmen's brother, had two more sons, bought the piece of land where they still lived, and became a market vendor. When I met her, two of her sons were married and had moved out of the house, and she continued to sell tortillas and tamales; actually, she explained, she worked on the outskirts of the market, because she couldn't afford the price of an official stall. She managed to bring in a little bit of money this way, supplementing her husband and younger son's incomes. Her husband and son both worked as waiters in Guatemala City and came home only on Wednesdays and Thursdays, their days off. The rest of the week, Florencia cooked, walked down to town on market days, and took care of her father-in-law. All of this was getting harder and harder, though, because she had lost the use of one eye and was having difficulties with her left leg.

Florencia's life had gone downhill since her American employers left without her. Her mother had recognized this only belatedly, apologizing to her daughter on her deathbed. By then it was too late, though. Florencia sighed once more: this was the kind of opportunity that presented itself once in a lifetime, and she had passed it up. As much as she worried about Carmen and everyone else she knew in the United States, she regretted heeding her mother's orders and continued to wonder about what might have been.

Florencia's hard-fought life and enduring remorse illustrate the other side of Carmen's experience, emphasizing what could have been and just what was at stake when individuals made the decision to migrate. It was against this predicament, ongoing poverty with little potential for advancement, that individuals like Carmen read their own successes and defined the American Dream, inconsistent and elusive though it remained. Florencia's life was a reminder of an *otherwise* that Carmen was thankful to have escaped.

Becoming American

More than financial gain, more than providing for her children (ungrateful though they often were), Carmen had experienced a radical transformation in herself. She had become somebody new, and in this way, she had managed to *superarse*. Along with her economic gains, she reveled in everything she had learned and become in the United States, in becoming "American." This change not only distinguished Carmen from the family and friends who remained in Guatemala, but also indicated the distance she had traveled since first arriving in LA.

She marked, and remarked upon, this progression in just about every conversation, as it was crucial to her sense of self. One of the first times I noticed this was at a birthday party for her friend Susana's ten-year-old son Daniel. From arrival to departure, she performed her expertise, enacting and narrating her "Americanness" for all to witness. The party was a few blocks from Carmen's house, but as anyone in possession of a car in Los Angeles would, we drove over. As we circled Catalina Street, between First Street and Beverly Boulevard, looking for parking, she briefed me on her friend Susana, whom she'd met about twenty-five years earlier on the bus when Susana referred Carmen to one of her employers. After ten minutes of driving around, we found a spot. Getting out of the car, Carmen spent a couple of minutes smoothing out her clothes, which were sticking to her body because of the tremendous heat. She had on white linen pants and a pink sleeveless button-down with little white flowers embroidered on it. Complaining that she was a mess, wrinkled after just fifteen minutes in the car, she sighed and said let's go.

We made our way toward the house, where we met Susana's husband Roberto. Seeing us, Roberto called Daniel over. We said hello, and Carmen handed him his present. She had brought him a backpack that she had originally purchased for her son, who didn't want it. It was expensive, she told me, and besides, Daniel could get a lot of use from it. She'd gone out of her way to dress up this gift, wrapping it in a paper bag emblazoned with the Metro's logo; she'd picked up this bag the previous week, on the Gold Line's first day of operations, and liked that it looked "*fina*" (fine/expensive/nice). Carmen had another present with her, two Avon lotions for Susana, placed in a paper bag from an Italian bakery that one of her employers frequented.

We went inside and found three women sitting at a card table near the front door, along with two other women at the dining table. Nodding to the women, Carmen led me into the kitchen in search of Susana, who was busy trying to get everything ready. The kitchen was tiny, just enough room for two people, so I stood at the door as Carmen and Susana exchanged greetings and news. Carmen offered to help, but Susana replied that there wasn't enough room and ushered us out of the kitchen.

In the living room, Roberto put on some marimba music, and Carmen started to dance. He joined her, and they danced together until the end of the piece. Sweaty and out of breath, Carmen sat down at the dining table, next to an open window. I joined her, and we struck up a conversation with Susana's aunt Pilar and her daughter María. María asked how she knew Carmen; Carmen looked very familiar. Carmen wondered if they had met on the bus, or, she said, she'd been on television a few times. Did María recognize her from the news? María gave her a quizzical look and shook her head. She had a lot of Guatemalan friends and had perhaps met Carmen through one of them. Carmen didn't think so; there were a lot of Guatemalans in LA. So many, she continued, because the city was so close to the border. Pilar disagreed, observing that, no matter what, the border was very difficult to cross. Carmen threw up her arms, as if to indicate that she wouldn't know. "Mi frontera fue" (my border was), she said, making an airplane motion with her hand. She informed us, and everyone within earshot, that she arrived by plane—"legally." No one responded; Pilar stared blankly, and María rolled her eyes. Carmen didn't notice; she went on, detailing her arrival at LAX and how she had convinced the immigration officer to stamp her passport.

At that moment, Susana came by to serve us. Carmen took only one tortilla with some beans; she wasn't going to eat because she had taken her son to Acapulco's this morning. It was his birthday, and he loved the ten-dollar buffet brunch ("el Brady Brunch," she called it) at this Mexican restaurant. She'd eaten a lot: mole, tacos, quesadillas, two margaritas, and three flans. Susana sat down with us, and the conversation shifted to employers. Carmen mused that rich employers were sometimes awful and sometimes a boon. She had worked for a horrible woman in Beverly Hills. Of course, she laughed, that was twenty years ago, when actors and other wealthy people still wanted to live in Beverly Hills. Now they all retreated to the mountains and outlying towns—even Bel Air wasn't acceptable anymore. Somehow this talk of rich people segued into a discussion about travel, with Pilar and Carmen lamenting how troublesome air travel had become. Visiting Honduras and Guatemala was too expensive, the flights were unpleasant, and with new restrictions, you could hardly bring anything anymore. María explained that she visited Honduras to see her family but for a more

relaxing time she liked Las Vegas. They all agreed—Las Vegas was ter-
rific, especially the buffets.

We chatted for a while longer, until it was time to sing "Happy Birthday" and blow out the candles. We ate cake, said our goodbyes, and left
with a plate that Susana had prepared for Carmen's sons.

I bring up this event as one moment, both singular and common-
place, in which to examine how Carmen constituted her "Americanness"
in the day-to-day. From her personal presentation, to her gifts, to her
familiarity with Los Angeles, to the relative nonchalance with which
she discussed travel, she underscored just how much she was of this
place. All of these revealed her transformation from ignorant, freshly
arrived immigrant to a more cosmopolitan self. In LA, she had become
a new type of person, an American. For instance, she had acquired mejores modales (better manners): before arriving in LA, she had been muy
peleonera (always getting into fights) and vulgar (vulgar). She had also
started to clothe herself differently. In Guatemala, she would never have
gone out without doing her hair, matching her shoes to her bag, and
getting her makeup done: "There, everyone is criticized, for the way
in which you dress, the way in which you conduct yourself."[24] Here she
could dress casually, although always in clean, well-ironed clothing, focused on the task at hand rather than on other people's opinions. She
appreciated this no-nonsense attitude, exclaiming that in LA, even the
ricachones (rich people) would don casual attire for parties.

Like American fashion, American food was also geared toward
people on the go: it was simpler to cook and easier on the digestive
system. And so Carmen had learned to eat accordingly:

Well, here you didn't use many spices, as you do in Guatemala.
Because sometimes in Guatemala, when I go to Guatemala, I have
to pack my medicine, because they serve me meals, but since they
are too spicy. . . . Here I only use scallions and a little bit of pepper;
I don't add so many things, because, yes, because before, oh, I had
to, I thought a meal wasn't good if it wasn't spicy. . . . A Guatemalan dish requires many ingredients. Here you can prepare the same
thing without as many ingredients, with less. It is more flavorful
there, but it's something that I've noticed that I'm used to the way it
is here. So when I eat a dish from there, either my stomach turns or
I get heartburn.[25]

She was irrevocably American now—her "Americanness" embodied, literally located in her body, so that she could no longer tolerate Guatemalan food. Bringing her "medication," Tums or Pepto-Bismol, when she visited relatives in Guatemala, she became the prototypical American tourist who could not handle the food or parasites to which Guatemalans are accustomed. Indeed, she realized just how total this transformation was on her first trip back to Guatemala. After nineteen years in LA, she did not know anyone anymore, and everything felt off—the food overly spicy, the streets too narrow, the streetlights surprisingly short. The visit made her see that she could never return permanently. "No me hubiera hallado" (literally, I would not have found myself), she insisted.

As well, she had awakened here, "me desperté," enthusiastically taking every opportunity to learn about the world. To this end, she became involved in a number of community activities. In the early 1990s, she joined a now-defunct immigrant organization called CIWA (California Immigrant Workers Association), through two of her friends. At CIWA, she took classes to be a health promoter and started doing theater, participating in a few productions. She also earned money for recruiting more members, in the same way that her friends had brought her to the organization. One year, she recruited eighty people and made so much money that she was able to travel twice to Guatemala. At CIWA, she encountered the Bus Riders Union and joined eagerly. Long after CIWA ceased to exist, she continued to go to BRU meetings, enthusiastically took part in its campaigns, and often volunteered to sort mail at the central office. She'd even appeared on TV, having been interviewed at BRU events a couple of time. In turn, the BRU connected her to the Domestic Workers Group, where she became an active member, especially in the group's theater unit. She wrote and staged a play about the plight of domestic workers. This piece re-created a run-in Carmen had had with an abusive employer and told the story of redemption that she found at the DWG, where she had learned about her rights. She also had the opportunity to travel to New York to participate in a two-week theater workshop.

Through these activities, she met an expanding network of people, from whom she learned, but whom she could also counsel about life in Los Angeles. Carmen regularly dispensed advice to younger, more recent immigrants and relished that so many people came to her for guidance. In seeking her wisdom, they not only recognized but expressed admiration for her expertise, for everything she had learned and become here.

Her crowning achievement, however, had been learning to read, finally, at age fifty. Prior to this, she'd never attended school, and she'd always felt inadequate: "My problem was, it continued to be, that I longed to know how to read, to know how to write, to be able to study."[26] Even so, learning to read in middle age was not easy—first she had to find a school where they taught basic literacy skills in Spanish, and then she studied for two years just to grasp the basics. More than twenty years later, she still struggled to write:

> So I dreamed of going to school, but there was something very hard for me. . . . I found a teacher, a man not a woman, who taught the classes, and he was older, and he did not teach Spanish. He only taught English. I didn't want English. I wanted Spanish—to read and to write, because if I didn't understand anything in Spanish I wouldn't be able to situate myself for English. . . . When they started some Spanish classes there in the school, then I took the opportunity to learn to read and write in Spanish. After that they switched me to an English *teacher* [in English]. . . . It was very hard, even with the Spanish teacher it was also hard because it was the first time I started something, writing—and, oh wow—and to learn to read and everything. The only thing I was never able to fix, sometimes I still do it over, where it was a problem that I could not retain, where there was a period . . . all those dots that go over the letters, like papá, mamá, the accents, periods, question marks . . . I could not retain that. And they repeated it and repeated it and I would say, "my god," I would say, will it be possible for me to learn to read and write? So yes, it was hard, because even now, reading I loved and I did it perfectly. Even now, I do it perfectly. What I didn't like, and I do because I have to, is to write, because it is very hard, even all these years later it is very hard. Now imagine that it is also very hard in English. In English you write one way and pronounce it another.[27]

Despite these frustrations, she persevered. In her seventies, as her work in homes dropped off, she began to go to school every morning, proudly earning certificates for perfect attendance for several school sessions in a row. She refused to stand still, determined to use her newly open schedule to learn English and to learn it well: "I think that if I retire completely, not doing anything. . . . I think I would die from inactivity, because I am someone who likes to be in motion, to be going out, waking up early, doing something, and so if I become an idle [*effete*] woman too early, I think I will die more quickly."[28] An early riser, someone always in motion, and allergic to idleness, she had taken on the attributes of a successful American, hardworking and persistent, always ready to learn and always moving forward. These qualities had led to all of her accomplishments, and together they retrospectively revealed that she was the right kind of person, in possession of the fundamental qualities of Americanness—discipline, determination, and a fierce work ethic. Indeed, she was delighted with everything she had realized: "And that's how we've gotten here. . . . I've been able to become an activist, to help when I can, to do my things, and then also later, in this country, I never imagined it, attaining my, first I got my residence and then seven years later I worked to study U.S. history to become a citizen of this country. And I feel very pleased, *happy* [in English] to belong."[29]

Citizenship Redux

In the above sections, I've used "Americanness" as indication of belonging, to highlight how material advancement and personal transformation combine to produce a sense of attachment to and social membership in this country. Citizenship, official recognition, remains a significant (and prized), but not necessarily the decisive, marker of this type of belonging. After all, Carmen did not become a citizen until 1994,[30] more than twenty years after her arrival, during which time she had grown immensely. Formal citizenship did not make her American, but instead revealed that she had already become American. More than dealing with paperwork and being savvy enough to navigate the bureaucracy—both markers of proficiency—she clearly possessed a certain type of American know-how. To become a citizen, you had to speak some English, learn American history, and understand how the U.S. government worked—every naturalized citizen had to pass a difficult exam, signaling her command of all things American.

I hadn't grasped the full gravity of this until hearing Carmen's reports about her friend Margarita, who was preparing for her final interview with immigration.[31] Becoming a citizen was hard, Carmen said; she had studied intensely, taking a twelve-week course. Because she prepared carefully, she passed on the first try. By contrast, this would be Margarita's third attempt, as she had failed the test on both of the previous occasions. According to Carmen, Margarita just didn't want to listen, refusing to follow Carmen's words. Carmen had counseled Margarita to study; she also advised Margarita to bring photographs to the interview, to make sure that she packed all the appropriate documents, and to have this paperwork translated into English. Beyond these logistics, Carmen had tried to prepare Margarita to act properly "American" and not like a clueless immigrant. For instance, she sent Margarita to the salon to get her hair colored and done for her passport photos. But she could only do so much if Margarita didn't want to help herself.

When Margarita finally passed her citizenship exam, Carmen declared that it was "un milagro" (a miracle). They had done Margarita a favor, Carmen asserted, because she couldn't remember a single thing, not even the big questions. Part of the problem was that Margarita got nervous: she didn't know how to handle herself in front of the American officials. Carmen, on the other hand, had had no trouble: she knew how things worked here. If anything, she held, Margarita had made it through only because José, Carmen's younger son, had helped her to study.

If Margarita's inability to pass the exam demonstrated just how American she wasn't, nothing was worse than refusing to try for citizenship. Given the satisfaction she derived from becoming a citizen, Carmen couldn't understand why others wouldn't pursue this opportunity. Other immigrants, she guessed, were lazy and not as motivated or hardworking as she. In particular, she was surprised that Yolanda, her friend Raquel's mother, had no interest in learning English or in becoming a citizen. Yolanda didn't think she needed English to work in a factory, and she was content with her situation. Yolanda and her son shared an apartment, which Raquel helped to finance, and rather than try to improve herself by learning English, looking for another job, or just aspiring for more, Yolanda relied on her daughter. To Carmen this was unthinkable—who wouldn't want a better life, to *salir adelante* and *superarse*? This lack of initiative signaled a real deficiency, a failure to become American; unwilling to make an effort, Yolanda would never progress. Yolanda's choices only served to underscore Carmen's Americanness, proof that she was exceptional. Indeed, Carmen had become a role model for Raquel; Raquel was always begging Yolanda to go to school and saying that she wished her mother were more like Carmen. Citizenship, then, gave official sanction to Carmen's hard-won successes, her transformation into an "American."

Conclusion

Claiming "Americanness," Carmen announced her individual accomplishments and also her value to this country, that she belonged. This was not a naïve identification, for its very content recognized the adversity of immigrant life and applauded the capacity not only to prevail but to triumph. The first time I visited her apartment, she showed me photos and mementos from her trip to New York City, among these a box containing images of the Statue of Liberty and an empty glass bottle. She had always felt a special connection to the statue, and this only intensified during her trip to New York. Unfortunately, she had not been able to visit it, because it was under repair. However, while in New York, she had participated in a theater workshop and had the opportunity to play the statue. On the final day of the workshop, she conceived a scene in which, as the statue, she stood atop a piano, holding the bottle for a torch, and laughed derisively at immigrants trying to cross the river and evade *la migra*.

This scene emphasized both hope and irony—the fantasy of a warm reception contrasted with the less-than-sunny reality of Carmen's experience. She had not been welcomed with open arms; she had not been welcomed at all, but had made her way in through years of drudgery and determination. She kept the bottle as a souvenir, a reminder of her particular affinity with the statue, which she frequently referred to as *mi consentida* (my special one) or *mi muchacha* (my girl). These fond recollections added a layer of admiration to the trenchant critique of the original performance, for every retelling allowed her to claim affiliation with the statue and thus to affirm her Americanness. She was proud of being American, pleased with everything she had attained and confident that she would continue to succeed.

For Carmen, as for the others, hope and despair, gratitude and criticism, material gain and oppression coexisted. In her experience, what the United States promised was the possibility that a better future, however open-ended or delayed, was achievable. Her hard-earned triumphs, in terms of advancing some of her individual potential and providing for her sons, produced an always-incomplete satisfaction, but one whose fulfillment was nevertheless imaginable. She was simultaneously living and working to fulfill the American Dream, an always-visible, always-near reality that kept possibility open.

Certainly, immigrant women's avowed faith in the American Dream fits squarely into the myth that success, in the form of economic mobility, reveals personal merit and in turn legitimates social membership, that "Americanness" is earned through effort. All the same, the experiences of the Mexican and Central American women I met in Los Angeles confound easy assumptions about the workings of hegemony. In this chapter, I have endeavored to show the ambiguity of these processes, how individuals simultaneously subscribe to an exploitative myth, even as their claims on it transform it from within. Locating themselves on the inside, they expand the boundaries of an "Americanness" that would define itself against them.

Conclusion

As I sit down to write this conclusion, the topic of immigration is once again making headlines, as it has almost continuously from the start of this project—indeed, as it has with regularity since the first mass migration from Eastern and Southern Europe began in the 1880s. The characters might change, but the content of these fears remains remarkably stable: Will (this batch of) immigrants ruin the nation, and how do we stop this from happening? What is inherent in this particular group that prevents its members from being fully assimilated, fully American?[1]

At stake in this discussion, in its every iteration, is the production of "America": Will social membership be defined as it has been or will it expand to accommodate the newcomers? Anti-immigrant constituencies refuse to consider the latter and blame the recently arrived for their failure to adapt—it is their fault that the American Dream is increasingly unstable and unachievable. These conversations turn on a flawed logic and confine how we think about immigration. Immigrants have always been crucial to nation-making, even as their contributions—and often even their bodies—remain invisible to the popular imagination. Therefore, a more relevant set of questions would inquire: How might new groups lay claim to their own Dreams? Will the prerogatives of "Americanness" swell to include them? And to what extent can we do this without upending the balance of inequality necessary to these processes?

Indeed, the issue is not whether the presence of immigrants curbs our prosperity, but rather, as the ten-chair exercise reveals, that there are not enough chairs and a very small number of people occupy the majority of them. This wealth gap only continues to magnify, thereby producing an amplified sense of insecurity and crisis. And as the future grows more precarious, so does the perceived vulnerability of both the individual and the nation. Hage's (2003) insights clarify the connections between escalating instability and paranoia about immigration. He explains:

> Societies are mechanisms for the distribution of hope, and . . . the kind of affective attachment (worrying or caring) that a society creates among its citizens is intimately connected to its capacity to distribute hope. The caring society is essentially an embracing society that generates hope among its citizens and induces them to care for it. . . . The defensive society . . . suffers from a scarcity of hope and creates citizens who see threats everywhere. It generates worrying citizens and a paranoid nationalism. (2003: 3)

To be sure, this is not novel. In the United States, there has been an almost continuous resurgence of this type of paranoia, one that turns on the very groups that make the Dream possible for everyone else. Its invariable recurrence highlights its necessity to the nation: marginality as central to "Americanness."

This book has endeavored to show that these processes are neither uncontested nor entirely predetermined. Beginning from the presumed difference and invisibility of immigrant women, moving through the erasure of reproductive labor within a middle-class understanding of value, to immigrant women's insistence on the value of such labor, the preceding chapters have traced alternative reckonings of belonging and "Americanness." I have discussed how both immigrant and native-born women fight against limited definitions of social worth, how they strive to make themselves visible and valued. I have also insisted that, as scholars, we must attend to these diverse renderings of "Americanness." If these remain unseen, it is precisely because of our own expectations about the confluence of work and self, the convergence between social membership and productive labor, and the temporal boundedness of the individual. In particular, we must be alert to the ways our work can reproduce the neoliberal logics we decry (cf. Gibson-Graham 1996, 2006). Accepting too-narrow renderings of success, we privilege foreclosure and neglect possibility (cf. Sedgwick 2003).[2] Rancière's notion of aesthetics is particularly useful here, for it urges us to look at what we can see and what remains invisible. He explains that aesthetics is "at the core of politics," defining this as "the system of a priori forms determining what presents itself to the sense experience. It is a delimitation of spaces and times, of the visible and the invisible, of speech and noise, that simultaneously determines the place and the stakes of a politics of experience. Politics revolves around what is seen and what can be said about it, around who has the ability to see and the talent to speak, around the properties of spaces and the possibilities of time" (2006: 13).

In this brief conclusion, I want to emphasize the potential of ethnography to shine a light on the distribution of the sensible, and therefore to illuminate alternatives—to show us an otherwise that we could not have anticipated. In particular, I want to analyze the potentialities of hope and its central role in the lives of the women I met in LA. Hope, whether waning or waxing, was vital to all of their experiences.

Hope and the Temporalities of Self

Miyazaki contends that hope is not "an emotional state," but rather "a method of radical temporal orientation of knowledge" (2004: 5). That is, thinking through hope allows us to get at what and how we know in the now. And so he urges scholars to examine our own "knowledge practices," along with those of the people we study. In this ethnography, I have sought to shift our temporal horizons through an emphasis on reproductive labor; limiting attention to paid employment allows us only a partial perspective on the possibilities available to both native-born and immigrant women. This view reads success in terms of capitalist time frames and fails to recognize that an individual's achievements can be projected onto subsequent generations, thereby exceeding the self. What happens if we consider past, present, and future as coeval?

Having (or losing) hope entails an imagined future, whether probable or increasingly unavailable. Either way, it is a subjunctive experience of the self, living as if.[3] The preceding chapters stressed how the future served as constant backdrop for the experiences of all the women I met in LA, immigrant and native-born. Their achievements in the present were inseparable from expectations about their children's futures. Tilted toward a someday, their reproductive endeavors nevertheless shaped their experiences of belonging in the now. Bridging present and future, hope helped to establish an individual's sense of personal worth and social membership. Still, as Hage points out, this can be both negative and positive, depending on whether hopes fade or persist. And so for middle-class mothers, this relationship remained vexed, while for Central American and Mexican women it seemed to offer more leeway.

Middle-class employers grappled with an erosion of hope, a fear that the future was shrinking rather than expanding. Further compounding this sense of future loss, the anticipation of less rather than more, they felt less than adequate in the current moment. Their individual definitions of success did not fit easily into received ideas of social and personal value, falling rather in the uncomfortable intersection of reproductive and productive labor. The conceptual separation between these, along with the ambivalences and erasures surrounding reproductive labor, rendered this junction untenable, creating an unshakable sense of failure. "Worry," then, characterized their relation to the nation, a type of attachment that "exerts a form of symbolic violence over the field of national belonging. It eradicates the very possibility of thinking of an alternative mode of belonging" (Hage 2003: 23). Thus, their views of success and belonging precluded full social membership, not just for the immigrants who worked in their homes but also for themselves.

Reading domestic employees through their jobs and meager incomes, employers reasoned that these women failed to achieve the Dream and, as a result, to become proper national subjects. However, immigrant women held fast to their hopes. From their vantage point, success encompassed both economic and personal advancement— for themselves and, more importantly, for their children. Locating success in their reproductive labor, making these endeavors visible and valuable, they predicated their current worth on the promise of their children's future accomplishments. Therefore, they experienced a more robust hope and a more capacious experience of the American Dream.

To be sure, hope can easily be read as a palliative of capitalist society, which uncannily maintains "its ability to maintain an *experience of the possibility of upward social mobility*" (Hage 2003: 13, emphasis in the original). Is the promise of a future, however elusive, enough to keep individuals going, to make them fall in line with the system? Or is it possible to read this differently, as both hegemonic and potentially transformative? Certainly, immigrant existence in this country is difficult, mired in poverty and increasingly subject to policing and moral panic. Nonetheless, as I have argued throughout this book, this does not define the totality of the immigrant life. Taking past, present, and future together, we can understand immigrant women's sense of advancement and optimism about what might come next. This might disrupt our conceptual frames, but it is precisely these unexpected turns that ethnography illuminates. Instead of verifying our preconceptions, it prompts us to look for the different and differing categories through which people structure their worlds. In so doing, it compels us to consider divergences, dissonances, and unexpected outcomes.[4]

If Carmen's experiences underscore anything, it would be the complicated and ambivalent nature of success, of a life. Having suffered both tremendous gains and losses, she remains, at seventy-seven, at the margins, struggling, still, to eke out a living and lead what she considers a dignified life. She continues to go to school, searching for ways to expand herself, to become "more." Through these very efforts she claims her right to be here, to belong, and to be considered a full human being. Not only has she learned and grown and outdone what she could only have dreamed of if she had not moved to the United States, but she was able to make a better life for her children. She fed, clothed, and schooled them, and brought two of them to the United States. One refused to migrate, and stayed behind. He has three children, lives in the town where Carmen grew up, and works as a waiter in the tourist town of Antigua. Of the two who came to the United States, both became citizens. One is an attendant at a country club and has numerous children in Guatemala with several different women. Unable to afford rent on his own, because he has to send the bulk of his income to his kids, he shares an apartment with his mother. Her third, and youngest, son lives around the corner with his wife and eight-year-old son. He works for an affiliate of the MTA, earning union wages, and his wife cleans houses a few days a week. Their son is in school, where he is learning to read and write in English.

This is not exactly the future Carmen imagined; like everyone's, her life path has turned in unexpected places, surprising her in both positive and negative ways. Thus we must consider the entire journey, beginning, middle, and end, to appreciate these complexities—the coinciding feelings of loss, gain, poverty, and upward mobility. We cannot discount the hopes that sustained and motivated her quest. Even if they did not leave a visible trace, they were vital to her process. Fully materialized or not, hope provided a forward view as well as a template for the present. It accompanied her through ups and downs, playing a key role in how she organized her life. Moreover, the prospects of a more ample future, for herself and as well as for her sons, solidified her attachments to this country, affording her a sense of success and belonging.

Belonging, Possibility, and the Politics of Immigration

Throughout this book, I have emphasized affective attachments, belonging, and individual senses of accomplishment and failure. These concerns remain crucial to any discussion of immigration, fleshing out the travails of daily life. They shed light not only on the ways in which alleged "outsiders" are essential to the nation, the hardships they endure, and their hard-won victories, but also on their remarkable similarity. Looking at native-born and immigrant women in the same frame, we find more parallels than differences. These groups shared overlapping concerns and desires, combining hope, reproductive labor, and paid employment in their pursuit of the American Dream.

And yet I can anticipate the ways in which this argument might be misread: to underscore optimism and hope is not to erase the violences with which immigrants deal on a daily basis. Their reality is delineated by both success and trenchant poverty. And so I am decidedly not making a case for the inherent fairness of the American Dream—that it will all shake out in the end, that immigrants should be grateful for what they can achieve here, and that everyone who deserves to prosper will do so. Attention to immigrants' hard-earned success stories does not let us off the hook for the damages we have inflicted or for continuing to fight for change. The battles for citizenship, a livable wage, and better working conditions continue and remain essential to producing the nation: will the prerogatives of "Americanness" expand to fit these newcomers, or will we continue to define ourselves through exclusion and exploitation?

What I am suggesting is that we must consider both foreclosure and possibility, achievement and pleasure, as much as frustration and loss.

Immigrant women are more than their work, more than their marginality; likewise, the native-born mothers who employed them are more than punishing employers. In their intersections, in their give-and-take, we see the unifying force of the American Dream, its hold on the imaginations of both groups, and the different, contradictory ways each experienced it. We also find the gendered dimensions of this Dream, for the devaluation of reproductive labor continues to squeeze both groups. Domestic workers earn scant wages, their labor invisible and undervalued, while employers juggle conflicting understandings of individual value and social membership. Yet homing in solely on productive labor provides but one definition of value, and fixes immigrant women as permanent outsiders. Juxtaposing these two groups of women and taking productive and reproductive labor as necessarily connected, I have sought to broaden the scope of inquiry—even more, to insist that the meanings and value of reproductive labor remain vital to making and remaking the very idea and possibility of "Americanness."

NOTES

Introduction

1. Liechty explains: "Over the centuries, slavery, steady influxes of vulnerable immigrant populations, and more recently, highly productive migrant labor populations . . . have all served as a kind of shifting human extractive frontier (hidden within the nation) that has helped make possible the 'classless' middle-class American lifestyle" (2003: 10).

2. Defining middle-class in the United States is a thorny endeavor. Some scholars use occupation rather than income to define the middle class, or sectors within it (e.g., Ehrenreich 1989; Ortner 2003; Devine 2005). Others argue that occupation is not necessarily a good indicator of class status, as the meaning of different occupations has shifted over time (e.g., Walkowitz 1999; Bledstein 2001). Moreover, even individuals whose occupations would position them as working class continue to identify as middle class (e.g., Halle 1984; Zussman 1985). I rely on self-ascription, since every employer I encountered placed herself in the middle class.

3. Ironically, many would also add that if I was interested in domestic service I should talk to "their" domestic worker, disregarding the relations of power that underlay this statement—could a domestic worker ever offer her employer up for an interview without a second thought? This suggestion also revealed that they could not imagine themselves as part of a study on domestic service, for what did domestic service have to do with them? They were ordinary—not worthy of study in and of themselves.

4. As Biehl and Locke observe: "People are not just the sum of the forces—however overwhelming—constructing and constraining them. Neither 'biopolitics' nor 'structural violence' is sufficient to account for the movements and meanings of their lives . . . just as often—more often—people curve around

impasses or push through anyway, carving out small life chances against the odds" (2010: 332–33).

5. A broad (and growing) literature illustrates the multiplicity of neoliberalism—how it shapes and threads its way through different types of systems; it is not singular or ahistorical, but always shifting and embedded within different types of politics (e.g., Ong 2006; Kingfisher and Maskovsky 2008; Kipnis 2008; Brenner et al. 2010; Ferguson 2010; Collier 2012; Goldstein 2012; Hilgers 2012, 2013; Peck and Theodore 2012; Jessop 2013; Ganti 2014). As Ferguson (2010) notes, broad discrepancies in the very meanings of the term allow for its efficacy (cf. Mirowski 2009).

6. Similarly, Beltrán (2015) explores how DREAM activists seek to "queer the politics of immigration—to operate successfully at the intersection of liberal inclusion and radical possibility" (2015: 81).

7. "Cultural citizenship" has provided an alternative lens for analyzing how marginalized groups assert legitimacy and demand rights, both within the nation-state and in diasporic contexts. In Ong's conceptualization, it is "a dual process of self-making and being-made within webs of power linked to the nation-state and civil society" (1996: 738). Ong's research on Chinese cosmopolitans and Cambodian refugees highlights the role of social institutions and state agencies in positioning and producing citizens/subjects; here citizenship functions "as less a legal category than a set of self-constituting practices in different settings of power" (2003: 276). In contrast, the Latino Cultural Studies Working Group highlights empowerment, defining cultural citizenship as "a broad range of activities of everyday life through which Latinos and other groups claim space in society and eventually claim rights" (Flores and Benmayor 1997: 15). Yet as Gálvez argues, both of these views "paradoxically reify the state's power as grantor of citizenship rights, even within arguments couched to celebrate the agency of individuals in asserting their rights irrespective of state acknowledgment" (2013: 724).

8. As I edit this in 2017, the national context has shifted radically, rendering the possession of legal status, especially of citizenship, more vital than ever. The intense urgency surrounding questions of citizenship must be acknowledged, and my argument above in no way seeks to deny or contradict this. Rather, I am saying that even as citizens, individuals are not insulated from the poverty, racism, and discrimination that mark their lives in the United States.

9. http://censtats.census.gov/cgi-bin/usac/usatable.pl?State=&County=06037&TableID=AAA.

10. *Gringo/a*, at times derogatory, refers to anyone from the United States.

11. Ortner argues that "what is called studying up is really 'studying sideways,' that is, studying people—like scientists, journalists, and Hollywood filmmakers—who in many ways are really not much different from anthropologists and our fellow academics more generally" (2010: 213; cf. Ginsburg 1995; Himpele 2002).

1. The tamales were most likely Mexican or Salvadoran, though I didn't speak to the vendor. *Atole* is a hot drink made from corn starch; *pan dulce* is sweet bread and often eaten for breakfast; *champurrado* is a thick hot chocolate spiced with cinnamon.

2. In 2002, bus tokens cost ninety cents, while a regular ticket cost $1.25.

3. A gourmet coffee chain much like Starbucks, the Coffee Bean is ubiquitous in wealthier areas but completely absent from the neighborhoods where most immigrants live. Prices start at $1.50 for a small cup of coffee and are higher than prices at local coffee shops, fast food restaurants, or 7-11s.

4. *Encerrada* is commonly used to mean someone who lives in, but it is literally translated as "locked up."

5. Here I am not referring to the "LA School" of urban studies (Dear 2002; Monahan 2002), whose adherents maintain that Los Angeles serves as a better contemporary model for urban theory than does Chicago (e.g., Scott and Soja 1996; Curry and Kenney 1999; Coquery-Vidrovitch 2000; Abbott 2002; Gottdiener 2002; Dear and Dahmann 2008; Shearmur 2008; Erie and Mackenzie 2009; Nicholls 2011). Rather, I use "categorically" to underscore how LA historically envisioned itself as exemplar, a city that would escape the problems that plagued older cities, countering these by attracting a white population.

6. Lefebvre asserts, "The whole of (social) space proceeds from the body" (1991: 405). It is through the body, and through movement, that individuals experience the "place-world" (Casey 1996: 24). Indeed, bodies and places are "interanimating" (Basso 1996), mutually constituting. Of course, places do not fashion uniform subjects; they craft specific types of bodies and selves, locating these in existing hierarchies (cf. Bourdieu 1977; Foucault 1977). Bodily experience and movement are therefore socially informed, shaped by a built environment that serves to naturalize the social order. Nevertheless, bodies and selves remain active agents, for bodies are both "technical objects" and "technical means" (Mauss 1973: 75)—the subjects, not merely the objects, of culture (e.g., Csordas 1994; Turner 1994). Thus bodies constitute and are constituted by/in place, and this occurs through movement and social interaction.

7. Literature on space and place does not present a definite picture of what these terms mean. There is a lot of slippage, as most authors take up one of the two terms without really explaining their choice. Casey's (1996) discussion is perhaps the most deliberate; he insists on the use of "place," arguing against the assumption that "space" exists prior to "place" (cf. Massey 2002). Even Casey, however, concedes that there is no single meaning attached to either term, explaining that "by 'place' I mean something close to what Soja . . . calls 'spatiality'" (2001: 693n38). Here I try to use the terms preferred by each author, but throughout the chapter I favor "place." Rotenberg notes that "in cities, people

force the spaces around them to take on meaning. No space is permitted to be neutral—or homogenous. . . . People's understandings transform space into place" (1993: xiii).

8. Peterson's (2010) analysis of LA's Grand Performances highlights how even attempts to harness a civic identity based on diversity demarcate suitable and unsuitable subjects, thereby reproducing difference.

9. There is some debate over just how to define the limits of Los Angeles, for "the city has no end, no middle and no limits" (Keil 1998: xv). Unless I specify, I use Los Angeles as shorthand for LA County. Soja delimits the Greater Los Angeles Area by drawing a sixty-mile circle with City Hall, in downtown Los Angeles, as its central point. This "covers the thinly sprawling 'built-up' area of five counties, a population of more than 12 million individuals, [and] at least 132 incorporated cities" (1989: 224). However, all the people I knew lived and worked in Los Angeles County.

10. U.S. Census data can be found at http://www.census.gov/quickfacts/table /INC110212/06037/accessible.

11. We can find the roots of this configuration in the late nineteenth century, when Los Angeles began its transformation from village to sprawling metropolis. From 1870 to 1910, the population of LA grew from 5,000 to 320,000 people (Wachs 1996: 108), and by 1930, LA County included 2,200,000 people (Wachs 1996: 113). The arrival of the railroad in the mid-1870s, several economic booms led by manufacturing and the discovery of oil, and real estate boosters who painted Southern California as a wholesome return to nature combined to create this "largest internal migration" in American history (Wachs 1996: 113). The majority of these new settlers were economically prosperous individuals who, above all, sought room to spread out. The desire for space, along with relatively affordable and widely available land, streetcars, and, eventually, cars brought about LA's dispersion. Initially, the creation of new housing tracts followed public transportation routes, but the growth of automobile ownership, which by 1915 was the highest in the country (Bottles 1987: 92), allowed for development of ever more outlying areas (Wachs 1996). From the start, this diffuse settlement pattern was also intentionally segregated, moving "Americans" away from foreigners—the Chinese, Japanese, and Mexican communities in the city's historical center (Sanchez 1993: 76–77; cf. Castillo 1979). As the population grew and suburbanization intensified, these unassimilable groups were regularly excluded from new tracts by real estate developers, banks, and existing homeowners (cf. Davis 1990; Scott and Soja 1996). Thus by the 1920s one could already see "a thorough, extensive, and permanent land-use segregation in the metropolis" (Fogelson 1967: 147). The establishment of discrete "Mexican" neighborhoods exemplifies this history. The term *barrio*, for instance, was not applied to specific sections of LA before the American takeover in 1848; in fact, it only gained currency in the 1870s, used to designate Spanish-speaking zones as the city's overall population exploded (Castillo 1979). In the 1880s, the number of these areas shrank as more Mexican Americans moved to the center of

town, spurred by poverty as well as a desire to maintain both their language and close family connections. By 1887, 55 percent of them lived in this central neighborhood, one of the poorest of the city (1979: 14). Early planners and boosters had imagined that as "leftovers," Mexicans would eventually disappear, and so they ignored this group. But even as the city's original population dwindled, migration from Mexico escalated. By the turn of the century, Mexicans were arriving in search of work, and their numbers ramped up significantly after the Mexican Revolution in 1910 (cf. Molina 2006; Scott and Soja 1996). If this (foreign) group could not be counted on to vanish, then spatial and social containment would help stave off its threat. Housing, planning, public health, and other city officials thus worked in concert to isolate Mexicans (cf. Deverell 2005; Molina 2006). The key was to keep this community at a comfortable distance—far enough away that individuals would be unrecognizable, disappearing instead into a faceless mass (Hise 2004: 552; cf. Sanchez 1993: 76–77).

12. Through the course of my research, I realized that employers came from different social classes and different sections of the city. There are definitely employers who are not wealthy; I knew a woman who was paid by the city to take care of an elderly neighbor. I spent a great deal of time with a cooperative that had customers who lived in East LA, a mobile home in Torrance, and other areas that are not considered wealthy. I use "employer neighborhood" to talk about parts of the city where the majority of residents either employ or can afford to employ some form of domestic service—neighborhoods where immigrant women would work but could not afford to live.

13. Lynch pioneered this concept to examine how the city is "perceived by its inhabitants" (1960: 3). He interviewed people in Boston, Jersey City, and LA about the places through which they passed daily and argued that people move their way through cities according to a "mental picture. . . . This image is the product both of immediate sensation and of the memory of past experience" (1960: 4). A few years later, the Los Angeles City Planning Commission, in conjunction with Lynch, conducted a study of Angelenos' perceptions of LA (Orleans 1967). They asked people in five different neighborhoods to draw a map of the city and found that residents of a wealthy white section had a much broader picture of the city than did the inhabitants of immigrant areas. The latter sketched a much smaller city and specified details only in their own neighborhood and around its adjoining bus lines, foregrounding "striking images of inequality of access to the city" (Hayden 1995: 27).

14. In 2003, the California legislature passed a bill allowing undocumented immigrants to have licenses. However, Arnold Schwarzenegger was elected governor a few weeks later and promptly vetoed the measure.

15. The Bus Riders Union's official denunciation of the Gold Line can be found in a press release at http://www.busridersunion.org/PressMedia/PDFs/7-25-03-mta-pasadena-line-bad-for-civil-rights.pdf.

16. Several scholars have written on restrictions on the mobility of domestic workers inside employer homes, as well as the differences in the rooms they can/should occupy (cf. Romero 1992; Gill 1994; Constable 1997; Stephenson 1999).

Chapter 2: Middle-Class Dreaming

1. As Bourdieu (1984) explains, class is not experienced as a particular position within a field, but rather by differentiating oneself from other players; class is a process (cf. Douglas and Isherwood 1979; Rapp 1992; Liechty 2003; Ortner 2003). Ortner further refines this idea, understanding class as a "project": "It seems more useful to think of people, groups, policy makers, culture makers, and so on, as engaged in 'class projects' rather than, or in addition to, being occupants of particular classes-as-locations. . . . We may think of class as something people are or have or possess, or as a place in which people find themselves or are assigned, but we may also think of it as a project, as something that is always being made or kept or defended, feared or desired" (Ortner 2003: 13).

2. These aspirations reveal a particular set of assumptions about childhood and what a successful child should look like. Zelizer discusses how ideas about children shifted in the late nineteenth century; she charts the process of "sacralization" whereby children were transformed from "'object of utility' to object of sentiment" (1985: 9), from children as economic actors to children as placed above economic considerations. She posits, however, that in the 1980s, changing family structures, namely working mothers and increasing divorce rates, could redefine the child as useful within the family. Among middle-class Angelenos, children remained objects of sentiment, childhood sacralized. Most parents spoke about childhood as a magical, ephemeral time that they should cherish. I was struck by everyone's explicit desires to enjoy and record every moment of this special period; for instance, one mother commented that she felt "melancholic" and "nostalgic" at the passing of every stage in her young daughter's life.

3. Berlant maintains "the affective fantasy of the normal requires activation of what Sedgwick calls 'the privilege of unknowing' the social costs to others of a general sense of personal freedom" (2008: 9).

4. As Lamont discusses, the workers she interviewed "dream the American dream [but] are quite critical of middle-class mores. . . . They construct the upper half as having a socioeconomic status to aspire to but values that should be rejected" (2000: 99–100).

5. The legal and ideological associations of whiteness with Americanness are long-standing (Haney-López 2006), and as Carla's words suggest, whiteness remains visual shorthand for Americanness. Whiteness, however, is not fixed but flexible, its content changing and changeable over time (e.g., Warren and Twine 1997; Yancey 2003; Zhou 2004). Scholars have shown that different ethnic groups have been "whitened" through economic integration and class mobility (e.g.,

Roediger 1991; Ignatiev 1995; Brodkin 1998; Jacobson 1998). I do not mean to elide the importance of race, or to reduce race to class; rather, I hope to emphasize how the Americanness of employers requires racializing the category of "immigrant" (e.g., Hondagneu-Sotelo 2001; Romero 2008).

6. Frankenberg (2001) asserts that the unmarked nature of whiteness emerged at a specific historical juncture and insists that we attend to the varying contexts in which whiteness is and indeed has been radically visible (cf. Hartigan 1999).

Chapter 3: Making Mothers Count

1. While time spent on housework seems to be evening out, this results largely from women spending fewer hours doing household work and men staying at the same level (Bianchi et al. 2012).

2. Rancière points out: "The distribution of the sensible reveals who can have a share in what is common to the community based on what they do and on the time and space in which this activity is performed. Having a particular 'occupation' thereby determines the ability or inability to take charge of what is common to the community" (2006: 12).

3. At the turn of the millennium, this trend was rising among mothers of infants: a 2002 Census Bureau Report showed that for the first time, labor force participation had dropped for this group (http://www.census.gov/prod /2003pubs/p20-548.pdf). And the trend persists: a 2014 Pew Research Center analysis reports that in 2012, 29 percent of mothers stayed at home, up from a low of 23 percent in 1999 (Cohn et al. 2014: 5). And, significantly for this book, 25 percent of the 2012 stay-at-home mothers were college graduates (2014: 7), many younger than thirty-five (2014: 8). Recently, Millennials' choices to stay home have come under increasing scrutiny (Miller 2015). Nevertheless, this movement is not necessarily significant when seen in absolute numbers. After all, the Census Bureau also reported that in 2000, 58 percent of American women engaged in paid employment (http://www.census.gov/prod/2005pubs/censr-20 .pdf), a trend that remains steady, a slower expansion resulting from the difficulty of finding work in the years after 2008. Further, as Pew reports, while most Americans believe that having a parent at home is important, in 2012, only 18 percent "agreed that women should return to their traditional role in society" (2013: 28).

4. That Matt Lauer would think to ask GM CEO Mary Barra in 2014 whether she could balance her job with her family life, along with the incensed reactions it provoked, signals once again how little the conversation has moved (Murray 2014). That is, are there other questions we could be asking that would reframe the debate, providing fresh ways to deal with the issue?

5. Generation X is broadly defined as those born between 1961 and 1981, the post–baby boom generation (Ortner 1998a: 416).

6. The use of "work" to define paid employment is problematic, for this term implies that housework and childcare are not really work at all, masking its value and rendering those who perform these tasks invisible. For the most part, however, the mothers in this group used "work" to define engagement in the paid workforce; at times, they acknowledged its problems, but they continued to use it. This slippage is significant, since the group recognized that this ideological division between work and home accounted for mothers' difficulties. Indeed, since the 1970s, feminist interventions have contested the putative separation of the public and private spheres, as this distinction classifies only work done in the public arena as valuable. Nevertheless, in the interest of following "native categories"—and brevity—I also use "work" to refer to paid employment.

7. According to the OECD, in 2000, American workers worked an average of 1,836 hours per year. Although by 2012 this number had decreased to 1,790 hours per year, U.S. workers labored more hours than the average for OECD countries (1,765). By contrast, in 2000 the OECD annual average (1,844) surpassed the U.S. figure (http://stats.oecd.org/Index.aspx?DatasetCode=LEVEL#, accessed July 9, 2014).

8. In 2012, women earned 84 percent of men's wages, while those women between twenty-five and thirty-four earned 93 percent of men's wages (Pew 2013). These gaps are often attributed to motherhood: "Most economists believe the gap between women's and men's wages does not stem primarily from employers paying women less than men for the same job. It occurs mostly because men and women take different jobs and follow different career paths. Part of this difference may be a result of discrimination in hiring and promoting. Much, though, is a result of the constraints of motherhood" (Porter 2012: B1).

9. For more about the debates, theoretical agendas, and historical conjunctures characterizing third-wave feminism, see Berger 2006; Heywood 2006a, 2006b; Gillis et al. 2007; Snyder 2008; Budgeon 2011; Reger 2012, 2014; Cobble et al. 2014; Dicker 2016.

10. In popular culture, Generation X is always tacitly white and middle-class (Liu 1994; Ortner 1998a, 2013; Shugart 2001; Springer 2002), obscuring the workings of privilege. Indeed, diversity remains a vexed issue for feminism (Reger 2012).

11. Although Gen X mothers were not necessarily aware of race and class privilege, these shaped their experiences. It is especially important to keep this in mind when specific groups claim to speak for all members of a generation, or all women, or all mothers, and so on. Feminists of the 1970s were roundly criticized by nonwhite writers for focusing solely on the concerns and experiences of white, middle-class, heterosexual women, neglecting the experiences of lesbians or women of color. For instance, while white women fought to break into the workforce, women of color continued to struggle for economic survival (e.g., Collins

1998). Similarly, attempts to represent the needs of all mothers ignore the effects of "stratified reproduction" (Colen 1995), processes that produce very different concerns for mothers from distinct groups.

12. Or, as Ho (2009) argues, a similar short-term emphasis on shareholder value shapes workplace demands and employee culture.

13. In his research among lifestyle migrants in the Midwest, Hoey (2014) explains that his informants viewed work almost as a religion and described their devotion to their jobs as cult-like; for many, it took a crisis of faith to shake this unquestioned acceptance of corporate lifestyles.

14. California was the first state to mandate paid family leave. This law took effect in July 2004 and provides six weeks of leave at 55 percent of salary (up to $728 per week) (Vrana and Banks 2004: C2). As of 2014, only three states provided such protections—while the United States remains one of only four countries that does not guarantee family leave for its workers (Sandler 2014).

15. This particular narrative style served as a marker of group identity. Telling their stories in a specific way signaled membership, for as individuals learned a new language for their problems, they also acquired the dispositions and identities required for participation in the group (cf. Ochs and Schieffelin 1984; Schieffelin 1990; Lave 1991).

16. The national group has a list of recommendations on its website; among the women I met, the most popular books were Ann Crittenden's (2001) *The Price of Motherhood*; Joan Williams's (2000) *Unbending Gender*, which details how the structures of the working world preclude a tenable balance between home and work; Edward McCaffery's (1997) *Taxing Women*, which shows how the tax system penalizes women at all income levels; and Nancy Folbre's (2001) *The Invisible Heart*, which explores the value of caregiving from an economic perspective. Through these books, members found the language to understand and categorize their experiences.

17. As Ginsburg explains, in the United States "the social forms that focus on making or remaking the self in new terms require association with like-minded others. In other words, the cultural system requires that the individual constitute himself or herself in order to achieve a social identity, and that the means available for achieving identity are through voluntary affiliations with others in a group that offers a comprehensive reframing of the place of the self in the social world" (1989: 221).

18. Significantly, while middle-class mothers want added respect for their care work, they continue to complain about the rising costs of childcare. Clearly, economic constraints play a role here, but this contradiction will only become more salient if the mothers succeed in their goal of making care work socially and economically rewarded. Meg pointed this out to me: "Part of the reason why we don't ever address the childcare needs of families is because we don't want to have to think about it, say how we value it, whether it's done by mothers or whether it's

done by professional caregivers. And so dealing with that would totally be huge, and then from a practical way, you have to talk about how do you finance higher wages for workers without burdening the family."

Chapter 4: Organizing, Motherhood, and Work

1. "Cuando uno quiere alguna persona ya no digamos a los hijos que es lo mas sagrado que uno tiene en la vida uno hace el tiempo."

2. Menjívar investigated Central American immigrants' perspectives on paid employment and found that the working-class women she interviewed "did not see their work in a liberating light but only as a way to meet the survival requirements of their families" (2003: 111). Scholars have also found that Mexican American working-class women similarly define their work through family obligations (e.g., Fernandez-Kelly 1990; Zavella 1991; Segura 1998).

3. "A mí todo el tiempo el diez de mayo me deprime, primeramente porque no esa una, no lo miran tan grande como en, como allá . . . y porque en México, los diez de mayo, no trabaja nada, la gente no trabaja. Pues yo siempre tengo que trabajar los diez de mayos."

4. Scholars have discussed extensively how migration affects gender dynamics in the household, particularly as the woman's earning power increases (e.g., Hondagneu-Sotelo 1994, 2003; Hurtado 1999; Hirsch 2003; Menjívar 2003; Gonzalez-Lopez 2005; Smith 2005; Kang 2010; Zavella 2011; Boehm 2012). For the immigrant women I knew in LA, however, this did not seem a central concern; most did not expect that men would be responsible for their children. While all of these women maintained that it was men's jobs to provide for their families, many were single mothers or the primary wage earners in their households. Those who did live with and could count on a man to supplement their earnings nevertheless relied on their own income to make ends meet. In fact, they had all worked in their home countries, where most of them had single-handedly supported their children, and they had all migrated to the United States to work, even the ones who came with a husband or boyfriend. Further, most of them affirmed that life was better without a man—those who lived alone explained that they would never go back to living with a man, especially as men would often intervene in a woman's relationship with her children.

5. Finding a job and a steady income took on even greater urgency for those women who had left their children in their home countries. For these "transnational mothers" (Hondagneu-Sotelo and Avila 1997; cf. Parreñas 2001; Gamburd 2008; Dreby 2010; Guevarra 2010; Abrego 2014), the money and presents they sent home substituted for the day-to-day aspects of mothering, tangible gifts that increasingly constituted a woman's relationship with her children.

6. Parreñas writes: "The deep-seated urgency of migrant Filipina domestic workers to leave Rome results in the hyperreality of making money. Everyone in the community maintains a sideline. . . . Thus, in Rome, the urgency of making

money among migrant Filipinos has reached a distortedly hyperstate. Migrant Filipina domestic workers turn to sidelines in response to the immobility of their life in Rome—socially, legally, and economically. Segregation and immobility intensify desires to expedite the accumulation of savings and in turn pressure them to produce surplus income. . . . Women seem to function on the basis that not a single day can ever pass without earning a profit. A day off is seen as a day to profit" (Parreñas 2001: 224–25).

7. "Me fui a la agencia, y ya fue, donde . . . me pusieron prácticamente en venta, ¿no? y allí donde me quede, porque dije, no aquí me quedo, ya no es tanto por amor [al trabajo]. . . . Si, en la agencia, me, me, me vendieron al trabajo, se lo vendieron a la señora, y la señora ya se sintió responsable de mí, *como que si me hubiera comprado a mí* y no mis servicios, sino a mí. Entonces allí me sentí como, me sentí muy humillada, pero que hacer. . . . Es la agencia, la agencia la que realmente ya tiene ese papel de vender esclavos. Poco te falta para que te levanten los labios y te revisen los dientes, de verdad."

8. "Me escogió por mi color. Me escogió porque era yo fuerte, y porque . . . era yo fuerte quizás, porque me vio a si entre, una edad pues buena, ¿no? Como, con experiencia y todo, y dice, 'a ella me la llevo.' "

9. Agencies are notorious for constructing/instilling racial/ethnic types and preferences, as well as for disciplining women in how to become appealing (e.g., Constable 1997; Bakan and Stasiulis 1995; Hondagneu-Sotelo 2001; Rosales 2001).

10. In her analysis of domestic workers in San Diego, Mattingly (1999) found that immigration laws after 1986, which make hiring an undocumented worker illegal, have narrowed considerably the types of jobs that immigrants can take, limiting individuals to domestic work or other informal jobs. In my experience, it was not only undocumented immigrants who wound up relegated to the margins of the labor market. Both documented and undocumented immigrant women held relatively few options as far as the type of work they could undertake.

11. Scholars have investigated various and varying attempts to organize paid domestic employees in the United States (e.g., Van Raaphorst 1988; Palmer 1989; Hondagneu-Sotelo and Riegos 1997; Boris and Nadasen 2008; Gupta 2008; Brown 2011; Shah and Seville 2012; Goldberg 2015; Nadasen 2015), Canada (e.g., Elvir 1997; Velasco 1997), and Latin America (Prates 1989; Schelleckens and van der Schoot 1989; Gill 1994).

12. In California, this process has been long and incremental, and the struggle continues. Following an expansion of the Fair Labor Standards Act in 1974 to include domestic workers, but not those who cared for the elderly or disabled, California's Industrial Welfare Commission passed the Household Occupations Wage Order Act in 1976 (Shah 2015). This bill extended overtime and minimum wage protections to domestic workers whose jobs entailed care of material goods, but not people (Shah 2015). Caregivers, designated as "personal attendants," finally received the right to the minimum wage in 2001 but remained ineligible for

overtime pay (Shah and Seville 2012). Since January 2014, the California Bill of Rights (AB241) has guaranteed overtime pay to all domestic workers, but this law is set to expire in 2017. The California Domestic Workers Coalition (CDWC), primarily constituted by groups in Los Angeles and the Bay Area, has been fighting for these protections since its inception in 2005. As of this writing, May 2016, the CDWC's efforts are focused on the 2016 Domestic Workers' Bill of Rights (SB1015), which would make these right guaranteed by AB241 permanent (http://www .cadomesticworkers.org/campaign-updates/).

13. Valentine illustrates how the category "transgender," so crucial for political mobilization, can exclude the experiences of the most vulnerable, least seen people it seeks to represent: "If the logic of representation in the 'politics of recognition' requires one to present a stable identity—this time consolidated in an understandable and marketable discourse about transgender as an identity based in gender variance—will it necessarily lead to a political movement where, also, whiteness, middle classness, and respectability are assumed? . . . It worries me that transgender itself (because of its institutional life, its implications in the agencies of the state, its racial and class entailments) may unintentionally become another tool of 'exclusion,' even as it promises to 'include,' to liberate, and to seek redress" (2007: 245).

14. As a rule, new women would work as "trainees" for eight dollars an hour and always accompanied by a member, who would train and observe them, for a three-month trial period. If at the end of this trial period the trainee was found acceptable, she would become a full-fledged member, get her own cell phone, and acquire insurance benefits.

15. According to Parreñas, in Rome, "the hyperreality of making money alienates migrant Filipina domestic workers from one another. It results in the commercialization of friendships and daily rituals in the community. With the hyperreality of making money, personal favors and visits to a friend's house are even attached with fees. Trust among friends is even further tainted by the threat of competition" (2001: 225). While Parreñas argues that the imperative to make money and the practice of making money from one another both unite and divide Filipino immigrants in Rome, Mahler finds pervasive distrust and conflict among Salvadorans on Long Island. Her informants so often stressed competition that she asks, "Do immigrants *believe* they are a community? Scholarly models and public opinions can easily omit the perspectives of the people they are describing. . . . My informants certainly do not see themselves as united. I have used their firsthand testimonies extensively to illustrate their point. In most texts on immigrants, however, readers are only privy to the author's analysis. . . . This leads me to suspect that portrayals of solidarity may reflect a romanticization of the immigrant experience" (1995: 225; cf. Myerhoff 1978).

16. T visas are granted to victims of human trafficking.

17. "Es mas bien aquí, porque allá, mucho trabajo, poco dinero . . . y aquí pues quizás no, no soy la gran cosa, no tengo las cosas que uno quiere tener, ¿no? Pero por lo menos no ando trabajando tanto como allá, que trabajaba de las siete de la mañana a seis de la tarde, siete de la noche y para vivir en miseria."

18. "Todos sacrifican para sacar a su familia adelante."

19. "Es como el marido malo que me está humillando ¿pero porqué no queremos dejarlo? ¿Porque entonces que nos vamos hacer? Nos vamos a morir de hambre."

20. "Yo acá sólo trabajando, y solo trabajar para mis hijos."

21. "Estoy agradecida con este país por la razón que he podido salir adelante, sacar adelante mis hijos. Puedo ayudarle a mis viejitos también. Me he sentido muy agradecida. Me ha gustado, porque aquí he podido, aunque no tengo dinero para mis felicidades poder ayudar a mi familia. Tengo mi casita donde yo puedo llegar un día . . . en el Salvador . . . y entonces digo yo, ¿que le puedo pedir a la vida? Dios me ha dado una casa, me ha dado hijos, que tanto los quiero, mi madre que todavía esta viva, mi papá."

22. I was never able to piece together the history prior to my arrival, as I received differing versions of the events from each participant. Thus, I focus on the time I spent there, emphasizing the difficulties the group had in attracting new members and in effecting its long-term goals.

23. "No me, no tomé tanto interés sobre las trabajadoras domésticas al principio pues porque yo ya en esa época yo ya estaba legalizada. Ya tenía todo, y yo decía, bueno porque voy a pelear. Pero después me puse a pensar de orientar a las otras mujeres como debían de, de vivir."

24. Temporary protected status (TPS) is granted to individuals who are unable to return to their countries because of war or natural disaster. This status was first extended to Salvadorans in 1991 in the aftermath of the civil war. In 2001, it was proffered once again in response to a series of earthquakes (Schmitt 2001).

25. This caravan traveled from California to New York, stopping at spots in between to rally. Its main purpose was to call attention to the plight of the undocumented and fight for "legalization" or amnesty. At least in California, it was the subject of much media attention, and, according to Josefina, they were met by large groups of supporters in every city, culminating in a march and rally in New York at the end.

26. "Yo quiero que las mujeres aprendan a defenderse. Esa es su herramienta. Yo quiero que las mujeres aprendan como es el curso de CPR, porque es herramienta de su trabajo, ¿si? Porque ese documento las va ayudar. Yo quisiera que yo lo que yo no tengo, quiero que lo tengan las mujeres, sin egoísmo: como es el ingles, como es la computadora, para que *ya no sean solo una mujer, solo un objeto, no quiero eso. Solo una empleaducha—no quiero eso.* Quiero más y más, pero educación, es lo que quiero. Porque acabando con la educación, se acaba la ignorancia. Acabando con la ignorancia, ya tienes las puertas abiertas."

27. "Las mujeres tienen que ser vistas, tienen que hacer publicidad. Tienen que darse a conocer, que existe la explotación, que tenemos necesidad, que tenemos necesidad de mover a la familia. Que tenemos necesidad de agarrar trabajo lejos, como no tenemos vehículo, no tenemos licencia, no queremos arriesgar lo poco que tenemos para comprar un, un vehículo, y que a la vuelta no los quiten, y no tenemos opción de como reclamarlo. Es dinero perdido. Entonces para que arriesgar, y agarramos el trabajo más pobre, menos trabajo, mal pagado, por lo mismo que es el más cerca, al alcance del bus, al alcance del movimiento, porque no puedes hacer más cosas. Entonces, allí nos estancamos. Entonces las mujeres tienen que, tienen que sentir cual es la necesidad, y yo ya agarro allí el tema de licencias, el tema de la legalización."

28. "Hay mucha necesidad; y con mis hijos yo pase muchas cosas y tuvo que pasarnos muchas cosas, ve'a. Me, me, me fui empoderizando y llegó un momento en que dije yo no, yo porque tengo que aguantar cosas. . . . Me puedo mantener de otra manera, vendiendo chicles, pero nadie me va humillar, nadie me va ofender. Vender chicles es trabajo muy digno. Empezaba yo a pensar de otra manera. Empecé a limpiar casas, ve'a, pero empecé a limpiar casas en otro, en otra forma. Yo llegaba yo y decía, esto es lo que te puedo hacer . . . ¿te conviene? Si no me voy. A si, ve'a. . . . Se me metió a si, ve'a. Si algo no le gusta usted me dice, yo lo trato de corregir si esta en mis manos, si no está en mis manos, 'tonces escoja a otra persona que venga."

29. "La doméstica no dejo de ser esclava; la doméstica entonces, em, todavía la seguían viendo como parte de eso, porque el hombre, por un lado, la familia de uno le decía que se tenia que preparar para ser esclava del esposo. No le decían eso—pero tienes que aprender para atender a tu esposo. Entonces nos enseñaron a servir. En la iglesia nos enseñan a servir también. En la iglesia nos enseñan a servir. En todas partes nos enseñan a servir. La mujer penitente es sumisa. Con eso no estoy de acuerdo yo; si soy de la iglesia pero soy muy liberal. Enseño a las mujeres a ser liberales. Me he encontrado lío, no, pero bueno, esa es parte de la vida, no? Todo, todo ese montón de mujeres en, en aquellas épocas eran mujeres que nunca habían tenido opción de estudiar nada, que solamente habían sido preparadas para ser amas de casa . . . en México. Aquí ya no tanto porque ya se creció otra forma de vida, pero la gente que viene a trabajar doméstica son de nuestros países. . . . Criadas para eso, ¿no?"

30. "Parte de mis metas es tener poder, ve'a, y que las mujeres tengan poder, ve'a. . . . Y haré todo lo posible por que las mujeres no pasen siete años como yo, bajo el poder de un hombre. Haré todo lo posible para que las mujeres no pasen bajo el poder de los patrones hombres. . . . ¿Y quienes son las que más necesitan eso? Las trabajadoras domésticas, ¿ve'a? Dejó de ser para mí la trabajadora doméstica como es trabajadora si no una lucha *como* mujeres . . . entonces empecé a reconocer que había mucho mas que hacer que hablarle de los derechos a las trabajadoras."

1. Of course, Carmen was fortunate, as she had legal papers that allowed her to access these benefits, but every woman I met experienced these contradictions in one way or another.

2. The 2006 immigrants' rights protesters, along with undocumented youth organizing on behalf of the DREAM Act, took this very tack in their assertions that "We Are America" (Reynolds and Fiore 2006). While protesters highlighted their labor and economic contributions to this country, DREAMers lay claim on a fundamental Americanness based on a sense of cultural assimilation, upstanding character, and future contributions to the country (e.g., Beltrán 2009, 2014; Galindo 2012; Olivares 2013; Torre and Germano 2014).

3. A wealth of scholarship has analyzed il/legality, the struggle for legal status, as well as varied and varying experiences of inhabiting different legal categories (e.g., Chavez 1992; Coutin 1993, 2000, 2013; Hagan 1994; De Genova 2005, 2013; De Genova and Peutz 2010; Dreby 2010; Hagan et al. 2011; Menjívar 2011, 2014; Menjívar and Abrego 2012; Gonzales and Chavez 2012; Abrego 2014; Pallares 2014).

4. As De Genova (2002) argues, illegality is neither self-evident nor naturally produced, but rather the effect of specific state policies that seek to regulate immigration and labor. He thus calls for further study of the category itself.

5. Ong reminds us: "A worker who is technically an American citizen may not enjoy basic rights because her conditions of existence are determined by work status and location rather than formal citizenship status" (2003: 283).

6. "Lo importante era que yo ya tenía mis papeles, ya podía ir a Guatemala, ir a ver a la familia. Lo único que hubo al principio, era que tenía los papeles para salir y entrar pero no tenía el dinero. . . . Eso es, a veces, usted tiene una cosa y no tiene la otra. . . . Pero lo importante era que yo ya no tenia miedo, ya no, bueno, yo nunca tuve miedo. Pero si andaba, siempre procure no hacer ningún problema para no tener problemas con migración ni nada de eso. Siempre estuve viviendo muy correctamente, muy, nunca hice problemas de nada."

7. "Aunque yo me quedara muriéndome de hambre, pero yo lo que hacía— mire lo que uno hace; yo lo hice. Yo cuando trabajaba en los restaurantes, no tenía tiempo de comer, pero cuando recogía las mesas. Usted sabe mucha gente no se come toda la comida, parten un pedazo de carne y dejan eso, y unseo . . . ay niña, yo agarraba los pedazos de carne mire, allí por el lavadero me los comía, mire. Yo tenía una desnutrición horrible. Yo tenía, yo me comía, lo que decimos las sobras, lo que quedaban en los platos. Pero yo decía, esta comida está limpia."

8. "Yo le dije no: no me molestan los niños. Yo lo que quiero es irme, porque tú sabes la vida que tengo aquí—una vida muy sufrida, una vida de hambre. Era un, era un calvario para mí. Entonces yo le dije que quería salir, y me dijo ella que estaba bien, que me preparara."

9. "Usted señora supiera, le dije, Marta que estar en Estados Unidos, le dije, es estar en el cielo. Se equivoca, le dije. Los Estados Unidos, si no se trabaja no se come. Usted no sabe le dije, lo que me costó, y ese dinero que yo le mandé a usted, le dije, yo lo debo. Yo lo presté, porque yo gano una miseria aquí le dije. No tenía todo ese dinero."

10. Mahler's (1995) study of Salvadorans on Long Island points to a distinct lack of solidarity among immigrants, as those who are more established regularly take advantage of new arrivals. Other scholars highlight how social networks do not always provide adequate or equal support for all immigrants; access to assistance is often determined by gender and other vectors of inequality (e.g., Hondagneu-Sotelo 1994; Hagan 1998; Menjívar 2000).

11. "La verdad, la verdad, todas tenemos necesidad. . . . Todas venimos a este país por una necesidad. Yo no voy a decir que no porque yo tuve necesidad en el momento que ya no tenía dinero, pero, pues, y también con personas afuera de la, de la cooperativa, que dicen que aquí se sufre mucho, que aquí se, se lloran, se lloran lágrimas de sangre por lo que uno está pasando. Y es la verdad, porque a veces, no hay trabajo tan fácil de encontrarlo."

12. "La gente, ya estando ganando dinero se vuelve más, se vuelve un poco más orgulloso. . . . Si porque a veces cuando uno llega, como los que ya están aquí, ya tienen trabajo como que no tratan de ayudar. Sienten que, que ellos son mejores que los que vienen y que no saben, que no saben como desenvolverse en este lugar y ya los que están aquí ya saben. Ya tienen experiencia, ya saben cómo es la vida aquí, cómo buscar el trabajo, cómo trabajar. . . . Y entonces la gente pues no, no en ves de ayudarlo como que se ríe de uno o así."

13. "Aquí hay muchas, muchas, muchas, muchas posibilidades. O sea que este país tiene oportunidades para el que lo aprecia y mala suerte para el que no lo aprecie. Porque hay quien esta en esta país y desprecia las oportunidades que el país le da. Porque para serte sincera el país da buenas oportunidades, muchas oportunidades, hasta beneficios. Aquí, la persona que no sale adelante es porque no quiere."

14. "Me quedo porque quiero pues, prepararme aquí, y ver qué, qué hago más adelante."

15. "Como toda la gente, como toda mujer me gusta la ropa, me gustan las diversiones, conocer lugares."

16. "Ahorita empecé a amar este país. Lo empecé a amar que no tienes idea, y, y por eso mismo, porque el país no tiene la culpa de mi situación. Me gusta de este país que hay muchas oportunidades, solo que no los [sic] sabemos canalizar, pero yo por eso digo, porque me ha dado mucho, la libertad de nacer nuevamente, porque vine a nacer nuevamente, porque aquí volví a nacer. Sufrí, me levante, pero todo, pero yo no le culpo al país."

17. "No me siento perseguida. Me siento bien. Me siento como que si estuviera en mi casa. Eso es lo que me gusta de acá: la libertad de expresión, ¿si? La liber-

tad, las leyes de acá me gustan, porque las leyes que están son justas. Y si te lo aplican es porque has violado realmente. Y lo que me gusta de acá es que no hay mordidas. No puedes comprar la ley. La ley es ley. Eso es lo que me gusta de acá. Eso es lo que me gusta de acá. Eso es lo que me gusta de este país. . . . Ya me di el lujo de sentarme en el capitolio y escuchar cómo se debaten los políticos por una ley y más por los inmigrantes. Es muy bonito estar allí, y eso es lo que a mí me gusta, de que nos permitan pisar a su casa, de que nos permitan allá."

18. "Pienso yo que eso, eso me ha ayudado a mi *bastante* a ser una persona muy abierta, y poder aprender, y sobre todo de tener amigas también de señoras que he conocido y de ellas también me dan valor, de decir, okay, es, es, se puede. O sea, si muchas pueden ¿porque no uno? Si es difícil, *si es difícil* porque, pues no sabes qué, qué complicaciones se te presenten verdad, pero en la mente mientras uno se enfoque en [esa meta] y quiera uno realmente de corazón lograrlo, venga lo que venga, pues eso es lo que te va, te va enseñar que tanto vas a valorar lo que tú quieres. . . . Aprender pues que si uno quiere algo pues, si tienes que, tú eres la única que tiene que salir de eso. . . . Con sacrificio si . . . porque no 'movies,' no televisión, ni nada. . . . Puedes sacrificar bastante como inmigrante y hacer sus, como se dice, sus sueños realidad pero tienes que saber cómo. Y sobre todo con tus amistades . . . saber con quién vas aquí y allá . . . saber gastar tu tiempo en lo que vale la pena realmente."

19. "Es una honra el trabajo, es la ley de todo lo Cristiano. La gente vaga sin ocupación, que le gusta ser gente mantenida, es lo peor."

20. "Ese es un sacrifico que cualquier gente que quiere superar lo hace. Porque todo, todo no le va llegar a uno de felicidad."

21. "Simplemente pensando en algún día tener una mejor vida, o no regresarme a lo mismo."

22. "Por eso me estoy sacrificando, verdad, para, para que ellos algún día, sean alguien."

23. "Aquí estamos pobremente pero estamos mejor que cuando nos estábamos muriendo do hambre en Guatemala . . . porque aquí, menos que mal, comida hay aunque sea, ya ve las tiendas de 99 y todo, puede uno comer latas o comer lo que sea, pero comida hay en este país. Y si uno bota la comida o ya no come es porque no quiere, pero comida hay. En cambio, como la situación que yo tuve, comer tres días pan en seco, tieso, pan duro y que yo me conservaba un pan, que no se me fuera terminar un pan, *eso* es duro. Por eso yo digo que yo sé lo que es la pobreza. Yo sé lo que es la miseria, y sé que es aguantar hambre."

24. "Allá todo el mundo es criticado, por la manera que se viste, la manera que uno se conduce."

25. "Pues aquí no se usaban muchas especies como se usa en Guatemala. Porque a veces en Guatemala, yo cuando voy a Guatemala, tengo que meter mi medicina, porque me dan las comidas pero como tienen mucho especie. . . . Es como aquí no más yo lo único que utilizo es cebollita de ensalada y muy poquita

pimienta, no le hecho el montón de cosas, porque, si porque antes, uy, yo tenía, según yo, una comida no estaba bien si no estaba llena de especies. . . . Muchos productos que lleva una comida Guatemalteca. Aquí se puede preparar lo mismo con menos ingredientes, con menos. Tiene más sabor allá, pero es algo que yo me he dado cuenta que ya me acostumbre a la de aquí. Entonces, cuando yo como una comida de allá o me da vuelta el estómago o me duele la boca del estómago."

26. "Mi problema era, que continuaba siendo, de que mi anhelo era saber leer, saber escribir, poder estudiar."

27. "Pues yo tenía toda la ilusión de estar en una escuela pero hay algo que si para mí fue muy difícil porque encontré un maestro que no fue señora que nos daba las clases, fue un hombre maestro y el era un señor grande y el no daba clases de español. El sólo daba clases de inglés. . . . Yo no quería inglés. Yo quería español—leer y escribir porque si no entendía nada en español no podía orientarme para el inglés. . . . Fue cuando abrieron unas clases de español allí en la escuela, entonces allí aproveche de poder aprender a leer y escribir en español. Entonces después fue cuando ya me pasaron la escuela con *teacher* de inglés. . . . Fue bastante difícil porque, pues, cuando fue con el maestro de español también era difícil porque era primera vez que yo entraba a una cosa, escribir—y híjole—y aprender a leer y todo. . . . Solo que lo que yo nunca pude componer, a veces si repito lo que hago, donde era un problema, que no se me quedaba, donde había punto . . . todo esos puntitos que van sobre las letras como papá, mamá, las tildes, los puntos suspensivos, los puntos de interrogación. . . . Todo eso a mí no se me quedaba. Y me lo repetían y me lo repetían y ay yo decía, 'dios mío' decía yo, ¿será posible que logre aprender a leer y escribir? Entonces eso fue duro para mi. Si fue duro para mí pues porque hasta la fecha leer me encanto y lo hacía perfectamente bien. Hasta la fecha lo hago perfectamente bien. Lo que no me gustó, y lo hago por necesidad, es escribir pero porque es bastante difícil aun años más tarde, es bastante difícil. Ahora imagínese que es bastante difícil también en el inglés. El ingles se escribe de una forma y se pronuncia de otra."

28. "Yo pienso que si me retiro del todo, no hacer nada. . . . Creo que me moriría antes de no estar en actividad porque yo soy una persona de que me gusta estar en movimiento, de estar saliendo, levantándome temprano, haciendo algo y entonces si me voy a volver una mujer inútil muy temprano creo que me voy a morir mas rápido."

29. "Y hasta allí es como hemos llegado nosotros . . . que he logrado pues hacerme activista, ayudar cuando puedo, hacer mis cosas, y después también mas tarde logre en este país, nunca me imagine, lograr mi, primero logre mi residencia y siete años mas tarde pues me preocupe en estudiar la historia de los estados unidos para lograr a llegarme hacer ciudadana de este país. Y me siento muy contenta, me siento *happy* de pertenecer."

30. Carmen was able to legalize her status through the Immigration Reform and Control Act of 1986. This law granted amnesty to over 2 million undocu-

mented workers who could show that they had been living and working in the United States since at least 1982. The relative ease of applying for a Social Security number in the 1970s allowed many long-term immigrants to prove their residency and contribution to this country. Patricia, for instance, got her Social Security number about two weeks after arriving from Mexico in 1974. Similarly, Carmen had been paying taxes since the mid-1970s, when a friend advised her that this would provide a paper trail that could eventually help her to arrange her papers.

31. The INS was abolished in 2003, and its functions were taken over by the U.S. Citizenship and Immigration Services, an arm of Homeland Security. Margarita became a citizen in 2003, in the midst of this transition, and I never found out which agency interviewed her.

Conclusion

1. This anxiety is foundational, woven into the very fabric of the nation. Before the United States was even born, Benjamin Franklin decried the presence of German immigrants in Pennsylvania: "Why should the Palatine Boors be suffered to swarm into our Settlements, and by herding together establish their Language and Manners to the Exclusion of ours? Why should Pennsylvania, founded by the English, become a Colony of *Aliens*, who will shortly be so numerous as to Germanize us instead of our Anglifying them, and will never adopt our Language or Customs, any more than they can acquire our Complexion" (1970 [1751]: 475, emphasis in the original).

2. Sedgwick terms this approach "paranoia" and encourages us to examine its performative implications. She argues that paranoid readings necessarily anticipate negative outcomes, thereby producing "an unintentionally stultifying side effect: they may have made it less rather than more possible to unpack the local, contingent relations between any given piece of knowledge and its narrative/epistemological entailments for the seeker, knower, or teller" (2003: 124).

3. I am indebted to Stephanie Sadre-Orafai for this phrase.

4. As Biehl and Locke maintain: "In learning to know people, with care and an 'empirical lantern' . . . we have a responsibility to think of life in terms of both limits and crossroads—where new intersections of technology, interpersonal relations, desire, and imagination can sometimes, against all odds, propel unexpected futures" (2010: 318).

REFERENCES

Abbott, Andrew. 2002. "Los Angeles and the Chicago School: A Comment on Michael Dear." *City and Community* 1(1): 33–38.

Abrego, Leisy J. 2014. *Sacrificing Families: Navigating Laws, Labor, and Love across Borders.* Stanford, CA: Stanford University Press.

Ahmed, Sara. 2004. "Affective Economies." *Social Text* 22(2): 117–39.

———. 2010. *The Promise of Happiness.* Durham, NC: Duke University Press.

Allen, Jafari S. 2011. *¡Venceremos? The Erotics of Black Self-Making in Cuba.* Durham, NC: Duke University Press.

Allison, Anne. 2013. *Precarious Japan.* Durham, NC: Duke University Press.

Andall, Jacqueline. 2000. *Gender, Migration and Domestic Service: The Politics of Black Women in Italy.* Interdisciplinary Research Series in Ethnic, Gender, and Class Relations. Aldershot, UK: Ashgate.

Anderson, Bridget. 2000. *Doing the Dirty Work? The Global Politics of Domestic Labour.* London: Zed.

Arnold, Jeanne E., Anthony P. Graesch, Enzo Ragazzini, and Elinor Ochs. 2012. *Life at Home in the Twenty-First Century: 32 Families Open Their Doors.* Los Angeles: Cotsen Institute of Archaeology Press.

Augé, Marc. 1995. *Non-Places: Introduction to an Anthropology of Supermodernity.* New York: Verso.

Avila, Eric. 2004. *Popular Culture in the Age of White Flight: Fear and Fantasy in Suburban Los Angeles.* Berkeley: University of California Press.

Bakan, Abigail B., and Daiva K. Stasiulis. 1995. "Making the Match: Domestic Placement Agencies and the Racialization of Women's Household Work." *Signs* 20(2): 303–35.

———, eds. 1997. *Not One of the Family: Foreign Domestic Workers in Canada.* Toronto: University of Toronto Press.

Barnes, Annie S. 1993. "White Mistresses and African-American Domestic Workers: Ideals for Change." *Anthropological Quarterly* 66(1): 22.

Basso, Keith H. 1996. "Wisdom Sits in Places." In *Senses of Place*, edited by Keith H. Basso and Steven Feld, 53–90. School of American Research Advanced Seminar Series. Santa Fe, NM: School of American Research Press.

Bell, V. 1999. "Performativity and Belonging: An Introduction." *Theory, Culture and Society* 16(2): 1–10.

Beltrán, Cristina. 2009. "Going Public: Hannah Arendt, Immigrant Action, and the Space of Appearance." *Political Theory* 37(5): 595–622.

———. 2014. " 'No Papers, No Fear': DREAM Activism, New Social Media, and the Queering of Immigrant Rights." In *Contemporary Latina/o Media: Production, Circulation, Politics*, edited by Arlene Davila, 245–66. New York: New York University Press.

———. 2015. "Undocumented, Unafraid, and Unapologetic: DREAM Activists, Immigrant Politics, and the Queering of Democracy." In *From Voice to Influence: Understanding Citizenship in a Digital Age*, edited by Danielle Allen and Jennifer S. Light, 80–104. Chicago: University of Chicago Press.

Berger, Melody, ed. 2006. *We Don't Need Another Wave: Dispatches from the Next Generation of Feminists*. Emeryville, CA: Seal Press.

Berlant, Lauren Gail. 2008. *The Female Complaint: The Unfinished Business of Sentimentality in American Culture*. Durham, NC: Duke University Press.

———. 2011. *Cruel Optimism*. Durham, NC: Duke University Press.

Bhimji, Fazila. 2010. "Struggles, Urban Citizenship, and Belonging: The Experience of Undocumented Street Vendors and Food Truck Owners in Los Angeles." *Urban Anthropology and Studies of Cultural Systems and World Economic Development* 39(4): 455–92.

Bianchi, S. M., L. C. Sayer, M. A. Milkie, and J. P. Robinson. 2012. "Housework: Who Did, Does or Will Do It, and How Much Does It Matter?" *Social Forces* 91(1): 55–63.

Biehl, João. 2013. "Ethnography in the Way of Theory." *Cultural Anthropology* 28(4): 573–97.

Biehl, João, and Peter Locke. 2010. "Deleuze and the Anthropology of Becoming." *Current Anthropology* 51(3): 317–51.

Bledstein, Burton J. 2001. *The Middling Sorts: Explorations in the History of the American Middle Class*. Edited by Robert D. Johnston. New York: Routledge.

Bobo, Lawrence D., Melvin L. Oliver Jr., James H. Johnson, and Abel Valenzuela Jr. 2002. *Prismatic Metropolis: Inequality in Los Angeles*. New York: Russell Sage Foundation.

Boehm, Deborah A. 2012. *Intimate Migrations: Gender, Family, and Illegality among Transnational Mexicans*. New York: New York University Press.

Bonilla-Silva, Eduardo. 2006. *Racism without Racists: Color-Blind Racism and the Persistence of Racial Inequality in America*. 3rd ed. Lanham, MD: Rowman and Littlefield.

Borden, Iain. 2002. "Another Pavement, Another Beach: Skateboarding and the Performative Critique of Architecture." In *The Unknown City: Contesting Architecture and Social Space*, edited by Iain Borden, Joe Kerr, and Jane Rendell, 178–99. Cambridge, MA: MIT Press.

Boris, Eileen, and Premilla Nadasen. 2008. "Domestic Workers Organize!" *WorkingUSA* 11(4): 413–37.

Bosniak, Linda. 2006. *The Citizen and the Alien: Dilemmas of Contemporary Membership.* Princeton, NJ: Princeton University Press.

Bottles, Scott L. 1987. *Los Angeles and the Automobile: The Making of the Modern City.* Berkeley: University of California Press.

Bourdieu, Pierre. 1977. *Outline of a Theory of Practice.* Cambridge: Cambridge University Press.

———. 1984. *Distinction: A Social Critique of the Judgement of Taste.* Cambridge, MA: Harvard University Press.

Brenner, Neil, Jamie Peck, and Nik Theodore. 2010. "Variegated Neoliberalization: Geographies, Modalities, Pathways." *Global Networks* 10(2): 182–222.

Brodkin, Karen. 1998. *How Jews Became White Folks and What That Says about Race in America.* New Brunswick, NJ: Rutgers University Press.

———. 2007. *Making Democracy Matter: Identity and Activism in Los Angeles.* New Brunswick, NJ: Rutgers University Press.

———. 2014. "Work, Race, and Economic Citizenship." *Current Anthropology* 55(S9): S116–S125.

Brooks, Jane E., and Christabel L. Rogalin. 2014. "Capturing Capital to Negotiate the Intersections of Motherhood and Work: Intersections of Motherhood and Work." *Sociology Compass* 8(6): 660–70.

Brown, Michael K., Martin Carnoy, Elliott Currie, Troy Duster, David B. Oppenheimer, Marjorie M. Schultz, and David Wellman. 2003. *Whitewashing Race: The Myth of a Color-Blind Society.* Berkeley: University of California Press.

Brown, Tamara Mose. 2011. *Raising Brooklyn Nannies: Childcare, and Caribbeans Creating Community.* New York: New York University Press.

Budgeon, Shelley. 2011. *Third Wave Feminism and the Politics of Gender in Late Modernity.* New York: Palgrave Macmillan.

Budig, Michelle J., and Paula England. 2001. "The Wage Penalty for Motherhood." *American Sociological Review* 66(2): 204–25.

Budig, Michelle J., and M. J. Hodges. 2010. "Differences in Disadvantage: Variation in the Motherhood Penalty across White Women's Earnings Distribution." *American Sociological Review* 75(5): 705–28.

Burnham, Linda, and Nik Theodore. 2012. "Home Economics: The Invisible and Unregulated World of Domestic Work." New York: National Domestic Workers Alliance. http://www.domesticworkers.org/homeeconomics/.

Caldwell, Kia Lilly, Renya K. Ramirez, Kathleen Coll, Tracy Fisher, and Lok Siu, eds. 2009. *Gendered Citizenships.* New York: Palgrave Macmillan.

Casanova, Erynn Masi de. 2013. "Embodied Inequality: The Experience of Domestic Work in Urban Ecuador." *Gender and Society* 27(4): 561–85.

Casey, Edward. 1996. "How to Get from Space to Place in a Fairly Short Stretch of Time." In *Senses of Place*, edited by Steven Feld and Keith H. Basso, 13–52. School of American Research Advanced Seminar Series. Santa Fe, NM: School of American Research Press.

———. 2001. "Between Geography and Philosophy: What Does It Mean to Be in the Place-World?" *Annals of the Association of American Geographers* 91(4): 683–93.

Castillo, Richard Griswold del. 1979. *The Los Angeles Barrio, 1850–1890: A Social History*. Berkeley: University of California Press.

Chaney, Elsa, and Mary Garcia Castro, eds. 1989. *Muchachas No More: Household Workers in Latin America and the Caribbean*. Philadelphia: Temple University Press.

Chang, Grace. 2000. *Disposable Domestics: Immigrant Women Workers in the Global Economy*. Cambridge, MA: South End.

Chavez, Leo R. 1992. *Shadowed Lives: Undocumented Immigrants in American Society*. Ft. Worth, TX: Harcourt, Brace, and Jovanovich.

———. 2008. *The Latino Threat: Constructing Immigrants, Citizens, and the Nation*. Stanford, CA: Stanford University Press.

Cheever, Susan. 2002. "The Nanny Dilemma." In *Global Woman: Nannies, Maids, and Sex Workers in the New Economy*, edited by Barbara Ehrenreich and Arlie Russell Hochschild, 31–38. New York: Metropolitan Books.

Childress, Alice. 1986. *Like One of the Family: Conversations from a Domestic's Life*. Boston: Beacon.

Clark, Clifford Edward. 1986. *The American Family Home, 1800–1960*. Chapel Hill: University of North Carolina Press.

Cobble, Dorothy Sue, Linda Gordon, and Astrid Henry. 2014. *Feminism Unfinished: A Short, Surprising History of American Women's Movements*. New York: Liveright.

Cohn, D'vera, Gretchen Livingston, and Wendy Wang. 2014. "After Decades of Decline, a Rise in Stay-at-Home Mothers." Social and Demographic Trends Project. Washington, DC: Pew Research Center.

Colen, Shellee. 1995. " 'Like a Mother to Them': Stratified Reproduction and West Indian Childcare Workers and Employers in New York." In *Conceiving the New World Order: The Global Politics of Reproduction*, edited by Faye D. Ginsburg and Rayna Rapp, 78–102. Berkeley: University of California Press.

Coll, Kathleen M. 2010. *Remaking Citizenship: Latina Immigrants and New American Politics*. Stanford, CA: Stanford University Press.

Collier, Stephen J. 2012. "Neoliberalism as Big Leviathan, or . . . ? A Response to Wacquant and Hilgers: Neoliberalism as Big Leviathan, or . . . ?" *Social Anthropology* 20(2): 186–95.

Collins, Patricia Hill. 1998. "It's All in the Family: Intersections of Gender, Race, and Nation." *Hypatia* 13(3): 62–82.

Constable, Nicole. 1997. *Maid to Order in Hong Kong: Stories of Filipina Workers*. Ithaca, NY: Cornell University Press.

Coquery-Vidrovitch, Catherine. 2000. "Is L.A. a Model or a Mess?" *American Historical Review* 105(5): 1683–91.

Corcoran, Mary P. 1993. *Irish Illegals: Transients between Two Societies*. Westport, CT: Praeger.

Correll, Shelley J., Stephen Benard, and In Paik. 2007. "Getting a Job: Is There a Motherhood Penalty?" *American Journal of Sociology* 112(5): 1297–1339.

Coutin, Susan Bibler. 1993. *The Culture of Protest: Religious Activism and the U.S. Sanctuary Movement*. Boulder, CO: Westview.

———. 2000. *Legalizing Moves: Salvadoran Immigrants' Struggle for U.S. Residency*. Ann Arbor: University of Michigan Press.

———. 2013. "In the Breach: Citizenship and Its Approximations." *Indiana Journal of Global Legal Studies* 20(1): 109–40.

Crenshaw, Kimberlé. 1991. "Mapping the Margins: Intersectionality, Identity Politics, and Violence against Women of Color." *Stanford Law Review* 43(6): 1241–99.

Crittenden, Ann. 2001. *The Price of Motherhood: Why the Most Important Job in the World Is Still the Least Valued*. New York: Metropolitan Books.

Csordas, Thomas J., ed. 1994. "Introduction." In *Embodiment and Experience: The Existential Ground of Culture and Self*, edited by Csordas, 1–23. Cambridge: Cambridge University Press.

Cuff, Dana. 2000. *The Provisional City: Los Angeles Stories of Architecture and Urbanism*. Cambridge, MA: MIT Press.

Cummings, Scott L. 2011. "Litigation at Work: Defending Day Labor in Los Angeles." *UCLA Law Review* 28: 1617–1703.

Curry, James, and Martin Kenney. 1999. "The Paradigmatic City: Postindustrial Illusion and the Los Angeles School." *Antipode* 31(1): 1–28.

Daniels, Roger. 2004. *Guarding the Golden Door: American Immigration Policy and Immigrants since 1882*. New York: Hill and Wang.

Davis, Mike. 1990. *City of Quartz: Excavating the Future in Los Angeles*. New York: Vintage.

Dear, Michael. 2002. "Los Angeles and the Chicago School: Invitation to a Debate." *City and Community* 1(1): 5–32.

Dear, Michael, and Nicholas Dahmann. 2008. "Urban Politics and the Los Angeles School of Urbanism." *Urban Affairs Review* 44(2): 266–79.

Deener, Andrew. 2012. *Venice: A Contested Bohemia in Los Angeles*. Chicago: University of Chicago Press.

De Genova, Nicholas. 2002. "Migrant 'Illegality' and Deportability in Everyday Life." *Annual Review of Anthropology* 31(1): 419–47.

———. 2005. *Working the Boundaries: Race, Space, and "Illegality" in Mexican Chicago*. Durham, NC: Duke University Press.

———. 2013. "Spectacles of Migrant 'Illegality': The Scene of Exclusion, the Obscene of Inclusion." *Ethnic and Racial Studies* 36(7): 1180–98.

De Genova, Nicholas, and Nathalie Mae Peutz, eds. 2010. *The Deportation Regime: Sovereignty, Space, and the Freedom of Movement.* Durham, NC: Duke University Press.

Deverell, William. 2005. *Whitewashed Adobe: The Rise of Los Angeles and the Remaking of Its Mexican Past.* Berkeley: University of California Press.

Deverell, William, and Greg Hise. 2010. *A Companion to Los Angeles.* Malden, MA: John Wiley.

Devine, Fiona. 2004. *Class Practices: How Parents Help Their Children Get Good Jobs.* Cambridge: Cambridge University Press.

———. 2005. "Middle Class Identities in the US." In *Rethinking Class: Cultures, Identities, and Lifestyles,* edited by Fiona Devine, Mike Savage, and Rosemary Crompton, 140–62. New York: Palgrave.

Dicker, Rory C. 2016. *A History of U.S. Feminisms.* Berkeley, CA: Seal Press.

Dill, Bonnie Thornton. 1994. *Across the Boundaries of Race and Class: An Exploration of Work and Family among Black Female Domestic Servants.* New York: Garland.

Doane, Ashley W., and Eduardo Bonilla-Silva, eds. 2003. *White Out: The Continuing Significance of Racism.* New York: Routledge.

Douglas, Mary, and Baron Isherwood. 1979. *The World of Goods.* New York: Basic Books.

Dreby, Joanna. 2010. *Divided by Borders: Mexican Migrants and Their Children.* Berkeley: University of California Press.

Ehrenreich, Barbara. 1989. *Fear of Falling: The Inner Life of the Middle Class.* New York: Perennial.

Ehrenreich, Barbara, and John Ehrenreich. 1979. "The Professional-Managerial Class." In *Between Labor and Capital,* edited by Pat Walker, 5–48. Boston: South End.

Ehrenreich, Barbara, and Arlie Russell Hochschild, eds. 2004. *Global Woman: Nannies, Maid and Sex Workers in the New Economy.* New York: Henry Holt.

Elvir, Miriam. 1997. "The Work at Home Is Not Recognized: Organizing Domestic Workers in Montreal." In *Not One of the Family: Foreign Domestic Workers in Canada,* edited by Abigail Bakan and Daiva Stasiulis, 147–56. Toronto: University of Toronto Press.

Emerson, Ralph Waldo. 1862. "American Civilization." *Atlantic Monthly* (April).

Erie, Steven P., and Scott A. Mackenzie. 2009. "The L.A. School and Politics: Bringing the Local State Back In." *Journal of Urban Affairs* 31(5): 537–57.

Esbenshade, Jill. 2000. "The 'Crisis' over Day Labor." *Working USA* 3(6): 27–70.

Ferguson, James. 2010. "The Uses of Neoliberalism." *Antipode* 41 (January): 166–84.

Fernández Kelly, M. Patricia. 1990. "Delicate Transactions: Gender, Home, and Employment among Hispanic Women." In *Uncertain Terms: Negotiating Gender in American Culture,* edited by Faye Ginsburg and Anna Lowenhaupt Tsing, 183–95. Boston: Beacon.

Fischer, Charles. 2010. *Made in America: A Social History of American Culture and Character.* Chicago: University of Chicago Press.

Flores, William, and Rina Benmayor. 1997. "Constructing Cultural Citizenship." In *Latino Cultural Citizenship: Claiming Identity, Space, and Rights,* edited by William Flores and Rina Benmayor, 1–23. Boston: Beacon.

Fogelson, Robert M. 1967. *The Fragmented Metropolis: Los Angeles, 1850–1930.* Cambridge, MA: Harvard University Press.

Folbre, Nancy. 2001. *The Invisible Heart: Economics and Family Values.* New York: New Press.

———, ed. 2012. *For Love and Money: Care Provision in the United States.* New York: Russell Sage Foundation.

Foucault, Michel. 1977. *Discipline and Punish: The Birth of the Prison.* London: Allen Lane.

Frankenberg, Ruth. 2001. "The Mirage of an Unmarked Whiteness." In *The Making and Unmaking of Whiteness,* edited by Birgit Brander Rasmussen, Irene J. Nexica, Eric Klinenberg, and Matt Wray, 72–96. Durham, NC: Duke University Press.

Franklin, Benjamin. 1970. "Observations concerning the Increase of Mankind, Peopling of Countries, Etc." *Perspectives in Biology and Medicine* 13(4): 469–75. (Originally published 1751.)

Fulton, William B. 1997. *The Reluctant Metropolis: The Politics of Urban Growth in Los Angeles.* Point Arena, CA: Solano.

Galindo, René. 2012. "Undocumented and Unafraid: The DREAM Act 5 and the Public Disclosure of Undocumented Status as a Political Act." *Urban Review* 44(5): 589–611.

Gálvez, Alyshia. 2009. *Guadalupe in New York: Devotion and the Struggle for Citizenship Rights among Mexican Immigrants.* New York: New York University Press.

———. 2013. "Immigrant Citizenship: Neoliberalism, Immobility and the Vernacular Meanings of Citizenship." *Identities* 20(6): 720–37.

Gamburd, Michele R. 2000. *The Kitchen Spoon's Handle: Transnationalism and Sri Lanka's Migrant Housemaids.* Ithaca, NY: Cornell University Press.

———. 2008. "Milk Teeth and Jet Planes: Kin Relations in Families of Sri Lanka's Transnational Domestic Servants." *City and Society* 20(1): 5–31.

Ganti, Tejaswini. 2014. "Neoliberalism." *Annual Review of Anthropology* 43(1): 89–104.

Gerson, Kathleen. 2010. *The Unfinished Revolution: Coming of Age in a New Era of Gender, Work, and Family.* New York: Oxford University Press.

Gibson-Graham, J. K. 1996. *The End of Capitalism (as We Knew It): A Feminist Critique of Political Economy.* Cambridge, MA: Blackwell.

———. 2006. *A Postcapitalist Politics.* Minneapolis: University of Minnesota Press.

Gill, Lesley. 1994. *Precarious Dependencies: Gender, Class, and Domestic Service in Bolivia.* New York: Columbia University Press.

Gillis, S., G. Howie, and R. Munford, eds. 2007. *Third Wave Feminism: A Critical Exploration,* 2nd ed. New York: Palgrave Macmillan.

Ginsburg, Faye. 1989. *Contested Lives: The Abortion Debate in an American Community*. Berkeley: University of California Press.

———. 1995. "The Parallax Effect: The Impact of Aboriginal Media on Ethnographic Film." *Visual Anthropology Review* 11(2): 64–76.

Ginsburg, Faye, and Rayna Rapp. 1995. "Introduction: Conceiving the New World Order." In *Conceiving the New World Order: The Global Politics of Reproduction*, edited by Faye Ginsburg and Rayna Rapp, 1–17. Berkeley: University of California Press.

Glenn, Evelyn Nakano. 1992. "From Servitude to Service Work: Historical Continuities in the Racial Division of Paid Reproductive Labor." *Signs: Journal of Women in Culture and Society* 18(1): 1–43.

Goldberg, Harmony. 2015. "Domestic Worker Organizing in the United States: Reports from the Field." *International Labor and Working-Class History* 88: 150–55.

Goldsmith, Pat Rubio, Mary Romero, Raquel Rubio-Goldsmith, Manuel Escobado, and Laura Khoury. 2009. "Ethno-Racial Profiling and State Violence in a Southwest Barrio." *Aztlan* 34(1): 93–123.

Goldstein, Daniel M. 2012. "Decolonialising 'Actually Existing Neoliberalism.'" *Social Anthropology* 20(3): 304–9.

Gonzales, Roberto G., and Leo R. Chavez. 2012. "'Awakening to a Nightmare': Abjectivity and Illegality in the Lives of Undocumented 1.5-Generation Latino Immigrants in the United States." *Current Anthropology* 53(3): 255–81.

González-López, Gloria. 2005. *Erotic Journeys: Mexican Immigrants and Their Sex Lives*. Berkeley: University of California Press.

Gordon, Jennifer, and R. A. Lenhardt. 2007. "Citizenship Talk: Bridging the Gap between Immigration and Race Perspectives." *Fordham Law Review* 75(5): 2493–2520.

Gottdiener, Mark. 2002. "Urban Analysis as Merchandising: The 'LA School' and the Understanding of Metropolitan Development." In *Understanding the City: Contemporary and Future Perspectives*, edited by John Eade and Christopher Mele, 159–81. Malden, MA: Blackwell.

Gough, Margaret, and Mary Noonan. 2013. "A Review of the Motherhood Wage Penalty in the United States: Motherhood Wage Penalty." *Sociology Compass* 7(4): 328–42.

Greenhouse, Carol. 2009. "Introduction." In *Ethnographies of Neoliberalism*, edited by Carol Greenhouse, 1–10. Philadelphia: University of Pennsylvania Press.

Guevarra, Anna Romina. 2010. *Marketing Dreams, Manufacturing Heroes: The Transnational Labor Brokering of Filipino Workers*. New Brunswick, NJ: Rutgers University Press.

Gupta, Monisha Das. 2008. "Housework, Feminism, and Labor Activism: Lessons from Domestic Workers in New York." *Signs: Journal of Women in Culture and Society* 33(3): 532–37.

Gutiérrez, David. 1995. *Walls and Mirrors: Mexican Americans, Mexican Immigrants, and the Politics of Ethnicity*. Berkeley: University of California Press.

Hagan, Jacqueline. 1994. *Deciding to Be Legal: A Maya Community in Houston*. Philadelphia: Temple University Press.

———. 1998. "Social Networks, Gender, and Immigrant Settlement: Resource and Constraint." *American Sociological Review* 63(1): 55–67.

Hagan, Jacqueline Maria, Nestor Rodriguez, and Brianna Castro. 2011. "Social Effects of Mass Deportations by the United States Government, 2000–10." *Ethnic and Racial Studies* 34(8): 1374–91.

Hage, Ghassan. 2003. *Against Paranoid Nationalism: Searching for Hope in a Shrinking Society*. Annandale, Vic.: Pluto Press Australia.

Halberstam, Judith. 2011. *The Queer Art of Failure*. Durham, NC: Duke University Press.

Hall, Stuart, and David Held. 1989. "Citizens and Citizenship." In *New Times: The Changing Face of Politics in the 1990s*, edited by Stuart Hall and Martin Jacque, 173–88. New York: Verso.

Halle, David. 1984. *America's Working Man: Work, Home, and Politics among Blue-Collar Property Owners*. Chicago: University of Chicago Press.

Haney-López, Ian. 2006. *White by Law: The Legal Construction of Race*. New York: New York University Press.

Harris, Dianne. 2013. *Little White Houses: How the Postwar Home Constructed Race in America*. Minneapolis: University of Minnesota Press.

Hartigan, John. 1999. *Racial Situations: Class Predicaments of Whiteness in Detroit*. Princeton, NJ: Princeton University Press.

Harvey, David. 2011. *A Brief History of Neoliberalism*. Reprint ed. Oxford: Oxford University Press.

Hayden, Dolores. 1995. *The Power of Place: Urban Landscapes as Public History*. Cambridge, MA: MIT Press.

Hayes-Bautista, David E. 2004. *La Nueva California: Latinos in the Golden State*. Berkeley: University of California Press.

Hébert, Karen. 2015. "Enduring Capitalism: Instability, Precariousness, and Cycles of Change in an Alaskan Salmon Fishery: Enduring Capitalism." *American Anthropologist* 117(1): 32–46.

Herd, P., and Madonna Harrington. 2002. "Care Work: Invisible Civic Engagement." *Gender and Society* 16(5): 665–88.

Heywood, Leslie L. 2006a. *The Women's Movement Today: An Encyclopedia of Third-Wave Feminism*, vol. 1: A–Z. Westport, CT: Greenwood.

———. 2006b. *The Women's Movement Today: An Encyclopedia of Third-Wave Feminism*, vol. 2: *Primary Documents*. Westport, CT: Greenwood.

Hilgers, Mathieu. 2012. "The Historicity of the Neoliberal State." *Social Anthropology* 20(1): 80–94.

———. 2013. "Embodying Neoliberalism: Thoughts and Responses to Critics: EMBODYING NEOLIBERALISM." *Social Anthropology* 21(1): 75–89.

Himpele, Jeff. 2002. "Arrival Scenes: Complicity and Media Ethnography in the Bolivian Public Sphere." In *Media Worlds: Anthropology on New Terrain*, edited by Faye Ginsburg, Lila Abu-Lughod, and Brian Larkin, 301–16. Berkeley: University of California Press.

Hirsch, Jennifer S. 2003. *A Courtship after Marriage: Sexuality and Love in Mexican Transnational Families*. Berkeley: University of California Press.

Hise, Greg. 2004. "Border City: Race and Social Distance in Los Angeles." *American Quarterly* 56(3): 545–58.

Ho, Elaine Lynn-Ee. 2009. "Constituting Citizenship through the Emotions: Singaporean Transmigrants in London." *Annals of the Association of American Geographers* 99(4): 788–804.

Ho, Karen Zouwen. 2009. *Liquidated: An Ethnography of Wall Street*. Durham, NC: Duke University Press.

Hochschild, Arlie Russell, and Anne Machung. 1989. *The Second Shift: Working Parents and the Revolution at Home*. New York: Viking.

Hoey, Brian. 2014. *Opting for Elsewhere: Lifestyle Migration in the American Middle Class*. Nashville: Vanderbilt University Press.

Hondagneu-Sotelo, Pierrette. 1994. *Gendered Transitions: Mexican Experiences of Immigration*. Berkeley: University of California Press.

———. 2001. *Doméstica: Immigrant Workers Cleaning and Caring in the Shadows of Affluence*. Berkeley: University of California Press.

———. 2003. "Gender and Immigration: A Retrospective Introduction." In *Gender and U.S. Immigration: Contemporary Trends*, edited by Pierrette Hondagneu-Sotelo. Berkeley: University of California Press.

Hondagneu-Sotelo, Pierrette, and E. Avila. 1997. "'I'm Here, but I'm There': The Meanings of Latina Transnational Motherhood." *Gender and Society* 11(5): 548–71.

Hondagneu-Sotelo, Pierrette, and Cristina Riegos. 1997. "Sin Organización, No Hay Solución: Latina Domestic Workers and Non-Traditional Labor Organizing." *Latino Studies Journal* 8(3): 54–81.

Hornstein, Jeffrey M. 2005. *A Nation of Realtors: A Cultural History of the Twentieth-Century American Middle Class*. Durham, NC: Duke University Press.

Huntington, Samuel. 2004. "The Hispanic Challenge." *Foreign Policy* 141(March/April): 30–45.

Hurtado, Aida. 1999. "Cross-Border Existence: One Woman's Migration." In *Women's Untold Stories: Breaking Silence, Talking Back, Voicing Complexity*, edited by Mary Romero and Abigail J. Stewart, 83–101. New York: Routledge.

Ignatiev, Noel. 1995. *How the Irish Became White*. New York: Routledge.

Ismail, Munira. 1999. "Maids in Space: Gendered Domestic Labour from Sri Lanka in the Middle East." In *Gender, Migration, and Domestic Service*, edited by Janet Henshall Momsen, 223–35. London: Routledge.

Jacobson, Matthew Frye. 1999. *Whiteness of a Different Color: European Immigrants and the Alchemy of Race*. Cambridge, MA: Harvard University Press.

Jessop, Bob. 2013. "Putting Neoliberalism in Its Time and Place: A Response to the Debate." *Social Anthropology* 21(1): 65–74.

Johnson, Kevin R. 2009. "The Intersection of Race and Class in U.S. Immigration Law and Enforcement." *Law and Contemporary Problems* 72(4): 1–35.

Kang, Miliann. 2010. *The Managed Hand: Race, Gender, and the Body in Beauty Service Work*. Berkeley: University of California Press.

Kaplan, Amy. 1998. "Manifest Domesticity." *American Literature* 70(3): 581–606.

Katzman, David M. 1979. *Seven Days a Week: Women and Domestic Service in Industrializing America*. New York: Oxford University Press.

Kefalas, Maria. 2003. *Working-Class Heroes: Protecting Home, Community, and Nation in a Chicago Neighborhood*. Berkeley: University of California Press.

Keil, Roger. 1998. *Los Angeles, Globalization, Urbanization, and Social Struggles*. New York: John Wiley.

Kessler-Harris, Alice. 2001. *In Pursuit of Equity: Women, Men, and the Quest for Economic Citizenship in 20th-Century America*. Oxford: Oxford University Press.

Kingfisher, Catherine, and Jeff Maskovsky. 2008. "Introduction: The Limits of Neoliberalism." *Critique of Anthropology* 28(2): 115–26.

Kipnis, Andrew B. 2008. "Audit Cultures: Neoliberal Governmentality, Socialist Legacy, or Technologies of Governing?" *American Ethnologist* 35(2): 275–89.

Knadler, Stephen P. 2002. *The Fugitive Race: Minority Writers Resisting Whiteness*. Jackson: University Press of Mississippi.

Lamont, Michèle. 1992. *Money, Morals, and Manners: The Culture of the French and American Upper-Middle Class*. Chicago: University of Chicago Press.

———. 2000. *The Dignity of Working Men: Morality and the Boundaries of Race, Class, and Immigration*. Cambridge, MA: Harvard University Press.

Lan, Pei-Chia. 2006. *Global Cinderellas: Migrant Domestics and Newly Rich Employers in Taiwan*. Durham, NC: Duke University Press Books.

Landsman, Gail H. 2009. *Reconstructing Motherhood and Disability in the Age of "Perfect" Babies*. New York: Routledge.

Lave, Jean. 1991. "Situating Learning in Communities of Practice." In *Perspectives on Socially Shared Cognition*, edited by L. Resnick, 63–82. Washington, DC: American Psychological Association.

Lefebvre, Henri. 1991. *The Production of Space*. Oxford: Blackwell.

Liechty, Mark. 2003. *Suitably Modern: Making Middle-Class Culture in a New Consumer Society*. Princeton, NJ: Princeton University Press.

Lipsitz, George. 1998. *The Possessive Investment in Whiteness: How White People Profit from Identity Politics*. Rev. and expanded ed. Philadelphia: Temple University Press.

Lister, Ruth. 2007. "Inclusive Citizenship: Realizing the Potential." *Citizenship Studies* 11(1): 49–61.

Liu, Eric, ed. 1994. *Next: Young American Writers on the New Generation*. New York: W. W. Norton.

Low, Setha M. 2000. *On the Plaza: The Politics of Public Space and Culture.* Austin: University of Texas Press.

———. 2008. "Incorporation and Gated Communities in the Greater Metro-Los Angeles Region as a Model of Privatization of Residential Communities." *Home Cultures* 5(1): 85–108.

Lowe, Lisa. 1996. *Immigrant Acts: On Asian American Cultural Politics.* Durham, NC: Duke University Press.

Lutz, Helma, ed. 2008. *Migration and Domestic Work: A European Perspective on a Global Theme.* London: Ashgate.

Luz Ibarra, María de la. 2000. "Mexican Immigrant Women and the New Domestic Labor." *Human Organization* 59(4): 452–64.

Lynch, Kevin. 1960. *The Image of the City.* Cambridge, MA: MIT Press.

Macdonald, Cameron Lynne. 2011. *Shadow Mothers: Nannies, Au Pairs, and the Micropolitics of Mothering.* Berkeley: University of California Press.

Mahler, Sarah J. 1995. *American Dreaming: Immigrant Life on the Margins.* Princeton, NJ: Princeton University Press.

Massey, Doreen B. 2002. "Don't Let's Counterpose Place and Space." *Development* 45(1): 24–25.

Mattingly, Doreen J. 1999. "Job Search, Social Networks, and Local Labor Market Dynamics: The Case of Paid Household Work in San Diego, California." *Urban Geography* 20(1): 46–74.

Mauss, Marcel. 1973. "Techniques of the Body." *Economy and Society* 2(1): 70–88.

McCaffery, Edward J. 1997. *Taxing Women.* Chicago: University of Chicago Press.

McClintock, Anne. 1995. *Imperial Leather: Race, Gender, and Sexuality in the Colonial Contest.* New York: Routledge.

Menchaca, Martha. 1993. "Chicano Indianism: A Historical Account of Racial Repression in the United States." *American Ethnologist* 20(3): 583–603.

Menjívar, Cecilia. 2003. "The Intersection of Work and Gender: Central American Immigrant Women and Employment in California." In *Gender and U.S. Immigration: Contemporary Trends,* edited by Pierrette Hondagneu-Sotelo, 101–26. Berkeley: University of California Press.

———. 2011. "The Power of the Law: Central Americans' Legality and Everyday Life in Phoenix, Arizona." *Latino Studies* 9(4): 377–95.

———. 2014. "The 'Poli-Migra': Multilayered Legislation, Enforcement Practices, and Can We Learn about and from Today's Approaches." *American Behavioral Scientist* 58(13): 1805–19.

Menjívar, Cecilia, and Leisy J. Abrego. 2012. "Legal Violence: Immigration Law and the Lives of Central American Immigrants." *American Journal of Sociology* 117(5): 1380–1421.

Miller, Claire Cain. 2015. "More Than Their Mothers, Young Women Plan Career Pauses." *New York Times,* July 22. www.nytimes.com/2015/07/23/upshot/more -than-their-mothers-young-women-plan-career-pauses.html.

Mirowski, Philip. 2009. "Postface: Defining Neoliberalism." In *The Road from Mont Pelerin: The Making of the Neoliberal Thought Collective*, edited by Philip Mirowski and Dieter Plehwe, 417–50. Cambridge, MA: Harvard University Press.

Mirzoeff, Nicholas. 2009. *An Introduction to Visual Culture*. New York: Routledge.

Miyazaki, Hirokazu. 2004. *The Method of Hope: Anthropology, Philosophy, and Fijian Knowledge*. Stanford, CA: Stanford University Press.

Molina, Natalia. 2006. *Fit to Be Citizens? Public Health and Race in Los Angeles, 1879–1939*. Berkeley: University of California Press.

Momsen, Janet Henshall, ed. 1999. *Gender, Migration, and Domestic Service*. London: Routledge.

Monahan, Torin. 2002. "Los Angeles Studies: The Emergence of a Specialty Field." *City and Society* 14(2): 155–84.

Muehlebach, Andrea. 2011. "On Affective Labor in Post Fordist Italy." *Cultural Anthropology* 26(1): 59–82.

———. 2013. "On Precariousness and the Ethical Imagination: The Year 2012 in Sociocultural Anthropology: Year in Review: Sociocultural Anthropology." *American Anthropologist* 115(2): 297–311.

Murray, Sara. 2014. "Matt Lauer Explains the GM Mom Question." *WSJ Blogs—At Work*, June 27. http://blogs.wsj.com/atwork/2014/06/27/matt-lauer-gm-ceo -mary-barra-mom-question/.

Myerhoff, Barbara G. 1978. *Number Our Days*. New York: Simon and Schuster.

Nadasen, Premilla. 2015. *Household Workers Unite: The Untold Story of African American Women Who Built a Movement*. Boston: Beacon.

Nader, Laura. 1972. "Up the Anthropologist: Perspectives Gained from Studying Up." In *Reinventing Anthropology*, edited by Dell Hymes, 284–311. New York: Pantheon.

Nelson, Margaret K. 2010. *Parenting Out of Control: Anxious Parents in Uncertain Times*. New York: New York University Press.

Newman, Katherine S. 1988. *Falling from Grace: Downward Mobility in the Age of Affluence*. Berkeley: University of California Press.

Ngai, Mae M. 2004. *Impossible Subjects: Illegal Aliens and the Making of Modern America*. Princeton, NJ: Princeton University Press.

Nicholls, Walter J. 2011. "The Los Angeles School: Difference, Politics, City: The Los Angeles School: Difference, Politics, City." *International Journal of Urban and Regional Research* 35(1): 189–206.

Ochs, Elinor, and Tamar Kremer-Sadlik, eds. 2013. *Fast-Forward Family: Home, Work, and Relationships in Middle-Class America*. Berkeley: University of California Press.

Ochs, Elinor, and Bambi Schieffelin. 1984. "Language Acquisition and Socialization: Three Developmental Stories and Their Implications." In *Cultural Theory: Essays on Mind, Self, and Emotion*, edited by R. Schweder and R. Levin, 276–320. Cambridge: Cambridge University Press.

Olivares, Mariela. 2013. "Renewing the Dream: Dream Act Redux and Immigration Reform." *Harvard Latino Law Review* 16: 79–125.

Ong, Aihwa. 1996. "Cultural Citizenship as Subject-Making: Immigrants Negotiate Racial and Cultural Boundaries in the United States [and Comments and Reply]." *Current Anthropology* 37(5): 737–62.

———. 2003. *Buddha Is Hiding: Refugees, Citizenship, the New America.* Berkeley: University of California Press.

———. 2006. *Neoliberalism as Exception: Mutations in Citizenship and Sovereignty.* Durham, NC: Duke University Press.

Orleans, Peter. 1967. "Urban Experimentation and Urban Sociology." In *Science, Engineering, and the City: A Symposium Sponsored by the National Academy of Sciences and National Academy of Engineering*, 103–17. Washington, DC: National Academy of Sciences.

Ortner, Sherry B. 1991. "Reading America: Preliminary Notes on Class and Culture." In *Recapturing Anthropology*, edited by Richard Fox. Santa Fe, NM: SAR Press.

———. 1998a. "Generation X: Anthropology in a Media-Saturated World." *Cultural Anthropology* 13(3): 414–40.

———. 1998b. "Identities: The Hidden Life of Class." *Journal of Anthropological Research* 54(1): 1–17.

———. 2003. *New Jersey Dreaming: Capital, Culture, and the Class of '58.* Durham, NC: Duke University Press.

———. 2010. "Access: Reflections on Studying Up in Hollywood." *Ethnography* 11(2): 211–33.

———. 2013. *Not Hollywood: Independent Film at the Twilight of the American Dream.* Durham, NC: Duke University Press.

Pallares, Amalia. 2014. *Family Activism: Immigrant Struggles and the Politics of Noncitizenship.* Latinidad: Transnational Cultures in the United States. New Brunswick, NJ: Rutgers University Press.

Palmer, Phyllis M. 1989. *Domesticity and Dirt: Housewives and Domestic Servants in the United States, 1920–1945.* Philadelphia: Temple University Press.

Parreñas, Rhacel Salazar. 2001. *Servants of Globalization: Women, Migration and Domestic Work.* Stanford, CA: Stanford University Press.

Pateman, Carole. 1989. *The Disorder of Women: Democracy, Feminism and Political Theory.* Cambridge: Polity.

Pazderic, Nickola. 2004. "Recovering True Selves in the Electro-Spiritual Field of Universal Love." *Cultural Anthropology* 19(2): 196–225.

Peck, Jamie, and Nik Theodore. 2012. "Reanimating Neoliberalism: Process Geographies of Neoliberalisation." *Social Anthropology* 20(2): 177–85.

Peterson, Karen. 2003. "Gen X Moms Have It Their Way." *USA Today*, May 7.

Peterson, Marina. 2010. *Sound, Space, and the City: Civic Performance in Downtown Los Angeles.* Philadelphia: University of Pennsylvania Press.

Pew Research Center. 2013. "On Pay Gap, Millennial Women Near Parity—For Now." *Pew Research Center's Social and Demographic Trends Project*, December 11. www.pewsocialtrends.org/2013/12/11/on-pay-gap-millennial-women-near -parity-for-now/.

Poo, Ai-jen, Ana Cristina Mercado, Jill Shenker, Xiomara Corpeno, and Alison Julien. 2013. "National Domestic Workers Alliance." In *The United States Social Forum: Perspectives of a Movement*, edited by USSF Book Committee, 155–69. Chicago: Changemaker.

Porter, Eduardo. 2012. "Motherhood Still a Cause of Pay Inequality." *New York Times*, June 12. www.nytimes.com/2012/06/13/business/economy/motherhood-still -a-cause-of-pay-inequality.html.

Povinelli, Elizabeth A. 2011. *Economies of Abandonment: Social Belonging and Endurance in Late Liberalism*. Durham, NC: Duke University Press.

Prates, Suzana. 1989. "Organizations for Low-Income Women in Montevideo: Reenforcing Marginality?" In *Muchachas No More: Household Workers in Latin America and the Caribbean*, edited by Elsa Chaney and Mary Garcia Castro, 271–90. Philadelphia: Temple University Press.

Pratt, Geraldine. 1999. "Is This Canada? Domestic Workers' Experiences in Vancouver, BC." In *Gender, Migration, and Domestic Service*, edited by Janet Henshall Momsen, 23–42. London: Routledge.

Preston, Julia. 2013. "Illegal Immigrants Are Divided over Importance of Citizenship." *New York Times*, November 20.

Ramirez, Renya K. 2007. *Native Hubs: Culture, Community, and Belonging in Silicon Valley and Beyond*. Durham, NC: Duke University Press.

Ramos-Zayas, Ana Y. 2012. *Street Therapists: Race, Affect, and Neoliberal Personhood in Latino Newark*. Chicago: University of Chicago Press.

Rancière, Jacques. 2006. *The Politics of Aesthetics: The Distribution of the Sensible*. New York: Continuum.

Rapp, Rayna. 1992. "Family and Class in Contemporary America: Notes toward an Understanding of Ideology." In *Rethinking the Family: Some Feminist Questions*, edited by Barrie Thorne and Marilyn Yalom, 49–70. Boston: Northeastern University Press.

Reger, Jo. 2012. *Everywhere and Nowhere: Contemporary Feminism in the United States*. New York: Oxford University Press.

———. 2014. "Debating US Contemporary Feminism." *Sociology Compass* 8(1): 43–51.

Regt, Marina de. 2009. "Preferences and Prejudices: Employers' Views on Domestic Workers in the Republic of Yemen." *Signs: Journal of Women in Culture and Society* 34(3): 559–81.

Repak, Terry. 1995. *Waiting on Washington: Central American Workers in the Nation's Capital*. Philadelphia: Temple University Press.

Reynolds, Maura, and Faye Fiore. 2006. "The Immigration Debate: Across the U.S., 'We Are America'; Immigrants and Their Supporters Call for Dignified

Treatment and, above All, Legalization. Some Recite the Pledge of Allegiance."
Los Angeles Times, April 11.

Rivers, Caryl, and Rosalind C. Barnett. 2000. "Wage Gap for Working Mothers May Cost Billions." *Women's Enews*, July 3. womensenews.org/2000/07/wage -Gap-Working-Mothers-May-Cost-Billions/.

Roediger, David. 1991. *The Wages of Whiteness: Race and the Making of the American Working Class*. New York: Verso.

Roitman, Janet L. 2014. *Anti-Crisis*. Durham, NC: Duke University Press.

Rollins, Judith. 1985. *Between Women: Domestics and Their Employers*. Philadelphia: Temple University Press.

Romero, M., V. Preston, and W. Giles. 2014. *When Care Work Goes Global: Locating the Social Relations of Domestic Work*. London: Ashgate.

Romero, Mary. 1992. *Maid in the U.S.A.* New York: Routledge.

———. 2008. "Crossing the Immigration and Race Border: A Critical Race Theory Approach to Immigration Studies." *Contemporary Justice Review* 11(1): 23–37.

———. 2011. *The Maid's Daughter: Living inside and outside the American Dream.* New York: New York University Press.

Rosaldo, Renato. 1994. "Cultural Citizenship in San Jose, California." *PoLAR: Political and Legal Anthropology Review* 17(2): 57–64.

Rosales, Grace A. 2001. "Labor behind the Front Door: Domestic Workers in Urban and Suburban Households." In *Asian and Latino Immigrants in a Restructuring Economy: The Metamorphosis of Southern California*, edited by Marta López-Garza, 169–87. Stanford, CA: Stanford University Press.

Rosales, Rocio. 2013. "Survival, Economic Mobility and Community among Los Angeles Fruit Vendors." *Journal of Ethnic and Migration Studies* 39(May): 697–717.

Rotenberg, Robert. 1993. "Introduction." In *The Cultural Meanings of Urban Space*, edited by Robert Rotenberg and Gary McDonogh, xi–xix. Westport, CT: Bergin and Garvey.

Rudd, Elizabeth, and Lara Descartes, eds. 2008. *The Changing Landscape of Work and Family in the American Middle Class: Reports from the Field*. Lanham, MD: Lexington Books.

Sanchez, George J. 1993. *Becoming Mexican American: Ethnicity, Culture, and Identity in Chicano Los Angeles, 1900–1945*. New York: Oxford University Press.

Sandler, Lauren. 2014. "How to Love Paid Family Leave." *Bloomberg Businessweek*, July 18.

Sanjek, Roger, and Shellee Colen, eds. 1990. *At Work in Homes: Household Workers in World Perspective*. Washington, DC: American Anthropological Association.

Sassen, Saskia. 2000. "Women's Burden: Counter-Geographies of Globalization and the Feminization of Survival." *Journal of International Affairs* 53(2): 503–24.

Scheiber, Noam. 2015. "U.S. Court Reinstates Home Care Pay Rules." *New York Times*, August 21. www.nytimes.com/2015/08/22/business/us-court-reinstates -home-care-pay-rules.html.

Schellekens, Thea, and Anja van der Schoot. 1989. "Household Workers in Perú: The Difficult Road to Organization." In *Muchachas No More: Household Workers in Latin America and the Caribbean*, edited by Elsa Chaney and Mary Garcia Castro, 291–306. Philadelphia: Temple University Press.

Schieffelin, Bambi B. 1990. *The Give and Take of Everyday Life: Language Socialization of Kaluli Children*. Cambridge: Cambridge University Press.

Schmitt, Eric. 2001. "Salvadorans Illegally in U.S. Are Given Protected Status." *New York Times*, March 3. www.nytimes.com/2001/03/03/us/salvadorans-illegally -in-us-are-given-protected-status.html.

Schultz, Vicki. 2000. "Life's Work." *Columbia Law Review* 100(7): 1881–1964.

Scott, Allen John, and Edward W. Soja. 1996. "Introduction to Los Angeles: City and Region." In *The City: Los Angeles and Urban Theory at the End of the Twentieth Century*, edited by Allen John Scott and Edward W. Soja, 1–21. Berkeley: University of California Press.

Sedgwick, Eve Kosofsky. 2003. *Touching Feeling: Affect, Pedagogy, Performativity*. Series Q. Durham, NC: Duke University Press.

Segura, Denise. 1998. "Working at Motherhood: Chicana and Mexican Immigrant Mothers and Employment." In *Families in the U.S.: Kinship and Domestic Politics*, edited by Karen V. Hansen and Anita Ilta Garey, 727–43. Women in the Political Economy. Philadelphia: Temple University Press.

Sennett, Richard, and Jonathan Cobb. 1973. *The Hidden Injuries of Class*. New York: Vintage.

Shah, Hina. 2015. "Notes from the Field: The Role of the Lawyer in Grassroots Policy Advocacy." NYU *Clinical Law Review* 21(2): 393–425.

Shah, Hina B., and Marci Seville. 2012. "Domestic Worker Organizing: Building a Contemporary Movement for Dignity and Power." *Albany Law Review* 75: 413–46.

Shearmur, Richard. 2008. "Chicago and L.A.: A Clash of Epistemologies." *Urban Geography* 29(2): 167–76.

Shugart, Helene A. 2001. "Isn't It Ironic? The Intersection of Third-Wave Feminism and Generation X." *Women's Studies in Communication* 24(2): 131–68.

Silvey, Rachel. 2004. "Transnational Domestication: State Power and Indonesian Migrant Women in Saudi Arabia." *Political Geography* 23(3): 245–64.

Smith, Robert C. 2005. *Mexican New York: Transnational Lives of New Immigrants*. Berkeley: University of California Press.

Snyder, R. Claire. 2008. "What Is Third-Wave Feminism? A New Directions Essay." *Signs: Journal of Women in Culture and Society* 34(1): 175–96.

Soja, Edward W. 1989. *Postmodern Geographies: The Reassertion of Space in Critical Social Theory*. London: Verso.

———. 1996. *Thirdspace: Journeys to Los Angeles and Other Real-and-Imagined Places*. Cambridge, MA: Blackwell.

Springer, Kimberly. 2002. "Third Wave Black Feminism?" *Signs: Journal of Women in Culture and Society* 27(4): 1059–82.

Stephenson, Marcia. 1999. *Gender and Modernity in Andean Bolivia*. Austin: University of Texas Press.

Stewart, Kathleen. 2012. "Precarity's Forms." *Cultural Anthropology* 27(3): 518–25.

Stiell, Bernadette, and Kim England. 1999. "Jamaican Domestics, Filipina Housekeepers, and English Nannies: Representations of Toronto's Foreign Domestic Workers." In *Gender, Migration, and Domestic Service*, edited by Janet Henshall Momsen, 43–61. London: Routledge.

Stoler, Ann. 1995. *Race and the Education of Desire: Foucault's History of Sexuality and the Colonial Order of Things*. Durham, NC: Duke University Press.

———. 2002. *Carnal Knowledge and Imperial Power: Race and the Intimate in Colonial Rule*. Berkeley: University of California Press.

Streeter, Kurt. 2003. "MTA Increases Most Fares, Cuts Some Bus Service." *Los Angeles Times*, May 2–3, sec. B.

Streeter, Kurt, Sharon Bernstein, and Caitlin Liu. 2003. "Mediation Plan Ends MTA Strike." *Los Angeles Times*, November 18, sec. A.

Streitfeld, David. 2003. "For Some, Strikes Are No Big Deal." *Los Angeles Times*, October 22, sec. A.

Stumpf, Juliet P. 2006. "The Crimmigration Crisis: Immigrants, Crime, and Sovereign Power." bepress Legal Series. Working Paper No. 1635, August 27. http://law.bepress.com/expresso/eps/1635.

Sullivan, Robert E. 2014. *Street Level: Los Angeles in the Twenty-First Century*. Burlington, VT: Ashgate.

Torre, Pedro de la, and Roy Germano. 2014. "Out of the Shadows: DREAMer Identity in the Immigrant Youth Movement." *Latino Studies* 12(3): 449–67.

Tucker, Susan. 1988. *Telling Memories among Southern Women: Domestic Workers and Their Employers in the Segregated South*. Baton Rouge: Louisiana University Press.

Turner, Terence. 1994. "Bodies and Anti-Bodies: Flesh and Fetish in Contemporary Social Theory." In *Embodiment and Experience: The Existential Ground of Culture and Self*, edited by Thomas J. Csordas, 27–47. Cambridge: Cambridge University Press.

Valadez Torres, Martin. 2005. "Indispensable Migrants: Mexican Workers and the Making of Twentieth-Century Los Angeles." In *Latino Los Angeles: Transformations, Communities, and Activism*, edited by Enrique Ochoa and Gilda L. Ochoa, 23–37. Tucson: University of Arizona Press.

Valentine, David. 2007. *Imagining Transgender: An Ethnography of a Category*. Durham, NC: Duke University Press.

Valle, Victor M., and Rodolfo D. Torres. 2000. *Latino Metropolis*. Minneapolis: University of Minnesota Press.

Van Raaphorst, Donna L. 1988. *Union Maids Not Wanted: Organizing Domestic Workers, 1870–1940*. New York: Praeger.

Velasco, Pura M. 1997. " 'We Can Still Fight Back': Organizing Domestic Workers in Toronto." In *Not One of the Family: Foreign Domestic Workers in Canada*, edited by Abigail B. Bakan and Daiva K. Stasiulis, 157–64. Toronto: University of Toronto Press.

Venable, Denise. 2002. "The Wage Gap Myth." Brief Analysis No. 392, National Center for Policy Analysis, April 12.

Vrana, Debora, and Gabrielle Banks. 2004. "New Parents Applaud Paid Family Leave Law." *Los Angeles Times*, June 30.

Wachs, Martin. 1996. "The Evolution of Transportation Policy in Los Angeles." In *The City: Los Angeles and Urban Theory at the End of the Twentieth Century*, edited by Allen John Scott and Edward W. Soja, 106–59. Berkeley: University of California Press.

Walkowitz, Daniel J. 1999. *Working with Class: Social Workers and the Politics of Middle-Class Identity*. Chapel Hill: University of North Carolina Press.

Walzer, Michael. 1983. *Spheres of Justice: A Defense of Pluralism and Equality*. Reprint ed. New York: Basic Books.

Warren, Jonathan W., and France Winddance Twine. 1997. "White Americans, the New Minority? Non-Blacks and the Ever-Expanding Boundaries of Whiteness." *Journal of Black Studies* 28(2): 200–218.

Webb, Cynthia. 2001. "US Workers Putting in Long Hours." *Washington Post*, September 4.

Weeks, Kathi. 2011. *The Problem with Work: Feminism, Marxism, Antiwork Politics, and Postwork Imaginaries*. Durham, NC: Duke University Press.

Weinstein, Richard. 1996. "The First American City." In *The City: Los Angeles and Urban Theory at the End of the Twentieth Century*, edited by Allen John Scott and Edward W. Soja, 22–46. Berkeley: University of California Press.

Werbner, Pnina, and Nira Yuval-Davis. 1999. *Women, Citizenship and Difference*. London: Zed.

Williams, Joan C. 2000. *Unbending Gender: Why Family and Work Conflict and What to Do about It*. Oxford: Oxford University Press.

Winarnita, Monika Swasti. 2008. "Motherhood as Cultural Citizenship: Indonesian Women in Transnational Families." *Asia Pacific Journal of Anthropology* 9(4): 304–18.

Yancey, George. 2003. *Who Is White? Latinos, Asians, and the New Black/Nonblack Divide*. Boulder, CO: Lynne Rienner.

Young, G. E. 1987. "The Myth of Being 'Like a Daughter.' " *Latin American Perspectives* 14(3): 365–80.

Young, Iris Marion. 1989. "Polity and Group Difference: A Critique of the Ideal of Universal Citizenship." *Ethics* 99(2): 250–74.

Yuval-Davis, Nira. 1997. "Women, Citizenship and Difference." *Feminist Review* 57(1): 4–27.

———. 2006. "Belonging and the Politics of Belonging." *Patterns of Prejudice* 40(3): 197–214.

———. 2007. "Intersectionality, Citizenship and Contemporary Politics of Belonging." *Critical Review of International Social and Political Philosophy* 10(4): 561–74.

Zavella, Patricia. 1991. "Mujeres in Factories: Race and Class Perspectives on Women, Work, and Family." In *Gender at the Crossroads of Knowledge: Feminist Anthropology in the Postmodern Era,* edited by Micaela Di Leonardo, 312–36. Berkeley: University of California Press.

———. 2011. *I'm Neither Here nor There: Mexicans' Quotidian Struggles with Migration and Poverty.* Durham, NC: Duke University Press.

Zelizer, Viviana. 1985. *Pricing the Priceless Child: The Changing Social Value of Children.* New York: Basic Books.

Zhou, Min. 2004. "Are Asian Americans Becoming 'White?' " *Contexts* 3(1): 29–37.

Zilberg, Elana. 2011. *Space of Detention: The Making of a Transnational Gang Crisis between Los Angeles and San Salvador.* Durham, NC: Duke University Press.

Zimmerman, Mary K., Jacquelyn S. Litt, and Christine E. Bose. 2006. *Global Dimensions of Gender and Carework.* Stanford, CA: Stanford University Press.

Zussman, Robert. 1985. *Mechanics of the Middle Class: Work and Politics among American Engineers.* Berkeley: University of California Press.

INDEX

California Domestic Workers Coalition, 195n12
California Immigrant Workers Association, 171
California's Industrial Welfare Commission, 195n12
capitalism, 10–11, 152–53, 179–83. See also neoliberalism; paid employment
Casey, Edward, 187n7
childcare: costs of, 56–57, 63, 92–94, 97, 193n18; domestic service and, 63–64, 74–79; middle class and, 64, 85, 92, 94–95. See also reproductive labor
children: of immigrants, 2, 11–13, 117–19, 130–34, 147, 159–64, 179–82; of the middle class, 51–64, 88, 179–80, 190n2. See also reproductive labor
Chinese immigrants, 14, 188n11
citizenship, 6, 12–16, 80, 151–52, 173–75, 182, 186nn7–8, 199n5. See also cultural citizenship; immigrants; social membership
class: creation of, 13–16, 25–26, 49–50; gender and, 25, 86; morality and, 2–4, 65–66, 69–74; privilege and, 5, 9, 192n11; as a project, 52–59, 64–69, 190n1; race and, 51, 85–87; rejection of, 50–51, 74–82; reproductive labor and, 12–13, 83–87; social membership and, 10–11, 25, 50; visibility of, 5, 26, 32–33, 69. See also middle class; race
Colen, Shellee, 12
Coll, Kathleen M., 162
color blindness, 81
Co-op. See Sparkle and Shine Cooperative
corporate culture, 90–91, 193nn12–13
counter-habitations, 44–46
crimigration, 151

Crittenden, Ann, 100, 193n16
cultural capital, 162–63, 167–76
cultural citizenship, 12, 158–63, 167–76, 181, 186n7. See also social membership

DASH bus system, 42
De Genova, Nicholas, 150, 199n4
deportation, 15, 120–24, 151
domestic employers: the American Dream and, 2–5, 25–26, 64–69, 82; "Americanness" and, 11, 48–51, 79–82, 149, 180, 190n5; class and, 16, 49–82, 189n12; spaces of, 5, 33–34, 37–38, 43–48, 64–69, 190n16. See also domestic service; Generation X; middle class
domestic service: the American Dream and, 2–3, 9–11, 25–26, 153–61; conditions of, 8, 119–27, 143, 153–58; gender and, 116–17, 142–47; immigrants and, 5–10, 143, 147, 194n2; middle class and, 51, 63–69, 82–83, 190n3; organizations and, 115–17, 124–47; power relations and, 5, 46–48, 74–79, 185n3. See also domestic employers; domestic workers; Generation X; immigrants; middle class
domestic service studies, 9–10, 12, 119–20, 190n16
domestic sphere, 4–5, 13, 83, 92–96. See also private spaces; reproductive labor
domestic workers: activism and, 27–30, 116–17, 125–26, 143–47; the American Dream and, 2–3, 6, 9, 25–26, 148–50, 153–61; "Americanness" and, 150–53, 167–73, 175–76; competition between, 123–26, 129–30, 134–37, 196n15; employment opportunities for,

116, 123–24, 147, 195n10; foreignness and, 5–6, 79–82; gender and,
116–17, 142–47; invisibility of,
31–37, 43–48, 83, 119–27, 139–42,
177–78, 190n16, 192n6; reproductive labor and, 114–19, 130–34,
147–49, 162–64, 179–82, 194n2. *See
also* domestic service; immigrants;
Mexican Americans
Domestic Workers' Bill of Rights, 125,
195n12
Domestic Workers Group, 7, 20, 27,
115–17, 121, 124–26, 137–47, 171
downward mobility, 96–102, 180
DREAM (Development, Relief, and
Education for Alien Minors) Act,
186n6, 199n2
DWG. *See* Domestic Workers Group

economic insecurity: immigrants and,
23, 115–25, 135–37, 142–47, 153–58;
middle class and, 1–2, 23, 51–59, 87,
109–10, 177–83
economic mobility: the American
Dream and, 2–4, 11, 50–51, 148–50;
immigrants and, 149–53, 158–67,
175–76; middle class and, 64–70.
See also American Dream; paid
employment
education: activism and, 107–12, 129,
137, 143–47; immigrants and, 8, 42,
118–19, 151, 159–63; middle class
and, 22–23, 52–59, 86
Emerson, Ralph Waldo, 2–4
employer-employee relationships, 5,
46–48, 74–82, 185n3
employer neighborhoods, 33–40,
43–46, 53, 189n12
erasure: "Americanness" and, 51,
149–50; immigrants and, 7, 13–16,
24–26, 31–33, 43–48, 82, 139–42; of
reproductive labor, 4–5, 25–26, 83,

96–107, 112–14, 178, 192n6. *See also*
invisibility
ESL (English as a Second Language),
161

factory work, 8, 116, 123, 126, 133, 156,
174
Fair Labor Standards Act (1974),
195n12
fall from grace, 97–105
feminism, 84–86, 192n6, 192nn9–11
Filipina domestic workers, 9, 194n6,
196n15
Fogelson, Robert M., 31
Folbre, Nancy, 193n16
food stamps, 165
foreignness, 5–6, 13–16, 79–82, 152. *See
also* othering; paranoid nationalism;
xenophobia
Frankenberg, Ruth, 191n6
Franklin, Benjamin, 203n1

Gálvez, Alyshia, 186n7
Gates, Bill, 109
GDP (gross domestic product), 4–5,
111–12
GED (General Educational Development), 8
gender: American Dream and, 3–6,
149–50, 182–83; class and, 25, 86;
domestic service and, 6–10, 48, 64,
116–27, 142–47; immigrants and,
194n4; invisibility and, 83, 96–105,
107–14; paid employment, 85–92,
117–18, 191n4; race and, 12–13, 86;
social membership and, 11–12, 63,
96–102; space and, 4–5, 32, 43–48.
See also gender roles; reproductive
labor
gender roles, 101–4, 112, 191n1,
194n4. *See also* gender; reproductive labor

sense of self: immigrants and, 6–11, 117–19, 126, 132, 139–52, 167–75, 178–82; middle class and, 13–16, 69–74, 83–86, 96–114, 117–18
slavery, 2, 143, 146, 185n1
social membership: the American Dream and, 11, 25–26; citizenship and, 12, 173–75, 186n7; immigrants and, 5–6, 9–16, 119–27, 149–53, 167–73, 177–83; middle class and, 50–69, 86–87, 149, 179–80; paid employment and, 4–5, 10, 25–26 118–19, 191n2; race and, 5–6, 12–13; reproductive labor and, 11–12, 83, 96–114, 117–18, 147–50, 193nn15–17. *See also* American Dream; "Americanness"
Social Security, 101, 111–12, 148–49, 151m 165, 202n30
Soja, Edward W., 187n7, 188n9
Sparkle and Shine Cooperative, 20, 36, 42–43, 71, 74, 80–82, 117–18, 124–39, 142–47, 151, 156, 163–64
spatial apartheid, 21
spatiality, 5, 25–48, 178–79, 187nn6–7, 188n11
spatial politics, 32
stock market crash of 1929, 15
stratified reproduction, 192n11
structural violence, 185n4
studying sideways, 24, 186n11
studying up, 24, 186n11
success: immigrants and, 2, 6–11, 26, 114–19, 147–53, 162–82; middle class and, 2, 5, 11, 26, 52–69, 97–98; neoliberalism and, 152–53, 178–79

Taxing Women (McCaffery), 193n16
temporary protected status, 151, 197n24
ten-chair exercise, 1–2, 108–9, 177
Toronto, 9

transgender, 196n13
transnational mothers, 132, 194n5
Treaty of Guadalupe Hidalgo, 13
trophy kids, 51–59
T visa, 131, 196n16

Unbending Gender (Williams), 193n16
undocumented migrants, 15–16, 35–36, 40, 120, 124, 143, 151, 159, 189n14, 195n10, 199n2, 202n30. *See also* immigrants; Mexican Americans
United States: citizenship in, 13, 119–20, 151–52, 173–75, 186nn7–8; immigration law and policy in, 6, 15, 23–24, 31, 150–53, 197n25, 199n4, 202n30, 203n31; income distribution in, 1–2, 49, 51, 86, 99, 108–9, 177–78, 192n8; tax policy in, 1, 93, 97, 104–5, 107–14. *See also* American Dream; "Americanness"
unpaid care work, 4, 83, 92–105, 111–14. *See also* domestic employers; domestic workers
upward mobility. *See* economic mobility
urban sprawl, 32, 188nn9–10
USA Today, 84, 92
U.S. Census Bureau, 186n9, 188n10, 191n3
U.S. Citizenship and Immigration Services, 203n31

Valentine, David, 126, 196n13

wage gap, 86, 98, 112, 192n8
wasps (White Anglo-Saxon Protestants), 14
whiteness, 3, 13–16, 80–82, 150, 190n5, 191n6. *See also* "Americanness"; middle class; race
Williams, Joan C., 193n16

women. *See* domestic employers; domestic workers; gender; immigrants; middle class; reproductive labor

work. *See* domestic employers; domestic workers; paid employment

workplace culture, 90–91, 193nn12–13

World War II, 15

xenophobia, 13–16, 79–82, 177–79, 203n1. *See also* anti-immigration sentiment; foreignness; paranoid nationalism

Zelizer, Viviana, 190n2

Zilberg, Elana, 32–33

Zoot Suit Riots, 15

CPSIA information can be obtained
at www.ICGtesting.com
Printed in the USA
JSHW060213150123
36251JS00002B/7